The Day the Catskills Cried

Wayne Beyea

iUniverse, Inc.
New York Bloomington

The Day the Catskills Cried

Copyright © 2008 by Wayne E. Beyea

All rights reserved. No part of this book may be used or reproduced by any means, graphic, electronic, or mechanical, including photocopying, recording, taping or by any information storage retrieval system without the written permission of the publisher except in the case of brief quotations embodied in critical articles and reviews.

iUniverse books may be ordered through booksellers or by contacting:

iUniverse
1663 Liberty Drive
Bloomington, IN 47403
www.iuniverse.com
1-800-Authors (1-800-288-4677)

Because of the dynamic nature of the Internet, any Web addresses or links contained in this book may have changed since publication and may no longer be valid. The views expressed in this work are solely those of the author and do not necessarily reflect the views of the publisher, and the publisher hereby disclaims any responsibility for them.

ISBN: 978-0-595-52286-6 (pbk)
ISBN: 978-0-595-51020-7 (cloth)
ISBN: 978-0-595-62342-6 (ebk)

Printed in the United States of America

iUniverse rev. date 11/03/08

Dedicated to Trudy Resnick Farber

"She was a kind, sensitive soul who wasn't interested in diamonds and furs. Her sole interest was people. She planted her garden with love." – Rabbi Herman Eisner

"The sunshine of her personality helped me to grow." – Roger Farber

Notice: *Although the characters portrayed in this true story are real, some names have been changed.*

Preface

The silence on the forest hillside was disturbed by the unmistakable sound of something or someone digging. The unmistakable ***thwack*** of an axe whacking at tree roots, and ***clunk, clang*** of a shovel making contact with stone was ample evidence that the animal digging was of human form. To anyone familiar with the rugged, heavily forested mountainside overlooking the Rondout Reservoir, the sound would seem incongruous and they would undoubtedly seek out its source. However, this day, the only witnesses to the disruption of pristine earth were trees and perhaps a few wary chipmunks and squirrels who watched from a safe distance. They likely later would excitedly warn kin not to go near the hole that the human had dug because it was probably a trap. They would have been nearly correct; however, the small pit, which would have a plywood cover when completed, had a far more diabolical purpose.

The tall young man digging the hole was not accustomed to manual labor, still, he was trim and in reasonably good physical condition as a result of having been a member of his high school and college track teams. Wielding a pick, shovel and axe – the tools necessary to dig a hole in ground mined with stone and laced with tree roots - was hard labor and within a short period of time his body was soaked with sweat. Tiny rivulets of salty water trickled from his forehead and burned his eyes. He paused from digging for a moment, removed a glove, and his steamed-over glasses, lowered his head, lifted the bottom of the white cotton tee shirt that covered his upper body and used its end to wipe the sweat off his brow. He stood for a moment staring down at his progress and decided to take a break to let his glasses clear. While resting he examined his surroundings with which he was quite familiar, as his parents had owned a large tract of these woods and he had explored the area as a young lad, searching for gold, pirate treasure and even the legendary Golden Fleece. Of course, they were never found, but what he did find was peace of mind and a treasure of disciples, with whom he could freely commune without fear of ridicule or embarrassment. Unlike deprecating humans Mr. Birch, Maple, Oak, and Pine, attentively listened in silence as he regaled them with self-aggrandizing tales inspired by the genius that dwelt within his mind. Occasionally these disciples even nodded their limbs in approval, or uttered sighs of approval and appreciation for sharing his future plans with them.

The thought of the drama that would soon unfold in this remote section of woods triggered the display of a sardonic smile. In a mocking, tone of voice, seasoned with a touch of bitterness, he said aloud, "This is perfect! No one will think to look here and it is unlikely that any hiker or hunter will happen upon this spot until long after the princess is freed from her dark, uncomfortable dungeon. Ron, you are an absolute genius!" Having patted himself on the back and re-assuring himself that this was the ideal location, he again wiped his brow with the tail of his tee shirt, donned his now clear horn rim glasses, picked up his shovel and continued digging. The excavation proceeded slowly and after only a few minutes of renewed digging, he was again soaked with sweat. However, the thought of the wealth he would soon acquire made the toil and sweat inconsequential. *Her old man will be eager to part with the pittance required to get his precious princess back. Pittance! Now what made me think of that word? It is so out of character of me to use an uppity word like that but I do like the ring of it. It is the sort of word rich people like her and her old man would use. Her old man thinks that just because he has money he is better than the little people he hires and fires at will. A million bucks is mere pocket change to Harry. It is a good bet he won't even call the police. As for you, Princess, a few hours of confinement in this hole will bring you down off your high horse and make you realize you are a mere mortal, just like me. You may have been raised with a silver spoon in your mouth and think you are hot shit, but this forest is my kingdom and while you are here you will grovel, cry and beg me to spare your life.* He envisioned the soft, blond haired woman groveling at his feet, begging him to spare her life. Having the power to give or take the life of a woman hitherto inaccessible to him was exciting and triggered arousal. Imagining what it would be like to feel her softness shifted a normally subdued libido into overdrive. He could not think straight while focused on such primal urges and knew that he needed to quiet the beast within so as to stay focused on his plan of attaining financial success. *Stay focused Ron*, he told himself. Taking several deep breaths, he removed his glasses, and once more wiped the sweat from them, using the tail end of his sweat soaked tee shirt, then used another equally wet part of the shirt to mop his brow and face. Having temporarily calmed the beast within him he replaced his glasses and resumed digging. Each small shovel of earth brought his dream of acquiring wealth closer to reality. With renewed digging, he mulled over the details of the plan that had slowly taken shape over the course of three years. Every detail had been fine tuned in his mind to avoid the possibility of mistake or error. He even recognized that the behavior of a person suddenly confronted with the possibility of death could be unpredictable, but he felt confident that his targets were weak personalities and would not resist. He had even toyed with the thought that they were so weak and fearful that they would heed his warning not to contact the police if they wanted to see their precious again. Of course that would make everything too easy. Logically, he had to assume that the police would be called and would play a game of cat and mouse to retrieve the princess and identify her abductor. This mouse will be difficult to catch, he mused with a feeling of superiority, and they will pay to get their princess back. Genius that he was (in his distorted and perverted mind) he had even devised a credible defense in the eventuality that something went awry and he was arrested. He told himself, yes, the plan is solid – as a matter of fact it is brilliant. This self-appraisal produced a sweaty glistening smile of smug satisfaction and inspired another pause from labor to massage his ego in a flourish of oratorical self-praise. It mattered not that his disciples were watching. He felt himself to be quite a powerful, commanding figure in their presence and they were a non-threatening audience. Ron, you are truly a genius! All that CIA training is about to pay off. They will never think to look here and your plan should go off without a hitch. These trees are my only witnesses. Having thought this, he studied the tall silent sentinels of Oak, Maple, Birch and Pine that surrounded him, then swept his arm in a circle to address them, in much the same manner an actor would address his audience. And why not, this was his theater - his stage and it would soon open with an exciting drama as its grand premier; a drama written, produced, directed and starring 'Nobody Ron' from the little 'no where' Village of Grahamsville. He chuckled at the notoriety the drama would receive, and the wealth it would bring to its creator who sadly out of necessity, would remain anonymous. The moment was stimulating and exciting, impelling him to address his audience and seek their adulation. "Ladies and gentlemen, you will soon witness the most exciting performance ever to grace this theater. The show you are about to see was written by, produced by, directed by and starred in by yours truly. Consider yourselves fortunate that you were selected as audience for this one-time, and one-time only performance. I thank you in advance for your appreciation, adulation – and silence." Introduction completed, Ron bowed to show his appreciation to his silent audience. He bent forward and swept his right hand in a downward motion from forehead to ankle. Then cupping a hand around one ear he called out, "What, no sound of appreciation from my captive audience? No murmur of moving limbs or whisper among leaves? Well, soon, you will be showing your appreciation for being granted the privilege of being the only audience to view a magnificent, unscripted and unrehearsed real life drama." This statement evoked a fit of hysterical laughter and again he spoke aloud. "Ron, you sure do know how to play on words."

Noting that the lens of his glasses had cleared, he put them back on, then inserted his hand into his glove and resumed digging. For the next several minutes the only sound emerging from the small glade was the faint unmistakable sound of excavation, accompanied by the labored breathing of the excavator. As the hole deepened in its progress toward hell, its creator paused, smiled, shook his head in satisfaction and muttered, "Perfect! Now all I have to do is apply the finishing touch and then we will be ready to start the performance." He leaned his tools against a log, sat down and stared at his handiwork again envisioning the terrified young woman who would soon occupy it. Once again, he could see the hitherto unapproachable, inaccessible rich bitch groveling beneath his feet begging him to spare her life. Tears would spew from those large blue eyes reflecting a mélange of confusion, pain and terror. *What is it you are trying to say Princess? Oh, you think I am going to rape you, kill you and then bury you here? Your fears are much exaggerated. I do not force myself on women and I don't want your life. Although I must admit that seeing you squirm and grovel is quite a turn on. What this is about Princess is money. Lot's of money! Your daddy has more money than he needs and I just want a little bit of it. If daddy truly loves you, he will quickly pay for your release and your short stay here will become just a bad dream.*

1

The rising sun began making its presence known in a juxtaposition of color proclaiming the dawning of a beautiful day. The dark shroud covering the eastern horizon was gradually penetrated and overpowered by a mélange of pink, coral, rose, orange, violet and yellow announcing the arrival of the smiling sun - a warm and friendly smile, that seemed to herald the early advent of summer.

Thirty year-old Trudy Farber was awakened by the probing rays of the sun and before getting out of bed, gave silent thanks to God for giving her so much happiness and prosperity. She gazed upon her sound asleep husband, smiled, tickled his earlobe with a finger and whispered in his ear, "Roger, you sleepyhead, it is a glorious morning. Don't waste such a beautiful day in bed."

Roger stirred from sleep, rubbed his eyes, then ran his fingers through his mop of dark hair and muttered, "What time is it?"

"Time for you to get out of bed and go make some money." Trudy responded with a laugh. "We'll toss a coin to see who gets to prepare breakfast."

"Yeah, as if toasting a bagel and pouring a glass of orange juice is such a difficult task," Roger muttered in reply, adding, "What day is this?"

"May 24th my dear, and I might add, a perfectly gorgeous day."

"No silly, I didn't mean the date. Is this Wednesday?"

"No, it's Tuesday and you are supposed to be at the Ellenville store at nine."

Roger yawned, stretched, and replied, "Thanks for reminding me. And I may be late getting home from work today because I've got to pick Harvey up at the Monticello store this afternoon and take him to the garage to pick up our van. What time I arrive home depends on what time the garage has the van ready for pick up."

Trudy smiled impishly and responded, "Such uncertainty certainly warrants you're taking me out for dinner tonight."

"Sounds good to me," Roger responded, "but we'll flip a coin to see who picks up the check."

"No way silly. You are definitely going to pay. Now get your butt out of bed and get going."

Blond, attractive, 30year old Gertrude "Trudy" Farber, nee, Resnick, was the eldest daughter of Harry and Marcia Resnick of Ellenville, New York. Handsome, curly-brown haired 30year old Roger Steven Farber was the son of Henry and Lily Farber of Monticello, New York. They had become husband and wife in June 1973, and by all outward appearances – according to family and friends – were very happy and devoted to each other. Six months after their wedding Roger and Trudy settled into a ranch style home constructed specifically for them, on Decker Farm Road, located near the eastern end of Sackett Lake, a mere five minute drive from the Village of Monticello. The happy couple had mutually decided to forego children until they had their careers on track, and in 1977 they were still laying career track. Roger – with business partner Harvey Kornblau – owned Catskill Electronics, headquartered on Jefferson Street in Monticello, New York. Catskill Electronics owned three Radio Shack stores located in Monticello, Ellenville and Monroe, New York. After graduation from Monticello High, Roger attended Albert Lea College in Minnesota and after graduation, remained at the university to complete post-graduate work that would prepare him for law school. After completion of studies at Albert Lea, he was accepted at St. Mary's University School of Law, in San Antonio, Texas. Realizing that he was not cut out for the rigors of law school and not being scholastically ambitious, he soon decided that he was not cut out to be a lawyer and dropped out of law school. Still young and unsettled as to what he wanted to accomplish in life, he returned to New York, and enrolled at State University New Paltz, hoping to discover a career that would interest and excite him. After completing a year at S.U.N.Y. New Paltz, he still had not found a career that he wanted to pursue for the remainder of his life. What he had decided was that he had had enough of college, so he dropped out of school and found employment as a law clerk for Attorney Murray Gaiman, in Woodridge, New York. Roger soon came to the realization that the work of a law clerk was confining, mundane and boring; he again searched his soul for the answer as to what he really wanted to do for the rest of his life. Enjoying freedom of movement and desirous of being his own boss, he decided that what he really wanted to do was own and operate his own business. That opportunity came in 1974, when he convinced longtime friend Harvey Kornblau to become his partner in Catskill Electronics. Together they bought into the management of three Radio- Shack Stores and by 1977, their business – although not booming – was pulling in a living for the two.

Popular, vivacious Trudy Resnick graduated from Ellenville High School, and was accepted at Rider College in New Jersey to pursue a degree in education. An intelligent and dedicated student, she left Rider with the post-graduate education degree. In the process of obtaining qualifications to begin teaching, she lost all enthusiasm and zeal to become a teacher and became fascinated with psychology. This motivated enrollment in New York University's School of Psychology located in New York City. Subsequent to graduation and conclusion of a brief internship, she was hired as a psychiatric therapist by Sullivan County Mental Health Clinic, with offices located in the hamlet of Ferndale, located just outside Liberty, New York. Trudy enjoyed her work and was grateful that her office was only a 15 –20 minute drive from home.

At around eight that May morning, Trudy kissed her slow starting husband goodbye and departed for work. She hesitated as she opened the door, turned back toward Roger and asked, "Have you heard anymore from that Ron Krom character?"

"No, I haven't," Roger responded, adding, "The last time I saw him, I told him that I was not interested in investing with him and after the way he upset you on the phone, I told him not to call us again. But I told you this before Hon, what brought this up?"

"I don't know. It's just that I keep recalling how weird and threatening he sounded during that phone call. He went from a polite soft-spoke individual to a bitter, angry sounding, threatening psycho so quickly. There is a side of him that is troubling. Perhaps it is my work that brings him so often to mind. Something, perhaps some sort of sixth- sense tells me we should be wary of him."

"You needn't worry about Ron, I have known him for a long time and although he sometimes has wild, grandiose ideas and is sort of strange acting, he is quite harmless."

"I certainly hope so. I just hope we don't have to deal with him again. Besides, this is too nice a day for anything to go wrong. I have an easy schedule today and should be home on time. I hope you don't run into any snags and are home waiting to greet me."

Roger smiled and nodded his head in agreement as he responded, "Getting our van back in service is the only glitch I have to deal with today.

The garage promised it would be ready by noon, so barring any unforeseen problems, I will be here to greet you, my love."

It is quite likely that in anticipation of a wonderful day, Trudy hummed or sang to herself as she drove to work that morning. It is also reasonably certain that she had no foreboding, no inclination, that in a mere ten hours she would come face-to-face with unimaginable horror. As a psychiatric caseworker, Trudy was used to confronting various types of mentally deranged personalities; however, this day she was on a collision course with a psychotic disciple of Satan, who would introduce her to terror never imagined – not even in her worst nightmares.

2

On May 24th Helen Redmond, a real estate broker employed by John Rogers Realty in Woodstock, New York was seated at her desk and observed a bright red/orange Chevrolet Corvette pull up in front of the building. She immediately recognized the tall, bespectacled young man exiting the car as Ron Krom. She would later explain to police that she had known Krom for about a year. One spring day in 1976 Ron came into the office and introduced himself as a realtor, working under the license of his family-owned agency located in Grahamsville. Helen related, "The polite, soft spoken, affable young man convinced both John and me that he was interested in developing property in Ulster County and wished to connect with our agency. Since that introduction, Ron periodically called or came in, always indicating that he had several deals working which might prove profitable to us." Therefore, Helen was not surprised by Ron's sudden appearance at around – as she remembered – about 10:30 on a Tuesday morning.

"Good morning Helen," Krom greeted as he entered the office. "How are you on this fine day?"

"Just great Ron. What brings you to Woodstock today?"

"Well, I came to ask you a favor."

"What sort of favor?"

"You know I love my 'vette but it will only accommodate one passenger and I have some clients coming in later today for a viewing of some property. I will need a bigger car to accommodate them. I have been giving serious consideration to buying a larger vehicle and possibly a Cadillac. I would like to try one out first, and I knew you drive an El Dorado. Would you consider swapping cars for the day? You could use my 'vette and I promise to bring your Caddy back tomorrow."

"I would consider that; however, at the present time my Cadillac is in the garage for repair."

"Gee, that's too bad. Do you suppose John would let me use his Caddy for the day? Some clients are flying into Sullivan International this afternoon and I'm going to show them some property for development. I want them to feel comfortable during the ride and if I close this deal it will mean millions."

"Why don't you just rent a Caddy for the day?"

"I thought about doing that, but it is too much money, and I immediately thought of my good friends in Woodstock. Maybe John would consider swapping cars for just today."

"I don't know, but John is in so you can ask him yourself." Turning her head toward a connecting office she called out, "John, Ron is here and wants to ask you for a favor."

John Rogers had overheard the conversation occurring in the front office, and responded by calling out, "Good morning. Come on in." Ron immediately walked into his office where they exchanged smiles and a handshake. "I heard you ask to borrow Helen's car, what's the matter, growing tired of driving a sports car?"

"No, but my 'vette isn't suitable for driving clients to showings. As a matter of fact, I am going to pick up some very wealthy investors from New York City this afternoon and show them a piece of property they are interested in developing, and I could use a larger car. Would you be willing to swap your Caddy for my 'vette – just until tomorrow?"

"I would, but my wife is using the Cadillac today and she has already departed for Kingston with it. She won't be home until this evening."

"Then how about loaning me your Firebird? It has a little more room than my 'vette, and I promise to return it tomorrow."

"Sounds like you have a big sale brewing? What property are you trying to sell these investors?"

"I would tell you, but they asked me to keep this whole deal hush-hush, to avoid competition. However, I can tell you that if I pull this deal off it will make me a wealthy man. I might even consider giving you a little piece of the action."

As he listened to Ron's proposal, middle-aged John – who epitomized the theory that upon reaching their 40-50's men purchase sports cars because of mid-life crisis – imagined himself tooling around Woodstock behind the wheel of the Corvette. "Okay," he immediately responded, "but let's agree that both cars will be returned with a full tank of gas."

Ron smiled, reached in his pocket, produced his car keys, handed them to John, then extended his right hand and as they shook hands said, "Thanks, I will return your Firebird tomorrow with a full tank of gas."

Ron departed Woodstock at around eleven that morning, driving John Roger's 1976 Pontiac Firebird, bearing vanity license plates JFR2. Whether coincidence or shrewd planning, the Firebird's color was nearly identical to Ron's 1976 Chevrolet Corvette. It was now time to proceed with the next stage of his carefully thought out plan, and it had nothing to do with the sale of real estate.

Standing at his office window, John watched Ron leave, then, turned his attention to the Corvette. As he stared at the attractive sports car he was struck by a sudden impulse. *It's such a perfectly gorgeous day, why not make the most of it?* He turned to Helen and said, "Helen, I don't have any appointments scheduled and it is such a beautiful day, I think I am going to take a spin down to Saratoga and check out the track. Please tell Ruth not to expect me home until late this evening."

3

It proved to be a routine business day for Roger. During mid-afternoon, the garage called to advise repairs on the company van had been completed and it was ready for pickup. At five he and Harvey departed the Monticello Radio Shack store and drove to the garage in Roger's car. It was decided that Harvey would drive the van, to the Farber residence to obtain some advertising display cases that were stored in the garage. He and Roger arrived at the house at around five or ten after five and immediately loaded the van. Roger would later explain to police that because it was a very warm afternoon, and having worked up a sweat, he invited Harvey into his home for a drink. Before entering the house, he walked to his mailbox located beside the road and retrieved the mail. Then he and Harvey went inside.

As they entered Roger invited, "You can wash up in the bathroom down the hall, and I'll use the one off our bedroom."

Harvey didn't verbally respond, but nodded and proceeded to the bathroom.

Roger entered his bedroom and was startled by its appearance. What in hell? The bed had been torn apart. Both pillowcases were missing, and a section had been torn or cut from the sheet covering the mattress. Someone has broken in and used the pillowcases to steal our stuff, he thought. He called out, "Harvey, come look at this mess! Someone has burgled us!"

Harvey joined Roger at the entrance to the master bedroom and stared wide-eyed at the condition of the bed.

"I'm going to check my bedroom to see what is missing. Please take a look in the other rooms and tell me if you see damage or anything appears missing," he asked. Of immediate concern was that guns, camera equipment and Trudy's jewelry might have been taken. A quick check, found nothing missing that he could account for. He was puzzled as to what the intruder was looking for as Harvey reported that he saw nothing out of place in the other rooms. As they discussed their findings, their attention was drawn to the sound of something or someone moving in the kitchen. Not knowing what to expect but dreading what they might be about to confront, Roger and Harvey moved cautiously toward the kitchen. Suddenly, a tall specter holding a rifle that was pointed at them came into view. They gasped aloud and shook with fear. The intruder's appearance and the rifle pointed at them left no doubt that he intended to harm or kill them. Despite the heat of the afternoon, their assailant was clad in heavy work clothes, wore a white ski mask to conceal his identity and gloves covered both hands. The individual did not speak, but motioned to them that they were to enter the kitchen.

"Please, don't shoot," Roger, pleaded. "You can take-have whatever you want, just don't hurt us."

The intruder did not verbally respond but motioned that both men were to lie face down on the kitchen floor. Roger and Harvey obeyed, and after both were prone, the mute intruder bound their hands and feet with a strong nylon string. When satisfied his victims were incapacitated, he produced a typewritten note and held it in a position for Roger to read. Roger would later recall that the note asked, "What time does Trudy get home, or, what time does your wife get home?"

Mind racing with fear and confusion, he did not immediately grasp the significance of the note, thinking that this home invasion thief did not want to be surprised in the act of his robbery. Roger responded, "Usually around five or five-thirty."

Remaining silent, the intruder tore a section from the Farbers daily newspaper and scrawled in felt tip pen the note, "Don't call the police or FBI. You will be released in one hour. Call Harry Resnick."

As Roger read the directive he heard a car entering the driveway and knew it was Trudy. The masked intruder also heard the car's arrival and rather than fleeing, seemed to look forward to Trudy's arrival. It suddenly dawned on Roger that the intruder had a much more diabolical crime in mind than robbery or burglary. Trudy was the intended target of this monster and she was about to walk in the door totally unprepared for the evil that was about to confront her. For a moment he thought of calling out a warning to her but fear of being shot prevented him from doing so and he remained silent.

Having observed Roger's car and the van in the driveway, Trudy anticipated that she would find her husband entertaining Harvey. She entered her home calling out, "Hello, I'm home. Where are you?" Sighting her husband and Harvey on the kitchen floor and confronted by the masked stranger, she gasped and shrieked, "Oh, no!"

Hearing Trudy shriek, Roger immediately called out, "Trudy, do not resist. Just do as he says."

Frozen by fear, Trudy commenced crying, and in a hoarse whisper begged, "Please, do not hurt me or my husband."

The intruder did not verbally respond but pointed to a chair, then pointed at her indicating that she was to sit down.

Crying hysterically, Trudy did as she was directed all the while begging that she not be harmed. "Take anything you want," she implored, "but please don't hurt us."

The gunman remained silent, and secured Trudy's arms together with a strip of sheet that had been cut from her bed. When she was bound, he took out his felt tip pen and once again scrawled on a piece of newspaper. When finished, he thrust the note in Trudy's face. Through tears she read, "If you do not want to be killed, you will do precisely as directed. If you resist or try to flee, I will kill you. Obey my instructions and you will survive. Do you understand?"

Numb with fear and her brain spinning with confusion, Trudy nodded her head in the affirmative.

Whether motivated by a perverse psychology or to emphasize his threat and further convince Trudy that he meant business, the silent assailant removed carving knives from the knife block that held them on the kitchen counter and proceeded to throw them – one by one - at her kitchen cabinets. Only one struck point first and stuck in the door. The others fell on the kitchen counter. Having completed this weird behavior, the masked gunman pointed toward the door, then pointed to Trudy and motioned that she was to accompany him out of the house.

Weak, and sobbing uncontrollably, Trudy arose from the chair and as she did, the assailant placed a pillowcase over her head, grabbed her arm and led her from the house toward the woods. She stumbled numbly along and the fact that she was wearing elevated wedge style shoes made walking through woods, with her vision hampered by tears, all the more difficult.

One of the knives thrown by the intruder had bounced off its intended target and fell onto the floor within Roger's reach. When he was sure the intruder was out of the house, he managed to get hold of this knife and used it to cut the rope that bound him. As soon as he was free, he looked out a kitchen window and would later tell police, "I saw my wife and her abductor disappear into the woods behind our house."

Roger's statement and the discovery that he owned a gun caused some of the state police investigators to question why he did not immediately arm himself and give pursuit. It was reasonable to believe that the abductor's flight from the house and through the woods was slow because of Trudy's hysteria and the fact that she was wearing platform wedge shoes, certainly not conducive for fast movement over rough terrain. Investigators were also curious as to how the lone intruder armed with a rifle, managed to bind two men with rope without placing the gun down and using both hands.

4

The tall, slender, silent abductor was strong and gripped Trudy's arm tightly as he led her from her home, across the back lawn and into a patch of woods. Not knowing where she was being taken, or why, yet fearing the worst, she tried to call upon learned psychotherapy skills, but panic depressed rational thought processes and all she could focus on was survival. The words scrawled on the piece of newspaper and thrust before her eyes echoed through cerebral passages repressing all other thought. Like a neon sign they flashed repeatedly through her brain, "If you resist or try to flee, I will kill you. Obey my instructions and you will survive." At a time calling for physical strength and rational thought, she felt only weakness, fear and confusion. Why is this happening? What are his intentions? Will he rape me? Will he kill me? Why doesn't he speak? Where is he taking me? He hasn't spoken. I must know him and that is why he won't speak. O God, please help me! Fear is a strong emotion and now caught and held in its grasp, Trudy stumbled along, sobbing aloud and pleading with her silent abductor, "Please, oh God please, do not hurt me. I can pay you – my father can pay you – whatever you want. Just don't hurt me."

Her abductor increased his grip on her arm and did not respond. They soon emerged from the small patch of woods, separating Decker Farm Road from Sunset Drive Extension, and approached a red/orange (sporty) looking car parked alongside the road. The silent gunman produced a set of car keys from a pants pocket, inserted a key into the trunk lock and opened the cover.

Having heard the trunk lid open, Trudy sensed she was about to be placed inside and sobbed, "Please, oh please, don't put me in there; I will not give you any trouble. Please, I beg you, don't put me in there. I have great fear of small dark spaces. Oh, God please…" Her entreaty fell on deaf ears.

 Knowing he could not tarry in the area, the mute abductor physically forced a compliant Trudy into the trunk and slammed the lid shut. Victim now secure, he got into the driver's seat, leaned the .22rifle against the front passenger seat, and - before starting the engine - removed his gloves and the stifling hot ski mask, placing them on the seat beside him, then started the car. He had planned his escape route carefully so as to avoid major highways where he would be at greater risk of being stopped by police. He reckoned that the flashy looking sports car would attract the attention of police, so he would take care not to exceed the speed limit or break any traffic laws along the way. It was a mere quarter mile to the end of Sunset, then a left onto Sackett Lake Road and a half-mile later, right onto Maplewood. His route would take him through the Hamlet of Loch Sheldrake, then over town roads to State Route 42, which he would take into the Village of Grahamsville. Upon reaching Grahamsville, he would turn right onto State Route 55, and shortly after entering Ulster County, make a right turn onto a desolate dirt road which ended in the woods just a few yards from his destination. During the trip, he silently commended himself for flawlessly carrying out the first phases of his diabolical plan. *I knew that Roger would not put up a fight. It is a good bet that he will follow my instructions precisely. Hey Roger, you know you are responsible for this. If you had not been so arrogant and shown some respect, I might have chosen someone else. It was not wise to anger me Roger boy, and you (glancing in the rearview mirror) conceited, condescending, spoiled, rich snob, how dare you look down your nose at me and order me around. No glass slipper for you blond princess. Consider your ordeal a lesson in humility. Ron, you are a true genius. By this time two days from now, you will be a rich man. Let's see, should I invest in a NASCAR racetrack named after me, or open up a resort as a front for training CIA operatives. I can see the look on old Harry's face when he learns his princess has been kidnapped; I hope he doesn't have a heart attack before getting the money together.* During the drive he frequently glanced in the rear view mirror, fully expecting at any moment to see Trudy appear, but she did not and seemed oddly quiet in the confines of the trunk. *At one point he thought, Maybe she is so scared that she passed out.*

 It is probable that at some time after being abducted from her home or during the half-hour to forty-five minute ride in the cramped trunk of the sports car, in a moment of lucidity, Trudy asked herself **Why hasn't he said anything? Why won't he speak? It has to be because he knows I would recognize his voice. He has to be someone I know, certainly not one of my patients, because none of them would do this to me.** It is also probable that she recalled Ron Krom's lurid accusations and threats when she told him not to call or come near her again. *It's him! He is sicker than imagined. He is angry with me for refusing to convince Roger to invest in his business. Will he let me go if my father gives him the money he wants?* If she did convince herself that Ron Krom was her abductor, it is also a good bet that she decided not to let on that she knew his identity out of fear that such revelation would result in her death. The message that she would survive if she obeyed instructions overwhelmed all thought of resistance or attempt to escape, and the wedgies on her feet made any attempt at trying to run impossible.

Trudy's five foot-five inch, medium build was crammed into the Firebird trunk compartment, but fortunately her assailant had tied her hands in front of her body and she was able to twist about. She pushed against the trunk lid and in the dark confines, groped about for a tool or object that could be used to pry open the lock. This proved futile as her assailant had carefully removed everything in the trunk - probably to provide room for his victim - the lock held, and the lid remained closed. It is a certainty that she was assailed by deepening feelings of helplessness, and despair during this ride to an uncertain fate. That morning, the promise of a very warm day had caused her to don lightweight dark cotton slacks and a sleeveless, striped open weave sweater. The sweater was already wet from perspiration and tears. When the car stopped, she would have sensed that it was parked on an incline, facing upward.

Before exiting the car Ron again donned the ski mask and gloves. Putting the ski mask on and taking it off was not an easy task because poor vision required his wearing glasses and so he had to adjust his glasses under the mask, to permit a good field of vision. He opened the trunk lid and stared for a moment at his prize.

Her trembling body was curled into a fetal position, and she had managed to remove the pillowcase from her head. My goodness, Ron said to himself, my arrogant blonde princess looks an absolute wreck. She needed this lesson in humility and when this is over she will be a much better person. Then he extended a gloved hand, pulling and lifting her out of the trunk.

Absolutely terrified, mind racing with confusion and dread, Trudy was eager to escape the dark, cramped confines of the vehicle's trunk; however, seeing that she was now in a remote forested area, her relief was short lived. Panic, fear and dread prevented her intelligent mind from forming any plan of defense or escape. However, she was a skilled psychotherapist and had convinced herself that – because her abductor remained silent and seemed to be carrying out some sort of plan with coolness and deliberation – he knew that if he spoke she would recognize him. Despite the great emotional trauma that was overpowering legitimate thought process, she reckoned that if she could get him to speak and respond verbally to her she would not only know who he was, but would also be able to diagnose his particular psychotic disorder. She also reasoned that her tormentor was already under mental health treatment and possibly a patient at the Sullivan County's Mental Health facility. Trudy was not physically strong and would not be able to put up a fight against this beast but she was intelligent and told herself that if she were to survive whatever ordeal this beast in a man's body had planned for her that she needed to penetrate his silence and get him to converse with her. Taking deep breaths to control her panic she called on the therapy procedures – referred to as Active Listening Skills – that were useful in establishing rapport and gaining the confidence of emotionally troubled people. These skills were the only weapon she possessed to prolong or, hopefully, prevent whatever horrible fate this man intended. Her blond hair was now disheveled and wet, salty strands, made so by an endless flow of tears had found their way into her mouth and made speaking difficult; she pushed the strands aside with her tongue and stated in a choking voice, "You seem very angry, did I make you angry?"

In most instances if this statement sounded sincere to an individual who was angry, it would trigger a response from them, something like, "You're damned right!" Or, "What the hell do you care?" Followed by, "You know damned well what this is about and now, you are going to pay."

However, Trudy recognized that the look he gave her through the holes of the ski mask seemed to portray excitement rather than anger. That look was more frightening to her than any look of anger. The blue eyes that studied her did not portray evil, yet their glow of excitement were as frightening to her as any emotionless stare from Satan would have been.

The canopy provided by tall trees blocked out the still bright, early evening sun, that was beginning its descent into the western horizon, but fingers of light probed for openings in the foliage and where there was an opening, a bright shaft of light streamed through to the forest floor. These lasers of light penetrated darkening shadows creating a diabolical resemblance to spotlights probing the dim light of a stage. The combination of lighting and dreadful silence, surely gave an eerie appearance to the wilderness scene.

Any relief that Trudy may have felt at being freed from the confines of the trunk immediately disappeared as she viewed her surroundings and had no idea where she was or what was about to happen to her. Displaying a look of terror, she fell to her knees and sobbed, "These woods - where are we? What are you going to do? Please, you promised that you wouldn't hurt me. Oh God, please, don't hurt me. I don't want to die here."

Her abductor did not respond, instead, he pulled and dragged her up an incline that led to a small clearing in the woods. They entered the clearing and he dropped her at the edge of a hole in the ground.

Realizing that she was about to be buried either alive or dead, Trudy screamed; however, overwhelming panic and terror were crushing her lungs and the scream came out as a strained whisper. Her body began shaking uncontrollably and she gasped for breath. "No, oh please, no," she begged. "I do not want to die."

The tormentor stared down upon his prey with the same sort of cold, quizzical look a raptor might display before swooping down upon a terrified mouse that was about to become his meal. The difference being, that this was no survival ritual by a creature of the wild, but the perverse plot of a beast in human form. A schizophrenic delusional beast who perceived himself as some sort of demigod engaged in wielding power over a mere human who had dared to tell him he was 'sick' and order him not to bother her again. He had brought her down off her high horse and reduced her to the pile of whining, quivering flesh that now groveled at his feet. The feeling of power in controlling the mortality of this woman was quite thrilling, exciting and stimulated sexual arousal. For a fleeting moment he considered taking advantage of her vulnerability but repressed that urge, telling himself, This sniveling mortal is unworthy of me and besides I want to be remembered by my benefactor as the compassionate genius who gave life when possessing the power to take it. Kneeling down beside his victim he whispered, "Consider this a lesson in humility, Trudy my dear. You are worth much more to me alive than dead, so I intend to keep you alive. Whether you live or die is now in the hands of your old man. If he pays quickly, you will be released." While speaking, he untied the fabric that bound her arms, then, with a heave, pushed her into the pit. For a long moment he stared down at the form of the writhing, choking woman below his feet. He smiled in satisfaction and hissed, "Now relax and enjoy your snug nest. Sorry it isn't lined with silk for someone of your importance and value, but eating a little dirt will make you a better person." Then he reached across the opening, and slammed shut the sheet of plywood designed as a cover for the makeshift tomb. Once closed, he secured the cover's metal hasp with a padlock and camouflaged the cover by covering it with leaves and twigs. When done, he placed the key for the padlock under a nearby stone. Phase 2 of his plan now complete, Ron sat on a log, removed his ski mask and gloves, stared at the sheet of plywood and listened.

It is reasonable to assume that Ron intended to terrorize Trudy, not kill her, for after constructing the makeshift grave he shot five twenty-two caliber bullets through the sheet of plywood to admit oxygen. A large drill would have better served that purpose because, although the small caliber bullets passed through the plywood, the minute holes admitted an insufficient supply of oxygen for someone in a state of panic, which increased their intake of oxygen.

As expected, Trudy's crying and screams were muffled and barely discernible. He propped his .22rifle behind the log, listened to Trudy's agony and savored the moment. Standing, he unzipped his pants, and urinated on a patch of moss beside the log. He had never heard a woman cry and moan like this before. It was exciting and stirred sexual arousal. For the first time in his life he had complete power and control over a woman and it was a wonderful feeling. At this time, place and moment, he was uninhibited and in full command and control. He could relieve himself without fear of embarrassment or rejection, and he did.

Why he didn't rape Trudy is unknown and open to conjecture. It is the opinion of the author that one of the causes of his perverse psychology involved an insecure and uncertain sexual identity. Perhaps some embarrassing moment – probably experienced as a teen – was imbedded in his sub-conscience and made him question his sexual identity. As an adult male, he was driven by the need to prove his masculinity; however, the fear of rejection caused him to seek the company of women with non-challenging personalities.

Lengthening shadows indicated it was time to put the next phase of his plan in action, and having satisfied the primeval urge that overwhelmed intelligent thought processes, he surveyed his handiwork one last time and leaving the rifle propped behind the log, headed for the car.

Trudy Farber was kidnaped at gunpoint from her home in Sackett La. Tuesday night. Her husband and a business partner were bound by their hands and feet inside, before they freed themselves to alert authorities of the crime.

Farber Home

5

Gertrude Resnick, made her debut into the world on July 30, 1946, as the firstborn child of Harry and Marcia Resnick. Gertrude was fortunate to be born into a hard working family, which in 1946, was on the cusp of achieving wealth and prosperity due to foresight and an intrepid investment by Uncle Joe Resnick.

The Resnick family arose from rather humble beginnings as a struggling farm family in mid-state New York, until Uncle Joe borrowed $7000 and founded Channel Master Electronics, which would manufacture components and antennas for a fledgling industry, which was starting to make its presence known. Joe wisely invested and started his business as WW II drew to a close and war weary, grateful citizens who enjoyed motion pictures and worshipped movie stars, commenced —what would become a love affair with a wonderful entertainment device named Television; which in essence was home theater. To obtain a clear picture on the magical box, an aluminum device resembling something from outer space and referred to as an antenna, was affixed to the roof of the home. This aluminum framework intercepted the electro-optics transmitted by the network and transferred them to a cathode-ray tube mounted in cabinets of varying size and design. In short order, millions of homes were sprouting television antennas and they were all manufactured at the Resnick manufacturing plant known as Channel Master, headquartered in Ellenville, Ulster County, New York. Ellenville was a small village located in the Shawangunk Valley, in the shadows of the Shawangunk Mountains and virtually had no industry until the Resnick brothers developed their business at the north end of the village. It was more noted as a popular summer vacation area for folks desirous of escaping the stifling heat of New

York City, without having to travel a long distance. In fact, many New York City residents owned cottages in the Ellenville area and in the summer, commuted daily or weekly from New York to Ellenville. Before the advent of ChannelMaster, the major industry of Ellenville was tourism and numerous hotels, such as the Neville, Fallsview, and nearby Homowack and Tamarack did a thriving business.

Joe Resnick promptly convinced brothers Louis and Harry to become his business partners and their combined intelligence and entrepreneurship quickly turned the original $7000 investment into millions of dollars. From the time it was founded until the mid 1960's, Channel Master was a successful industry producing television components and antennas. The business provided employment for hundreds, and during its tenure, the population of Shawangunk Valley grew and prospered – thanks to Channel Master, and the Resnick family. Appreciative and thankful for their good fortune, the Resnicks became active philanthropists contributing large sums of money to various charities, civic organizations, schools and private citizens. The family soon became widely respected and admired for their generosity and concern for their fellow man.

A life long Democrat, Joe Resnick contributed much time and money to the party and believing he could make a difference, accepted his party's nomination for Congress. The popular philanthropist was elected in a landslide and if fate had not dealt him a cruel hand, he would probably have had a long, distinguished career in government. Joe Resnick was elected to his first term in Congress in 1965 and immediately started making a name for himself as a dynamic, hard-working force within the Democratic Party. Emulating brother Joe, Lou Resnick also enjoyed being in the public eye and supported government programs he felt beneficial to Ulster County. Unlike Joe, Lou was content to seek a more local political office and accepted his party's nomination for a seat on the Ulster County Legislature. As popular as his brother, he too won in a landslide, and would continue to hold that office until advanced age convinced him to retire. Brother Harry harbored no ambition for political office and preferred to stay out of the public limelight. Recognizing that the demands of holding political office detracted from their ability to manage a large corporation, Joe and Louis convinced Harry that he should take the helm of the family business. Thus in 1950, Harry was named President of the corporation. He continued in that capacity until 1967 when the company was sold to Avnet, Inc. and then became an officer on the Avnet Board, as part of the sale agreement. The Resnick family had a sense of indebtedness and gratitude toward the community that had given them so much and Harry was heard to say, "This is my town. I owe a lot to Ellenville and its people."

The Resnick brothers had prospered during Channel Master's tenure and the three were multi-millionaires at the time of its sale to Avnet. Sadly, Congressman Joe Resnick would pass away in 1969 at the young age of 44. Harry and Louis were named executors of their brother's estate, which remained unresolved in 1977.

It did not take long for family members to tag little blonde, precocious Gertrude with the nickname "Trudy" and throughout the remainder of her life she preferred being addressed by family and friends alike as Trudy. Despite wealth and the ability to place their daughter in a private school, Marcia and Harry – having personally evolved from a middle-class background and not wishing to separate her from adolescent friends – decided to enroll Trudy in Ellenville's public school system. Intelligent, thirsting for knowledge and aspiring to become a teacher Trudy studied faithfully and achieved good grades, while still finding time to engage in many extra-curricular activities and enjoying the reputation as one of the most popular girls in school. Young Trudy had many childhood friends; however, she spurned the attention given to her by a dark-haired neighbor boy by the name of Ronald Krom, telling her friends, "He's weird."

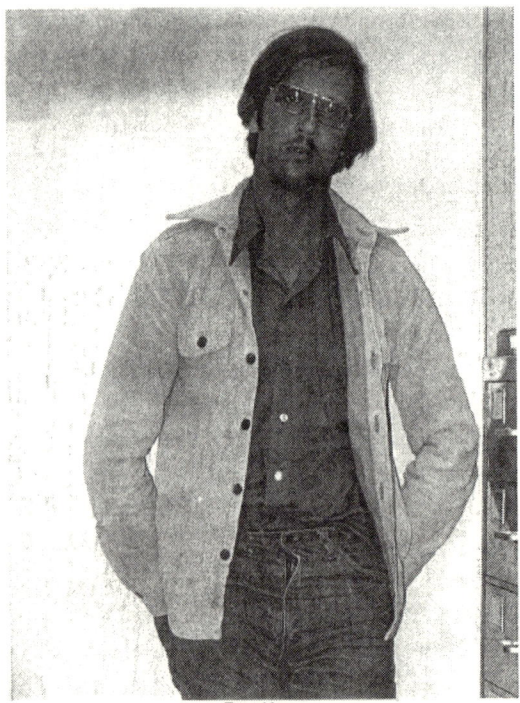

Ron Krom

6

During the late afternoon and into the evening of May 24th young BCI Investigators Paul Muhlig and John Gallagher interviewed all residents living in the vicinity of the Farber home. They would report, "Susan Katz, residing on Sunset Drive Extension with husband Ron and three children, told us that at around 3:35 p.m., she drove to the intersection of Sunset Drive and Osborne Road to pick up her son Peter, age 12, who would exit his school bus there. While driving east on Sunset Extension, she drove past a car parked on the north side of the road. As this is a rural area and her home had been burglarized in October 1976, the presence of the vehicle caused suspicion as to its purpose for being there. She reported that the parked car was vacant and she did not see anyone in its vicinity. Mrs. Katz described the car as a red/orange sporty looking car. She could not recall the number on the car's license plate but was certain it had a maximum of 4 characters. Her suspicions were further aroused because the driver side window on the car was closed and this seemed strange on such a hot day. She was also certain that she had never seen this car before it appeared parked on the side of Sunset Drive Extension."

7

During the early evening of May 24th, Harry Resnick was talking on the telephone with plumber Stan Carlson of Stone Ridge, who had worked on his water well the previous day. Their conversation was suddenly interrupted by a female voice who stated, "Excuse me, this is the operator. I have an emergency call for a Mr. Resnick from Roger Farber."

Harry tensed and the hand holding the telephone receiver commenced trembling as he responded, "This is Harry Resnick."

"Mr. Resnick, I have Roger Farber on the line. Go ahead Mr. Farber."

"Roger, what is the matter?" Harry worriedly asked.

It was immediately obvious to Harry that his son-in-law was greatly upset and excited, as he spoke much too loud and his words were disjointed and hurried. Roger opened by shouting, "The house – we were robbed, he had a gun, took Trudy, his note said call you. Harry, Trudy has been kidnapped!"

Hardly calm himself, but trying to sound so, Harry responded, "Calm down Roger and tell me what happened."

Roger took a deep breath and, after exhaling slowly, replied, "Harry, an armed intruder was in our house when we came home from work this afternoon, and he abducted Trudy. He showed me…"

"Abducted Trudy! My God, I can't believe you are telling me this!" Harry interrupted, immediately regretting having done so, because Marcia, his wife, was standing by his side.

Hearing her husband's response to the telephone caller, Marcia placed a hand over her mouth and wailed, "What is this you are saying? My Trudy abducted, how can that be? Harry, who is telling you these terrible things?"

"It's Roger." Harry responded. "Hold on Roger, I've got to calm Marcia before she collapses."

A minute seemed an eternity; however, Roger's brain was spinning with confusion as to what he should do and surely his ever intelligent, cool-headed father-in-law would offer the right course of action. Therefore, he was relieved to hear Harry's voice again.

"Okay, I'm back. Please try to speak slowly and explain what happened."

"The guy was in the house when I arrived home from work. He had a rifle and I was afraid he would shoot me. He tied us up and put a note in front of me that asked what time Trudy would arrive home from work. Then he wrote another note on a piece of newspaper, which said I was to call you. The notes and his disguise convinced me that his intent was to kidnap Trudy. It has to be someone we both know, Harry, because he knows you and he was dressed to conceal his identity. Had on a ski mask and wore dark glasses under the ski mask to conceal his eyes. He was in our bedroom before I got home and cut out a piece of bed sheet that he used to tie Harvey and me up…"

"Harvey was with you?" Harry interrupted.

"Yes, Harvey came up to the house in the business van to pick up some advertising stuff that we had stored in the garage. After we loaded the stuff, I invited him in for a drink. We were both…"

"What did he say his intentions were and what did he sound like?"

"He never spoke, and that makes me all the more certain that he is someone I know and he was afraid I might recognize his voice. He just showed me the note asking about Trudy, and the note telling me to call you. Right after he finished tying me, and Harvey up, Trudy arrived home. I was on the kitchen floor when she came in and heard her say, "Honey, I'm home." But he had me lying face down on the floor and I couldn't see her because he put a pillowcase over my head. The guy had a gun and, and I couldn't warn her because I was sure that if I did he would shoot her or me. I heard her scream "Oh, My God, no, or Oh, God, no," when she came into the kitchen and not wanting her to get hurt, I told her not to resist and everything would be all right. He took her Harry! As soon as they left the house I managed to get hold of a kitchen knife and cut myself free. Then I cut Harvey loose and told him to go down to the road and look for any vehicles leaving the area. When Harvey went out, I immediately called you."

Harry Resnick felt as if he had been hit in the chest with a hammer and although portraying calmness, he was forced to take deep breaths to avoid collapsing. The impact of Trudy's reported abduction triggered panic that he knew had to be kept under control. "Roger," he calmly directed, "I want you to call the FBI immediately and report this. I know you are upset so make careful note of everything they tell you to do then, come to my house. I am going to call the State Police. I will do whatever I have to do to have Trudy returned home and avoid harm to her. Now make the call and get yourself over here."

"Okay," Roger dutifully responded. Then he asked, "Should I call or tell anyone else?"

"No, not yet. Just tell the FBI, then come over here."

Upon concluding his conversation with Roger, Harry called the home of his attorney Louis Berger. Lou was not home so he left a message asking that Lou come to his home when he received the message because of a most urgent matter. Then he dialed 0 and when the operator answered, asked to be connected with the state police. The nearest state police station, referred to as the Ellenville Barracks was located on Route 209, only a short distance from Ellenville; however, as it was a patrol station, the desk was not manned 24/7. When SP personnel were not in the station, dispatch was assigned from zone 3 headquarters located in Kingston, which was about 30 miles north of Ellenville. Harry Resnick's call was routed to the Kingston state police barracks, and after identifying himself and explaining his reason for calling, the trooper on desk advised that a patrol would be immediately dispatched to his home. Approximately 15 minutes later, a uniformed trooper arrived at the Resnick home and introduced himself as Trooper John Schetzel from the Ellenville barracks. Schetzel listened to Harry's summary of the telephone call he had received about a half-hour earlier from his son-in-law, made some notations in a notebook and explained that he would remain at the Resnick home for support and security until receiving new orders. The Resnick telephone commenced ringing at 6:45 p.m. Trooper Schetzel lifted an extension to his ear at the same moment Harry lifted the receiver of his home office phone.

Trying to sound calm, Harry answered, "Hello, this is Harry Resnick."

He was greeted by the voice of a male who spoke slowly and quietly. "I have your daughter. Is this call being recorded?"

"There is no recorder here," Harry responded. Trying to give the impression that he was unaware of Trudy's abduction, he added, "I don't know what you are talking about. You have to be kidding. Perhaps you are out of your mind."

"No," the caller hissed in a serious, threatening voice, "I am not out of my mind and I am not kidding. You had better get in your Rolls Royce and drive up to Sunset Drive, then you'll know this is no joke."

"I'll send a neighbor over there," Harry replied.

"Fine. Do you have any money?"

"I have a thousand or two thousand here at the house."

His answer was greeted by diabolical laughter.

"What do you want? What are you looking for in terms of money?" Harry asked.

"Listen carefully," the male voice whispered tersely in reply. "If you want to see your daughter again, you must do precisely as directed. We want one million in fifty and hundred denomination bills."

"Look, please don't harm my daughter. I can comply with your request but it will be difficult to get that much money together," Harry responded, trying to sound calm, despite the fact that his heart was pounding and his brain was awash with confusion.

"Contact your two brothers for assistance. You can negotiate with them to come up with the money. Transfer some funds."

"I have only one brother, my other brother passed away some time ago."

"Look, we want the million and understand that it will take some time. Listen carefully! You are not to call the police or FBI. If you do call the police we will know it because we have people watching your home and we have your telephone tapped. We know a lot about you. Your house is on top of the hill above Johnny's Shell station and the pay phone there is 9419."

"Okay, so how can I get in touch with you when I have the money?"

"We will call you tomorrow relative to future negotiation."

"What time should I expect your call tomorrow?" His question went unanswered, as the caller had terminated the call.

He turned to Trooper Schetzel and asked, "What do we do now?"

"Mr. Resnick, all you can do now is wait and let us do our investigation," Schetzel replied.

In conversation with state police detectives, arriving later that evening, Schetzel and Resnick agreed that the caller was quiet, articulate, soft-spoken, uttered no profanities, and seemed quite cool. Neither had heard any background noise during the call. Harry had tried to connect the caller's voice to someone known to him, but came up empty in that regard. After obtaining Harry's signature on a telephone eavesdropping consent form, an investigator connected a recorder to the Resnick phone line. When it was learned that family maid, Mary Gonzales, lived on the premises and had her own telephone, she was asked for consent and a recorder attached to her telephone as well. The Resnick home gradually took on the appearance of a police station, as uniformed police and detectives from the state police and FBI converged on the premises. The distraught parents would get no sleep that night, nor the following day as they waited anxiously for a return call from their daughter's abductors. As the hours dragged on without word of Trudy's fate, every ring of the phone was greeted with hope, only to be followed by despair when the caller proved to be a concerned relative or friend and not the kidnapper. Only those who have personally experienced the confusion, despair and hopelessness of waiting to learn the fate of an abducted loved one could imagine the ongoing emotions Harry and Marcia shared. As the seconds, minutes and hours ticked slowly by, with no word, they tried to busy themselves in conversation with the police massed around them. They kept apologizing – when no apology was needed – for being such poor hosts. During the night Harry and FBI agents discussed how the million dollars in ransom would be raised and how the money would be processed. Harry's attorney stayed through the night and agreed to aid Harry in getting the money together the next morning. Agents Steve Holbrook and Bruce Ponzio attached to the FBI's New York City office had arrived in Ellenville. During the early morning hours of May 25th, they accompanied Attorney Louis Berger in obtaining $1 million cash comprised of an almost equal quantity of one hundred and fifty dollar denomination bills. The group worked feverishly to photo copy the money and wrap it for placement in a package that would conceal a transponder. The ransom money was ready for delivery by noon. The agents also concealed a transponder in Harry's Rolls Royce, under the assumption that the vehicle would be used to make the ransom drop.

Twenty-nine hours would click slowly off the clock, before the kidnapper called again and this time the call was answered by, Roger Farber. He had gone to his in-laws home after reporting Trudy's abduction, and had remained there.

Police recorders hummed and an FBI agent picked up an extension at the same moment Roger lifted his receiver. Roger had answered several calls since the previous evening, and not knowing when the kidnapper would call, he had been prompted by the FBI to answer with a simple "Hello."

A recognizable male voice responded, "Is this Resnick?"

"No, this is Farber."

Upon hearing this response the caller terminated the call.

Roger slowly replaced the receiver in its cradle, then turned to on-looking police investigators and stated, "I think I recognize that voice."

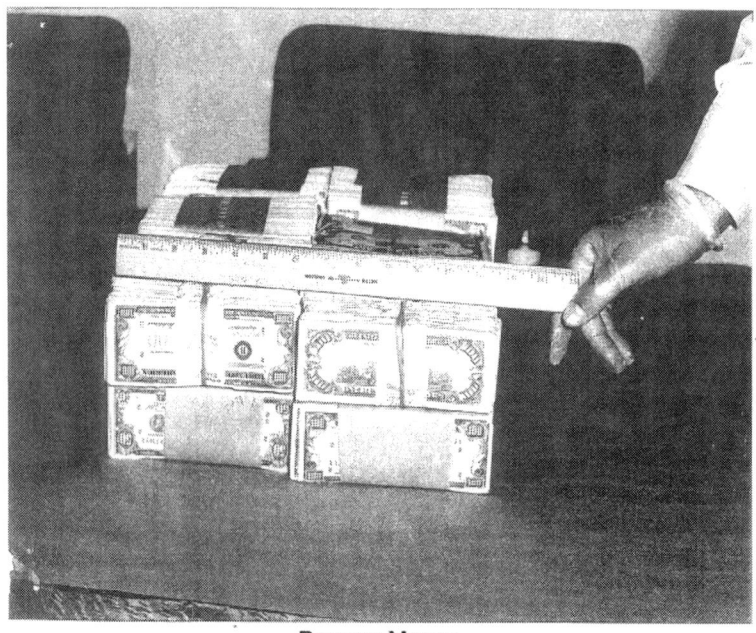

Ransom Money

8

The hours passed with no additional calls received from Trudy's kidnapper(s). Her location and fate remained unknown and police investigation thus far had failed to develop any suspects. At around 10:00 a.m. May 25th, the trooper working the desk at the Ferndale State Police barracks received a call from Harvey Kornblau, who asked to speak with the BCI. Unit supervisor Don Scherpf answered the page from the front desk and picked up his telephone.

"Mr. Kornblau, this is Don Scherpf. Do you have some information for us?"

"Just a hunch; well, more than a hunch really. I got a feeling that the person who took Trudy is Ron Krom."

"And who is Ron Krom? Please tell me more about him and why you believe it is him?"

"Well, Krom is about the same height and build as the man who tied 'us' up and took Trudy. He also wears glasses and Roger and I both know him and he knew that we would recognize his voice if he spoke and that is why he didn't say anything. Also, I know he had an argument with Roger and Trudy about five months ago about some sort of money deal. Roger told me that Trudy told him that Krom was weird and she was afraid of him. Roger also told me that he warned Krom not to bother his wife again, and that he didn't want anything to do with him. Roger can tell you more about that. Anyway, my gut feeling is that Krom was the guy in the house."

"We will ask Roger," Scherpf replied. "How old is Ron Krom?"

"I am pretty sure he is in his mid-twenties."

"Where does he live?"

"I'm not sure. You will have to ask Roger."

"How well do you know this Krom?"

"Not well, but I was introduced to him when he came into the store to speak with Roger, and he came in a couple of other times looking for Roger."

"Do you know what sort of vehicle he drives?"

"Yes, it's hard not to notice. He's got a reddish orange Corvette, and it's fairly new."

Scherpf thanked Harvey for the information and concluded his conversation with Kornblau. He then assigned Investigators Larry Topping and William Whalen on surveillance duty at the Resnick residence, to question Roger Farber who was at the residence, about Ron Krom.

"Yes, Harvey could be right." Roger responded after being told about his business partner's suspicion. "As I told the officer's at Harry's house last night, when I took that call, the voice asking for Harry sounded to me like Ron Krom's voice. I, too, immediately thought about Krom, but have been reluctant to tell anyone because he is crazy and I am afraid if he is holding Trudy, and you go looking for him, he will hurt or kill her."

"How do you know Ron Krom?" one of the investigators asked.

"Well, I first met Ron about 12 or 13 years ago. Harrison Krom, his father, had attended real estate school with my parents and they opened a Realty business together in 1970 or 71. We got to know each other through our parent's business relationship. I am a few years older than Ron and we lost touch after I went off to college and our parent's ended their business relationship. Then, a few months ago, Ron came into our Monticello store looking for money. He wanted me to become his business partner in operating a bar and wanted me to put up the money. I told him that I did not have any money to invest at the time and wasn't interested in owning a bar. I thought that was the end of that, but then a few weeks later, Trudy called me at work and I could tell she was upset. She told me Ron had called her and wanted her to convince me to put up the money for the bar. She told him that she did not get involved in my business and that she didn't want to be bothered about it. He responded by accusing her of being a spoiled, rich, stuck-up snob, disdainful of common folk like him. As you know, Trudy is a psychotherapist, and knows how to deal with angry people. She informed Ron that he was demonstrating inappropriate anger and needed to calm down. That made him flip out and she said he became irrational to the point of becoming threatening and incoherent, which caused her to terminate the call. Ron's call upset her so much, she felt the need to call and inform me that he frightened her and that I should be wary of him, as he was emotionally unstable. About a month later, Ron came into our store again and he seemed normal. He wanted to either rent or sell a billboard to me for advertising my business. I declined the offer and took the opportunity to ask him why he called my wife and upset her. He answered that he had only tried to conduct business and that Trudy must have misunderstood him and over-reacted to something he may have said. He invited me to look at his Corvette, and after that, he left and I haven't seen him again."

"Please describe Krom?" one of the investigators asked.

"Ron's about my height, six foot, but he's not as heavy as me. He wears glasses, the kind with the lenses that seem to change color in different light. His hair is about the same color as mine (brown) and it comes just over his ears. He also has a mustache that sort of resembles those of Mexican bandits seen on TV."

"Is he married?"

"No, and I think he still lives with his parents over in Grahamsville."

"Anything else you can tell us about him?"

"Well, he's always trying to make out he has some sort of big business deal in the works and that he is connected to important people. I think he has a vivid imagination and sometimes when carrying on a conversation – out of the clear blue sky - he says something totally out of perspective and inappropriate. He is quite soft-spoken and I don't think he has ever done anything criminal or violent but he is strange and oh, yes – I remember now – when he was in high school something happened and his parents had him committed to a mental hospital. He wasn't there long, though and I'm pretty sure he graduated from high school."

When the kidnapper aborted his second call into the Resnick home because Roger Farber had answered the telephone, the action was greeted with mixed emotion. On the plus side, they now had a suspect. On the down side, it was likely he would not call again decreasing the odds of Trudy's survival. Throughout the remainder of the night the gathering of police and family tried not to stare at the telephone, while hoping in their hearts that it would ring again. However, the night dragged on and the telephone remained silent. Investigators theorized that the lack of a return call indicated Roger and Harvey were probably correct in their assessment that the caller was Ronald Krom.

9

As an awakening sun began pushing away the darkness of night, with no word received as to Trudy's fate, Harry and Marcia were on the verge of mental and physical collapse. Family members and the police gathered around them offering words intended to provide optimism and bolster their morale; however, the words seemed hollow and without meaning. In truth, the investigators offering encouragement knew that as time passed without receiving a renewed ransom demand, any chance of rescuing Trudy diminished. By dawn, all concurred that a suspect had been identified and it was time to stop playing cat and mouse with him. BCI supervisor Don Scherpf passed the word that a briefing would take place in the Ferndale station at 7:30 a.m.

Tall, broad shouldered, physically imposing Senior Investigator Don Scherpf typified the men who enlisted in the New York State Police during the 1950's era. Despite having a tough, no nonsense reputation, in truth he was a gentle giant possessing a warm, likeable personality. He was highly regarded and respected by all who knew and worked with him.

Under normal circumstances, the Ferndale station was crowded and a beehive of activity but when a major crime was under investigation, the building seemed it would burst at the seams. Personnel from various police agencies and BCI investigators from other areas of the troop descended on the facility, with everyone eager to participate in solving the crime. Members of the Resnick family had reported Trudy's abduction to the State Police, FBI and Sullivan County Sheriffs Department, and representatives from those agencies were invited to the briefing. Sullivan County Sheriff Robert Flynn (a retired state police lieutenant), lacking manpower and resources to investigate a crime of this magnitude, readily acquiesced to the state police while offering limited assistance. On the other hand, the FBI was having pressure applied from a Resnick family member, politicians and influential citizens, to take charge of the investigation. Thus far, they had aided Harry Resnick in getting together the $1 million in ransom money, had the money under their control, and offered assistance where they could, but the state police were in charge of the investigation.

Before providing a summary of the briefing on the morning of May 26th, your author will digress to provide some interesting insight into the working relationship that existed between members of the state police and FBI during that era. Crimes having overlapping jurisdiction – meaning both federal and state statutes had been violated – resulted in an investigative response from the FBI and local police, each working within their established criteria to crack the case and bring the perpetrators to justice. Sometimes there was investigative harmony, but all too often a clash of strong egos, each ego desirous of recognition for breaking the case, and not troubled by taking credit for something the other agency did, fueled resentment and anger. There was a perception by some members of the FBI that they were superior to state and local police, and when they entered an investigation, the "locals" should acknowledge their superiority, and be relegated to roles of support. In contrast, there were members of the state police who felt the initials FBI stood for "Federal Bureau of Incompetence" and each could relate an instance where an FBI agent had "screwed up an investigation." In truth, a lot of the conflict resulted – not for the sake of P.R. - but a contrast in prescribed investigative procedures established as a result of federal or state court rulings determining how warrants would be executed, how evidence was to be gathered and how suspects were to be treated under federal law, as opposed to the requirements under state law. The differences were often quite profound and in many instances diametrically opposite to how each agency conducted business.

During mid-afternoon of the second day into the investigation, an FBI supervisor appeared at the Ferndale station and asked to speak with the Officer-in Charge. It is a certainty that the confident, vain G-man anticipated the state police would relinquish control of the investigation. However, he was probably unprepared for the possibility that he would confront a veteran state police officer having as strong an ego as his, and who held the FBI in contempt.

Their verbal exchange would remain etched in the memory of those who witnessed it, but propriety and the danger of damaging later prosecution dictated that nothing about the confrontation reflect on written record.

The state police lieutenant displayed a sardonic grin as he greeted, "I understand you want to speak with me."

Hostility recognized, the G-man responded with a stern look and asked, "Are you the officer in charge of the Trudy Farber investigation?"

"Why?" The lieutenant responded, then in expectation of receiving an answer he did not want to hear, folded his arms across his chest and assumed a defensive posture.

"Because members of the Resnick family have contacted our New York office insisting that we take the lead role in this matter," the FBI supervisor snapped in reply.

Jaw jutted forward, the lieutenant responded in a voice rife with sarcasm, "Is that a fact? Well, Harry Resnick seems perfectly satisfied with our handling of the case, and last I knew the criteria for turning kidnapping cases over to the Feds was passage of 24 hours, or reason to believe the victim or perpetrator had left the state." He pointed at the clock on the station wall and added, "Seems you are jumping the gun."

Face turning red, the G-man responded, "Look Lieutenant, I would also tell you that high ranking members of Congress have been putting pressure on the Director insisting that the FBI take charge of the investigation. I am sure that the Governor of New York, and State Police Superintendent would not want to alienate the Director of the FBI, or members of Congress. It would be in your best interest to cooperate and let us take charge of the investigation."

Face now white with anger, the lieutenant curtly responded, "In my best interest! My best interest is that you get to hell out of my station!"

The FBI supervisor angrily shot back, "How dare you speak to me in such a contemptible manner! I have the force and authority of the federal government behind me, and kidnapping is a federal crime! I am no longer asking you to turn over control of this investigation, I am ordering it!"

The Lieutenant angrily responded, "Your orders don't mean shit to me!" He pointed toward the door and commanded, "Get to hell out of here, before I throw you out!"

Although seething with rage, the FBI supervisor recognized that trying to force the issue at this time and in this place was a losing proposition. Deciding that discretion was better than valor, he responded, "Lieutenant you are making a big mistake." Then he turned and exited the building.

It is a certainty that telephone lines between high-ranking members of the FBI and New York State Police became very busy after the Ferndale incident. One can expect that the exchange of conversation was cordial but strained. Only those involved in the exchange remain privy to the details, which if known would make interesting reading. However, airing dirty laundry in public served no purpose and any such release was sure to sound a death knell to the career of the foolhardy whistleblower. Therefore, the conversations remained secret. In any event, cool heads prevailed and a compromise struck. FBI agents would continue to work alongside BCI investigators and after Trudy was found and the perpetrator(s) apprehended, the decision would be made as to whether to prosecute under federal or state statutes.

We return to the briefing of May 26th.

Seeming out of character for a man who smiled easily and often, Senior Investigator Scherpf greeted the gathering with a somber, sober face. "Good morning everyone. First a recap and then I will bring you up to date. As you know, Trudy Resnick Farber was abducted from her home in Sackett Lake at around 5:30 p.m. Tuesday." He held up a sheet of 8 x 11 copy paper bearing the victim's photograph and description then continued, "You should have received copy of her photo and description. If not, stop in my office and pick one up. A ransom demand for one million dollars was phoned into the Resnick home in Ellenville about one and one half hours after her abduction. It was left that Resnick would receive another call providing him the time and place of delivery. That call came into the Resnick home at eleven twenty-six last night and was answered by Roger Farber – the victim's husband. When Farber identified himself, the caller immediately terminated the call. Farber believes he recognized the voice of the caller as belonging to 25 year old Ronald Harrison Krom, who resides in Grahamsville. Earlier this morning I received a call from Harvey Kornblau who told me that he is convinced Trudy's abductor is Ronald Krom. Kornblau is coming into the station to provide a deposition explaining why he believes the perpetrator is Krom. No more ransom calls have come in and the victim's circumstance and fate remain unknown. We are now going to focus on finding Krom and hope that he leads us to the victim. Upon conclusion of this briefing, stop into my office to pick up a description of the suspect and you will be given your assignment. Any questions?"

Most of those gathered had obtained little sleep over the course of the prior two days and displayed signs of frustration and exhaustion, but as professionals they were determined to stay the course. They knew what needed to be done, and if they did have a question, kept it to themselves. Upon closing the briefing, Scherpf told Investigators Ralph Fuente and Jim Chandler that he wanted to see them in his office.

Veteran detectives Fuente and Chandler were muscular and nearly as tall as their supervisor, but when standing beside him, both seemed small in comparison. The investigators entered their boss's office carrying a cup of freshly brewed, strong coffee containing the caffeine that repressed exhaustion and kept their brains wired and ready for action.

Scherpf greeted the men with a nod. Then, immediately explained their assignment beginning his conversation by commending them. "I am giving this assignment to you because you are both excellent interrogators, noted for your expertise in getting confessions. It has been forty hours since Trudy Farber was taken from her home, gentlemen, and although Ron Krom has emerged as a suspect, at best, we have only circumstantial evidence. We know he owns a car that matches the description of a car seen in the vicinity of the crime and a 'gut' feeling by Farber and Kornblau that Krom is responsible. That suspicion doesn't add up to probable cause for his arrest. The lack of another call for ransom concerns me greatly. Either Farber's voice on the telephone spooked the scumbag or Trudy is dead. We can only hope that she is still alive and it was fear of recognition of his voice by her husband that prevents 'him' from calling again. We have got to locate Ron Krom and hope he either leads us to 'her' location, or confesses and takes us to her. I want you to go to Grahamsville, find Ron Krom, and use your expertise to get him to talk. I am assigning other teams to dig into Krom's background and find out everything about him and what makes him tick. If anything is learned that will aid you in questioning him, I will let you know. Gentlemen, we need to find Trudy A.S.A.P and if Krom is our guy, I am confident that you will find a way to crack him." Intentionally saving the hardest part of their assignment until last, Scherpf concluded, "and I want you to accomplish this without the feebs. You will have to duck them while finding and cracking Krom."

To lesser men it would seem their supervisor had just placed a huge burden on their shoulders; however, Scherpf, Fuente and Chandler were members of a semi-military organization that prided itself on excellence and were accustomed to dealing with pressure and overcoming odds to get the job done. The two knights in business suits were fully focused on rescuing a damsel in distress and capturing or slaying the dragon holding her.

10

Fuente had had previous dealings with Wayne Krom, the suspect's older brother, and had given him a break. Having dealt with Wayne, Fuente felt he might be cooperative and provide information helpful to the investigation, so the decision was made to locate Wayne Krom before moving on his brother. They located Wayne at Finch's Restaurant in Grahamsville, where he was having breakfast. After introducing his partner, Fuente informed Wayne that they were investigating the abduction of Trudy Farber, and were interested in speaking with Ron who might have information as to who might be responsible. They did not indicate their suspicion that Ron was directly responsible.

Although not as tall as his brother, 28year-old Wayne resembled Ron in having dark hair and brown eyes. "I believe Ron might be over at the office," he advised. By office he was referring to Green Hills Realty, the family business. "I'll take you over there."

Ron was not at Green Hills when they arrived; however, in looking around the office a photograph attached to the front of a refrigerator door caught the investigators attention. The photo depicted Ron standing beside an orange Chevrolet Corvette. Chandler pointed at the photo and asked, "That Ron?"

"Yeah," Wayne replied, "that's his car. He leased it from a dealer in New Jersey. It is a real eye-catcher."

"Where would we find Ron now?" Fuente asked.

"He's probably at the house. He works as a salesman here but he usually comes in late in the morning and then disappears for the rest of the day.

He isn't overly ambitious. I can give him a call and tell him to come down because you want to speak with him."

"Yes, that's fine." Fuente replied. "Give him a call but don't tell him we are here. If he knows anything about this it might upset him. Just ask him when he intends to come in to work."

Wayne called his parents home and learned that his brother had just awakened.

"Yeah, what's up?" he inquired still groggy from sleep.

"Are you coming into work today?" Wayne inquired.

"Why, do you need me?"

"Well, a couple of guys are here and they want to see you?"

"I don't have any appointments scheduled for today. Who are they and what do they want?"

"They're from the BCI, Ron, and they want to ask you some questions about a missing girl."

"Look, I just got up. Tell them I'll be down in about forty minutes. Ask them if they can wait that long?"

"Okay, Ron. See you later."

Upon cradling the telephone receiver Wayne turned his attention to the detectives and said, "Ron told me he just got out of bed and it will take him about forty minutes to get here. You want to wait?"

"Well, this is really an urgent matter that can't wait," Fuente responded, disgruntled that Wayne had revealed their identity. "If you give us directions, we could go up to your parents house and speak to him there."

"I can do better than that. They live up on Moore Hill Road and I can take you there in my car."

Fuente and Chandler pondered Wayne's offer for a moment and thought Why not. If we arrive at his house with his brother, it will be less threatening and he might be more cooperative. "Thanks we would appreciate that." Fuente replied. "Let's go."

During the short drive to the Krom home, Wayne asked the identity of the missing girl.

Assuming there was a possibility that he could be involved with Ronald in Trudy's abduction, Fuente was reluctant to provide him information. He responded, "Do you know Gertrude Farber?"

"Of course," Wayne responded, "she lived across the street from me when we were kids and I know her husband Roger, because his parents and my parents were involved in real estate together. Is Trudy the girl that's missing?"

"Yes," Fuente responded, immediately asking, "can you tell us anything that would help in locating her?"

"No," Wayne replied without making eye contact. He added, "I haven't seen Trudy in quite some time. I believe she and Roger live over around Monticello, and Roger manages the Radio Shack store in Monticello. Do you think my brother has something to do with Trudy being missing?"

Purposely avoiding providing Wayne any information that would give him cause to alert his brother, Fuente nonchalantly replied, "Well, apparently Ron has been trying to work some sort of business deal with Roger and we have some questions to ask him." Changing the focus of conversation, he asked Wayne in return, "Does Ron own or possess any guns?"

"We are here," Wayne responded, indicating they had arrived at his parent's home and then added, "Yeah, he has several rifles."

As Wayne pulled to a stop in his parents driveway the investigators attention was drawn to the orange Corvette parked in the open bay of a two-car garage. One of them opened his notebook and jotted down the New Jersey plate number on the car. Not wishing to appear aggressive or pushy, Fuente and Chandler agreed that they would remain outside while Wayne went into the house to get his brother. Within a minute, Wayne and Ron came out of the house together and approached the investigators who were examining the exterior of Ron's Corvette. Both detectives studied Ron as he walked toward them seemingly unconcerned. They noted that he was – as Roger and Harvey had indicated – about six feet tall, slender build and wore glasses. They would later agree that if not for his dark mustache and the beginning growth of a goatee, their suspect could easily be presumed - in physical appearance - to be a teenager. They also noted that he was not an imposing figure and spoke politely and in a soft voice.

As he drew near he asked, "Are you interested in my car?"

"As a matter of fact, if you are Ron Krom we are." Fuente responded.

"Yes, I am Ron. What did you wish to see me about?"

The size of both men and the fact that they were wearing dress slacks, dress shirts with tie and sport blazers readily identified them as police detectives, and would be confirmed when they produced state police identification. Fuente opened conversation, "Ron, Investigators Fuente and Chandler from state police Ferndale. We are investigating the kidnapping of Gertrude Farber and your name came up as a suspect. You drive an orange sporty looking car and a car of that description was observed parked near the victim's home when she was abducted. Also, the victim's husband, Roger Farber, told us that he recognized your voice on the phone when you called the Resnick home last night. You hung up when he identified himself. But, before I ask you any questions, I must advise you of certain rights. First, you have the right to remain…"

If Ron was upset or concerned about his situation, he did not physically or emotionally show it. He calmly interrupted Fuente and stated, "I know my rights. I could have been a lawyer."

"Never-the-less Ron, I am required to advise you that you have the right to remain silent. That should you give up the right to remain silent, anything you say can be used against you in a court of law. You have the right to consult an attorney before answering questions, and if you are unable to afford an attorney, one will be provided to represent you without charge. Do you understand these rights?"

"Sure, as I told you, I was going to law school and could have become a lawyer. I don't need a lawyer and am interested in helping you out. I might be able to help you find Trudy Farber." Having said this, he turned suddenly to his brother and screamed, "Why didn't you tell me the state police were looking for me and what did you bring them here for?" Not waiting for an answer, he turned and walked toward the house, entering his bedroom through a sliding glass door on the side of the house.

Startled and not knowing what their suspect was going to do, Fuente and Chandler followed after him and entered the bedroom right behind their quarry. They did not move to restrain him but cautiously watched as Ron went directly to a closet, opened it and reached in. As he did both detectives unfastened the safety straps that secured revolvers in their holsters, gripped the weapon and prepared to draw it if needed. Their tension eased somewhat when - rather than a weapon - Ron produced a small toy safe from the confines of the closet. However, not knowing what he intended to take out of the safe caused both detectives to keep their hand on the grip of their weapons. The safe appeared too small to conceal a weapon, and curious as to its contents the detectives remained wary. They made no move to restrain Ron thinking that he might have something in the safe pertaining to the crime and he was about to give it to them.

Ron removed a small piece of paper from the safe, looked at it and began cursing. "Damned plans were all screwed up. I tried to tell the bastards but they wouldn't listen." He placed the paper back in the safe, turned to the detectives and said, "Look, I work for the fucking CIA. If you don't believe me, you can contact Donovan in CIA headquarters in Washington. Of course the son-of-a-bitch probably won't tell you shit. Everything is very secret with those assholes, and wouldn't bother them in the least to hang me out to dry."

Fuente and Chandler exchanged puzzled, confused looks and Fuente responded, "Ron, what has all that to do with the kidnapping of Trudy Farber?"

Ron did not respond and startled them by dashing back out the sliding glass door and running toward the garage. Both investigators immediately gave chase. Ron ran into the garage, got into his Corvette and started to back it out of the garage. Both investigators came to a running halt behind the Corvette, stood in the garage door to block the car's exit and shouted for him to stop.

"Get to hell out of the way," he shouted in reply, "or I will run you over!"

Fuente held his position while Chandler ran up beside the car, reached in the open driver's window and removed the keys from the car's ignition.

Ron made no move to physically resist and responded by getting out of the car and starting to walk away.

However, Fuente blocked his path preventing him from leaving the garage and in a forceful voice stated, "Ron cut the shit. We are willing to work with you but we've got to find Trudy. You said you might be able to help find her. We want that help. Now let's do it. Where is she?"

"Okay, I can help you find her but before I do, Resnick will have to give me three hundred thousand dollars, and another hundred thousand for Roger Farber. You see, Roger needs money and he planned the kidnapping of his wife, because he really doesn't give a shit about her. He knew I worked for the CIA when I was attending Vassar and that I was let go when I called Nixon a crook. He was guilty as shit but he didn't go to jail and because I complained his honchos kicked me out. But while I was an agent, I learned a lot of secret - how to - stuff and Roger needed someone with my talent to pull it off for him."

The veteran detectives were accustomed to dealing with suspects exhibiting bizarre psychological behavior – sometimes legitimate, more often contrived to minimize responsibility – and wisely did not challenge Ron's illusions, instead ignoring them to address the issue at hand. "Ron, where is Trudy?" Fuente responded.

"I will need the money first, three hundred thousand for me and a hundred thousand for Roger. I am sure Harry Resnick can afford that to get his daughter."

"Ron, do you know her location and is she safe?"

"I believe she is safe and someone is watching over her."

"Ron, we will work on getting the money, but we need your help in gaining Trudy's release. Where is she being held? Where can we find her?"

Calm and seemingly unperturbed by his untenable situation, Ron quietly replied, "I am quite adept at poker, gentlemen and know when to call a bluff. Although I hold the winning hand, if I tell you where she is it won't be worth shit and I will get nothing. If Harry wants to see his precious Trudy again, he will have to pay. I want him to pay for shitting on me, and my family, for five years. You know I wasn't invited to Trudy's grand wedding because 'they' looked upon me as a loser and nobody, and that caused my girlfriend to leave me. My uncle lost his job when Channel Master closed down and moneybags

Harry could give a shit less. Now it is get even time and Harry can pay up or forget about seeing his precious daughter again."

Ron's sudden venting of frustration triggered Fuente to ask a question that might result in obtaining a motive for the kidnapping. "Sounds like you took Trudy because you are angry with the treatment you and your family received from the Resnick family. Is that why you took her?"

"I didn't say I took her!" Ron snapped in reply. "Roger doesn't give a shit about his wife and wants his father-in-laws money. I helped him plan this for five years. I don't give a shit about anything but the money. You get a hold of Harry and tell him I can help if he pays. You don't have to worry about Trudy because Roger knows where she is. She could be sitting in an air-conditioned room right now eating chicken and watching television. You tell Harry to pay the money, then I will confront Roger and make him tell where his wife is."

"Okay then. Ron, we would ask that you accompany us to the Ferndale station where we will reach out to Harry Resnick and let him know your demand." Fuente replied, adding, "It will be easier to convince Mr. Resnick to come into the station to meet with you. I'm sure you won't mind that, and if Mr. Resnick declines to come in, we'll bring you home."

"Well ah, yeah, ah, I guess so." Ron replied.

The short return drive to the real estate office was made in silence as the investigators wanted to let Ron ponder his situation, and as he was angry with his brother, he had nothing to say to him. After transferring Ron to the BCI car, one of the investigators advised, "Ron, Roger called the FBI and there are 75 FBI agents scouring the area looking for Trudy. They are eager to grab a piece of your ass and aren't going to buy your allegation that Roger is behind his wife's kidnapping. We can believe it though and are willing to listen, but we need to locate Trudy and make sure she is all right. Think about your situation and when we get to our office, we'll do our best to work with you, but you've got to help us out."

11

When they arrived at the state police station Ron was escorted to the station interview room for continued interrogation. One of the detectives invited, "Have a seat and make yourself comfortable. Feel free to smoke and if you would like I can get you a cup of coffee or a soda."

Ron stared curiously at the two tall men and responded, "I don't smoke. It's bad for your health. As a trained CIA agent I am fully acquainted with interrogation tactics and know how witnesses are unwittingly drugged. No thanks, I don't need anything at the moment."

Both detectives smiled at Ron's paranoia and Fuente flashed him a smile of assurance as he stated, "I assure you we do not use drugs, make threats, or use force to get at the truth. We just want to get Trudy, Ron, and you have already indicated that you can help us in that regard. So help us, while at the same time helping yourself; tell us where we can find her."

"I previously stipulated the conditions." Ron answered. "Get Harry Resnick in here to speak with me. When he pays the money to me and Roger, I will tell you her location."

"We will call him, Ron, but it will be necessary to convince him that you are part of the plot and can lead us to his daughter, or he isn't going to pay you any money. What should we tell him that will convince him you can do this?"

Ron smiled as he responded, "Tell Resnick that I am the one who called and asked for a million dollars ransom to be paid in fifties and hundreds. Ask him if he remembers that I told him to contact his brothers and have them liquidate assets to raise the money. Tell him that I am the one who called his house last night and spoke to Roger Farber. Tell him that I hung up because it was obvious that Roger was pulling some sort of shit on me. Tell him that I want to know how police got involved when I told him not to contact them. Tell him that his daughter is fine and Roger knows where she is. Tell him…better yet, take me up to Resnick's place and I will tell him myself."

"We cannot do that Ron; however, we will give Mr. Resnick a call and ask him to come down to the Ferndale station to see you."

"He will be shocked to learn that his son-in-law has been planning this for three years. You know Roger could tell you where she is why don't you ask him?"

"We will deal with Roger, but we need to speak with Trudy, and you know where she is. How about it Ron? Where is she?"

Folding his arms across his chest Ron answered, "Not until I speak with Harry Resnick."

"Okay, I'll give Mr. Resnick a call and see if I can convince him to come here." Fuente replied, and then left the room.

Investigator Chandler encouraged, "It won't be long before we know Mr. Resnick's answer, but in the meantime we can chat about your relationship with Roger Farber. Tell me how this kidnapping scheme came about?"

Ron did not immediately respond and as he pondered the question, his eyes and body language seemed to reveal he was searching for a believable plot. He would prove adept at creating a scenario to match any and every troublesome question or situation. After examining his hands and looking around the room he began, "We – Roger and me – started planning this about three years ago. Started even before he married Trudy. Roger said it would be an easy way to get some of Resnick's money. It took a long time to plan it out because we had to make sure that no one would ever know that Roger was involved. How do you think it was so easy for me to get into the house? I cut the screen in a back window that Roger left open for me. It was all prearranged. I didn't hurt her and hurting her was not part of the plan. Yeah, she's alive and well and probably eating chicken in a motel room and watching television. Roger knows where she is."

"Okay, I can buy that Ron, but you also know where she is. Every moment that passes without us finding her makes it more difficult for you, now I need to know where she is."

"Where is Resnick? No deal unless I get the money. I guess he isn't going to show, so I guess I will be going now." Then he arose from his chair.

Chandler faced him and displaying a stern look firmly stated, "You are not going anywhere! You are now under arrest for the kidnapping of Trudy Farber!"

The look the detective gave him made it clear that fabrication and bullshit were no longer going to buy him time nor produce any money. He responded, "If that's the case, I want to speak to my attorney."

"Who is your attorney?" Chandler snapped in reply.

"Barry Martin. I want to speak with Barry Martin, he is my family attorney."

"Come with me." Chandler directed. He led Ron into one of the BCI offices pointed to a telephone and invited him to use it to call his attorney.

Barry Martin was a well-known attorney with office located in Monticello. Barry, as, he was referred to by Ron, had performed legal work for Harrison Krom, Ron's dad. Martin agreed to come to the Ferndale station. He arrived about a half hour later, spoke briefly with Ron, and then excused himself to speak with the investigators. After learning the details of the kidnapping and his client's admissions to the detectives, he decided to call Harrison Krom before deciding that he would represent Ron. Harrison refused to pay the retainer demanded by Martin in order to have him take the case, and informed the attorney that his son was old enough to stand up for himself. Upon completion of his telephone conversation with Harrison Krom, Martin informed Ron that he would not represent him without receiving a retainer. Ron was unable to put up the money required, so Martin advised him to request legal aid. Martin then left the station. While Ron sat in the interview room pondering what to do about legal representation, a trooper appeared with a gift of hamburger, French fries and milkshake purchased at the local McDonalds. Fuente and Chandler re-entered the room after delivery of the food.

Fuente smiled and opened, "We thought you might be getting hungry. How's the stuff from McDonald's?"

A full mouth made his response sound garbled. "Danks, it's goo."

Fuente continued, "Martin told us that he won't represent you. Is there another lawyer that you would like to call?"

Ron swallowed, wiped his mouth with the back of his hand and responded, "I don't need a high-priced mouthpiece, and I don't want some flunky from legal aid. I will represent myself."

"Okay Ron, I would point out that the best thing you can do for yourself is tell us where Trudy is. The District Attorney will take into consideration your cooperation and it will work favorably for you. So do yourself a favor and tell us where she is."

Ron gave his inquisitor a smug look and responded, "Here is the way it is: I want one million dollars from Harry Resnick, and a promise from the district attorney that he will let me cop a plea to a reduced charge in return for telling you where to find Trudy. Let me see Resnick, personally talk to him, and I will surprise everybody. I want to talk to the D.A. and have him give me a typewritten agreement that I will be given consideration for my cooperation. Those are my terms!"

"We have spoken with Mr. Resnick, and he is coming to the station," Fuente replied. "Also, District Attorney Gellman is here and we will see if he wants to speak with you." As Fuente addressed Krom, Chandler left the room and returned accompanied by Sullivan County District Attorney Emmanuel Gellman, who had been summoned to the police station and was standing by for just such legal decision.

"Hello Ron," the young attorney greeted. "I understand you are willing to tell the investigators the whereabouts of Trudy Farber in return for consideration from our office. We can discuss terms but first I am going to again advise you of your Miranda rights."

Ron displayed a bemused smile and studied the young attorney reading him his rights. When he concluded Ron responded, "I could have been an attorney and am fully aware of my rights. Now what are you prepared to offer for the safe return of Trudy Farber?"

"Our office will recommend to the court that you not get a maximum sentence."

"That is not good enough. In order for me to tell you her whereabouts, you must agree to release me without placement of criminal charges."

The District Attorney shook his head in the negative as he responded. "That is not a possibility and out of the question. If you want to be given consideration at sentencing you will cooperate and tell these gentlemen where they can find Trudy. If not, I assure you that our office will prosecute you to the fullest extent of the law and insist that you be given the maximum sentence. Now what is your decision?"

"A contract. You are an attorney and know that a contract is a binding document. Give me a legal pad and I will write out a contract of agreement. If you agree to my terms, I can help you find her."

Wrinkling his brow and tilting his head, Gellman silently studied Ron with a look of curiosity and finally replied, "What terms are you setting forth in this contract?"

"I want three hundred thousand from Harry Resnick and, in exchange, I will tell you where to look for Trudy."

"You can write out your contract but that would be something Mr. Resnick would have to agree to, not the District Attorney's office."

Ron smiled at Gellman and answered, "While I am writing out the contract, you can convince Harry to come here and sign it. If he wants to see his precious daughter again, he will be happy to sign it."

Gellman gave Ron a return smile and directed, "You write out your contract and I will give Mr. Resnick a call." Then he gave a nod to the investigators indicating that he wanted to speak with them outside the room. After exiting the room, he shook his head from side to side while speaking. "That asshole is not working with a full deck gentlemen. We can let him prepare his contract with any terms he wants and sign it, because a contract signed under duress isn't worth crap. If it makes him give up Mrs. Farber's location we'll give him his contract and he can wipe his ass with it later. I will give Mr. Resnick a call and ask him to come here, and if he agrees, I suggest we let him speak with the defendant and play along with his terms."

Krom had now been at the state police station for about seven hours and although frustrated, the two veteran investigators were confident that given more time they would get him to crack and give up Trudy's location. As they stood in the hallway discussing strategy they, were joined by Senior Investigator Scherpf.

"Gellman is using my phone to call Resnick," he advised. Then in a disgusted tone of voice he added, "The Major called from troop headquarters. We have been directed to permit the FBI access to Krom. It is still our case, though and we are taking the lead. Agent Leo McGillicuddy is here from the New York office of the FBI and will be joining you. Do you think his appearance will spook Krom?"

Fuente and Chandler were astute enough to recognize that their boss had no choice in the decision to involve the FBI, and as both appreciated rapport between the two agencies, their response was, "No, boss. If he starts throwing his weight around or gets out of line, we'll send him packing," Chandler added. "I think Harry Resnick is the key that will get him to reveal 'her' location. This guy is so loony-tunes he believes in his mind that Resnick will give him the money and he will get to keep it. We'll introduce the 'feeb' and make it clear to Ron that he was called by the Resnick family and only wants to help them."

Scherpf smiled and replied, "I have the utmost confidence in you both and know that you will keep his Irish reined in."

Shortly before six in the evening, Investigators Fuente and Chandler re-entered the station interview room accompanied by FBI SA Leo McGillicuddy.

Ron gave the G-man a curious look as he was introduced but the look quickly changed to a confident smile as McGillicuddy insisted on once again providing him his Miranda Rights. His schizophrenic mind was busy creating a delusion that the gullible-appearing federal agent would believe, and why not, for once said, Ron would believe it himself.

McGillicuddy displayed a warm friendly smile, as he asked, "Mr. Krom, do you fully understand these rights I have explained to you?"

"Of course," Ron answered, smiling in return. "As I told Ralph and Jim, I took law and could have been a lawyer if I wanted to. That's why – at the moment – I am representing myself. I'm also quite familiar with the interrogation tactics used by the FBI because I was subjected to that while I was in the CIA. We had to be prepared you know, in case we were captured by the enemy. When I got the goods on Nixon, the FBI protected him and I had to get out or risk getting killed. So Agent McGillicuddy, are you going to give me some sort of truth serum or are you a hypnotist?"

Smiling convincingly, McGillicuddy replied, "Mr. Krom, you have nothing to fear from me. However, I want you to know that kidnapping is a very serious federal offense, presenting the possibility of a life sentence upon conviction. That is why it is very important to your future that you cooperate and tell us where Trudy Farber is. Cooperation is the key to a favorable sentence by the court."

"Ron motioned toward the state police investigators as he responded, "Like I told them, this was Roger Farber's idea. He needs money and knew he could get it from his wife's old man. He asked me to help because of my CIA training. I can help you find her but not until I speak with Harry Resnick, have a guarantee of getting released on bail, legal expenses paid and provided a cash reserve. Look, I wrote out a contract. Resnick needs to sign it to have me show you where Trudy is being held. No contract, no deal."

May 26th, 8:00 p.m. A distraught but determined Harry Resnick entered the interview room and gazed upon his daughter's abductor for the first time. He fought against any display of hatred and anger and calmly stated, "Mr. Krom, I want my daughter back and I will offer any assistance necessary to accomplish this. What must I do to have you tell where my daughter is being held?"

Ron seemed bemused that powerful millionaire Harry Resnick now stood before him, humble, and ready to acquiesce to his demands. He savored having this moment of personal power over the wealthy, influential business owner and stared at Harry with an inquisitive smile as he stated, "Mr. Resnick are you aware that your son-in-law is behind the kidnapping of your daughter?"

If by this statement Krom hoped to confuse and upset Harry to make him more vulnerable it did not reflect on his face or in his response. "I have been advised of your allegations about Roger and I will deal with that later," he replied in a calm voice. "All I care about at this time is having my daughter returned. If it is proven that Roger is involved – as you claim he is – I will deal with that later. Right now, I would offer him the same assistance that I am willing to offer you to have Trudy returned. So what is it you want from me?"

"I want $400,000 dollars, and another $100,000 for Roger."

Fuente interceded before Resnick could reply, stating, "Ron, that is not what this contract that you wrote out calls for. You keep changing…"

"Investigator," Harry Resnick interrupted, "I am prepared to meet his demand for this amount of money if it means my daughter is returned. Mr. Krom, if you take these gentlemen to my daughter, I will pay what you ask."

May 26th, 8:45 p.m. Ron suddenly arose from his chair in the small interview room and blurted out, "Let's go, I'll take you there."

It had taken almost nine hours of interrogation to get Ron to this point and the appearance of the victim's father had accomplished that which hours of psychological combat had been unable to do. Yet realizing that Ron had been diagnosed as a delusional schizophrenic, capable of surprise behavior, the experienced detectives were wary that he may not intend to take them to the victim but was pulling some sort of ruse to get away or stall for time. However, they were not about to waste the opportunity. "You have made the right decision Ron." Fuente replied. "Jim, Agent McGillicuddy and myself will go with you and this had better be for real. If you are pulling any bullshit, all deals are off and you can forget about getting any money." Then turning his attention to Harry Resnick he stated, "Mr. Resnick, would you like to wait here at the station or go home and await our call?"

"I will wait here and pray that my daughter is alive and has been unharmed."

12

May 26th, 9:15 p.m. The Catskill Mountains were enveloped in darkness and anticipating their need, the three detectives brought along powerful flashlights. Krom was directed to Chandler's unmarked bureau car and placed in the rear seat. Fuente sat beside him and Agent McGillicuddy joined Chandler in the front. Before leaving the station parking lot, Chandler asked, "Okay, where to Ron?"

Krom responded, "Go to Grahamsville, and head into Ulster County on fifty-five. I'll tell you when to turn after you go across the county line."

During daylight the stretch of state route 55 that paralleled the south shore of the Rondout Reservoir was a beautiful but lonely stretch of highway that attracted tourists, hunters and fishermen. Forested mountainside teeming with deer and black bear bordered the south side of the highway and stately trees protected the steep bank separating highway and reservoir from erosion. Only non-power watercraft were allowed on the waters of the reservoir and then only by special permit issued by the New York City Water Authority. Infrequent pull-offs and parking areas along the north side of the highway provided travelers a place to leave their vehicles while enjoying the beauty of the area. A proliferation of deer constantly crossing the highway presented a constant hazard to motorists, especially at night, as they suddenly bolted from the forest on both sides of the highway. The pristine, clear blue body of water stretching eight miles between the Village of Grahamsville on the west end and Hamlet of Lackawack at the east end was magnificent to behold. Despite its size, the Rondout is actually one of the smallest of the six

Catskill/Delaware Reservoirs providing water to New York City. Begun in 1905, these reservoirs are considered one of the greatest public works projects and civil engineering marvels of all time. Most people would be surprised to learn that New York City's water travels hundreds of miles through a series of aqueducts and is constantly monitored and tested for purity.

On the evening of May 26, 1977, the history and beauty of the reservoir was far removed from the minds of the four occupants of the State Police bureau car driving along its shore. The experienced detectives had an ominous dread that Trudy would not be found alive.

The detectives thought it bizarre that after holding out for nearly nine hours, Ron now seemed eager to take them to Trudy. During the twenty-thirty minute ride he talked freely about the crime, repeating much of what he had already related to the investigators. "You know Roger Farber could have told you where his wife is. How do you think I knew which screen to cut and which window would be open? When I arrived at his house, the window was open like he said it would be."

Knowing how desolate the area Ron was taking them into was, Chandler asked, "Ron, are we going to find Trudy alive?"

"You will find her scared and a little dirty, but she should be fine. She will be really upset when she finds out Roger is responsible for what happened to her." As he spoke these words, they entered Ulster County-prompting Ron to call out, "Slow down, it's just a little way(s). As soon as you go by South Hill Road, take the next dirt road that goes into the woods. Drive up the hill to where the road forks, then stop; we will have to walk a short distance to where she is. Here, turn here and go slow because it is very rough."

Chandler turned onto the dirt path that seemed more a logging trail than a road and was grateful that after driving about a quarter of a mile the road ended.

"Here," Ron directed, "stop here and we walk the rest of the way."

Surrounded by darkness and trees caused Jim to ask, "What made you chose this location?"

Ron nonchalantly replied. "This property belonged to my parents and Roger Farber's mother until about six weeks ago, when I sold it to an out of town buyer," Not waiting for a response, he jumped out of the car and without the aid of a flashlight, dashed up the steep incline calling out as he ran, "Come on, she's right up here."

Aided by the beam of their flashlights, the three detectives hurried up the hill behind him. For a moment it crossed their minds that Ron had brought them here on a ruse and was attempting to flee; however, the chase ended on a level patch of ground about seventy-five yards from where the car was parked. Their flashlights illuminated Ron standing still and pointing at the ground.

"Here! She's here!" He called, then stooped and used his hands to sweep away leaves that concealed a sheet of plywood appearing to be a cover over a hole in the ground. The sheet of wood was held in place by an iron bar inserted in hasps and locked with a padlock. Ominously, no sound emitted from below the cover in response to Ron's loud cry. "Give me a flashlight," he directed, "and I will unlock the padlock."

One of the detectives handed over his light and Ron immediately directed the light's beam onto a nearby rock. Reaching down, he lifted the rock and retrieved a key from beneath it. Then he used the key to unlock the padlock. After removing the lock, he slid the iron bar out of the hasps that secured it and opened the trap door.

The beams from three flashlights were directed inside the hole, illuminating the specter of horrific death!

Darkness hid the look of panic on Ron's face as he realized Trudy was dead "Aggh!" he choked and gagged, trying to keep down stomach contents that demanded expulsion.

The three veteran police detectives, who had confronted many different faces of death during the course of their careers, were stunned and horrified by the scene portrayed below their feet. It is likely all three felt a cold shiver run up his spine as they studied the scene in silence. Trudy's wide-open blue eyes stared up at them from a distorted face frozen in terror. Although on her back, the grave was too small for stretching out, causing her to be cramped into a fetal position. It was immediately obvious that she had fought desperately to escape her tomb. Her clenched hands were locked in an upright position, above her shoulders, giving the appearance that even in death she fought the cover that imprisoned her. Torn fingernails and readily noticeable abrasions on her hands and fingers were further evidence of her desperate struggle.

Overcome by revulsion and panicked by the sudden realization of what he had done, Ron continued gagging and choking; then, suddenly he turned away and ran towards the log that hid his rifle. Whether intending to shoot himself, or the detectives would remain open to conjecture, for as he grabbed the rifle, Investigator Chandler hit him with a body block knocking him to the ground. Consumed by panic and fear Ron squealed, screamed and fought to escape; however, the sound he emitted came out in a high-pitched screech.

Chandler quickly overpowered the panic stricken kidnapper responsible for brutally taking his victim's life. When subdued, he forced Ron to put his hands behind his back and secured his wrists with handcuffs.

Having observed the death mask of suffering and horror on Trudy's face Chandler now felt utter contempt for her tall, slender killer. "Stop struggling asshole," he hissed, "or I will put you in that hole and seal you in. You are now under arrest for Murder, and I hope 'they' lock you in a cell and throw the key away!"

13

"Ferndale on F161," the Ferndale state police dispatcher responded. He recognized the voice on the radio as that of BCI Investigator Ralph Fuente.

"One-six-one Ferndale, ask Senor Investigator Scherpf to come to the radio."

"Stand by one-six-one."

After a short pause the big Senior Investigator's powerful voice boomed out, "Ferndale to one-six-one, this is Scherpf."

"Ferndale, we have located the victim and will need the Coroner and someone from the I.D. Bureau."

"Received one-six-one; what is your location?"

"We are in the woods, a short distance off fifty-five on the south side of Rondout Reservoir. We are about a half-mile into Ulster County. We will light a flare and place it at the turn-off on fifty-five."

"Received one-six-one. Will have required personnel respond A.S.A.P. Do you require anything else?"

"Not at this time, Ferndale."

Scherpf displayed a solemn look as he walked down the hallway separating dispatch from the BCI offices, dreading having to inform Harry Resnick that his daughter was dead.

Investigator Chandler grasped the now quiet and compliant defendant by one arm and pulled him down the path to the BCI car.

This man who had dashed up the path in total darkness only short minutes previous, now stumbled over the same path and whined, "I didn't think this would happen. I only wanted to make her suffer a little before she went home."

"Shut up!" Chandler commanded. "We will talk about it later. Right now, I am pissed and don't want to listen to your whining."

Shortly after the radio conversation, various police personnel from Ferndale, Ellenville and Middletown commenced arriving at the crime scene. All who gazed at the ghastly scene that night would forever carry etched in their mind this brief introspection of hell.

Ron was driven back to the Ferndale station by uniform troopers and made the trip in silence. On arrival at the station he was escorted to the interview room and directed to sit in the same chair he had previously occupied for most of the day. Fuente, Chandler and Agent McGillicuddy soon joined him in the room. None of the three were men to be trifled with; however, all were astute interrogators and recognized that this was a time to conceal their contempt for Ron, as a pretense of understanding and compassion could result in a truthful confession. They also knew Ron had been diagnosed as a schizophrenic and was quite capable of manufacturing a tale that – once told – he would believe as true. They would focus on trying to obtain details that could later be proved or disproved by witnesses and evidence.

Chandler forced a warm smile and spoke in a quiet friendly tone of voice. "Ron, you have been provided your Miranda Rights, and told us that you understand them and would represent yourself. Is that still your choice?"

"Yeah, I guess so," Ron meekly replied, then asked, "What's going to happen to me now?"

"That will be up to the District Attorney and court. We have a rock solid case against you, Ron, and the only thing you can do to lessen the severity of your sentence is cooperate. We need to know what really happened, Ron. We can understand taking Trudy to get money, but why did you bury her in that hole?"

During his return ride to the station Ron had created the answers to the questions he anticipated being asked. The answer was obvious and would diminish his culpability in Trudy's death. "Look, like I told you," he began, sounding sincere because in his mental state he probably believed it true, "this was Roger's idea. He has been planning this for five years, even before he married Trudy. I showed him the hole while we were hunting and when I told him I had dug it for the purpose of someday kidnapping someone, he suggested that I should take Trudy, and it would be easy because he would help me. I wasn't too keen on the idea but when he told me how easy it would be and how much money we could get from Harry, I agreed to do it. We planned it for a long time. After I dug the hole, I slept in it one night to see if it was big enough to hold someone. It took me longer to build the cover than it did to dig the hole. We just wanted to get Harry to pay and didn't intend to hurt her. If you check the cover, you will find holes that I shot through it to let air in. Like I said, this was really Roger's idea and he left the window open for me so that all I had to do was cut the screen to get in."

"Ron, that doesn't make sense. If Roger planned to have you tie him up so as to convince his wife he was also a victim, why would he involve Harvey?"

"Roger is smart, and he thought having Harvey there would be even more convincing."

"Okay, but what if Harvey had resisted? Were you prepared to shoot him?"

"Ah, well, maybe Harvey was in on it with Roger. He didn't tell me that Harvey would be there, but Harvey didn't do anything."

"Yes, but what if he had? If he had tried to grab your rifle or fight with you, would you have shot him?"

"Well, if he tried to get physical, I suppose I would, but I'm pretty sure he was in on the plan with Roger, because he didn't try nothing."

"What time did you arrive at the Farber home?"

"It was about two-thirty."

"What were you driving when you went to take Trudy?"

"I was afraid that my 'vette would be too noticeable, so I borrowed a friend's car."

"Please describe the car and give us the name of your friend?"

"It's a Firebird, almost the same color as my 'vette. It belongs to John Rogers, and it is his second car. I tried to borrow his Cadillac but his wife was using it, so he let me take the Firebird."

"Where does John live?"

"Most everybody knows John. He is the owner of Rogers Realty located up - just outside of Woodstock. We have been friends for a while. He let me borrow his car and I left my 'vette with him. I returned his car that night."

"Where did you park the car when you went to the Farber house?"

"On the side of the road up there – out of sight of the house. I think the road name has Sun in it."

"What were you wearing when you went to the Farber home?"

"Just some old clothes and (pointing to the jacket he was wearing) this coat."

"What were you wearing on your feet?"

Ron responded with a one word reply, "These," and pointed to the green athletic shoes on his feet.

"We know you wore a mask and gloves, Ron. Describe them and tell us where they are now."

"Well, it was part of the plan. We had to make it look like I was a stranger in order to pull it off. So, I wore a ski mask and a pair of light work gloves." Anticipating that he would be asked their disposition, he added, "I stashed them in a metal box up in the woods near where you found her."

"Why did you remove pillowcases from the bed and cut the bed sheet? What did you intend to do with those?"

"Roger told me to make the house look as if someone had broken in looking for valuables, and I used a piece of sheet to tie Trudy's hands and I put a pillow case over her head so she wouldn't see my face when I took the mask off."

"What about the rifle? Where did you get it?"

"I purchased it from Woolworth's in Middletown about two weeks ago."

"Why did you leave the rifle behind that log?"

"I don't know. I guess I thought it might come in handy in case I needed it."

"Was this the same gun that you had at the Farber house?"

"Yeah."

"What did you intend to do with the gun after you grabbed it tonight from its hiding place?"

"Ah, I don't know. I freaked out when I saw her – Trudy – and wasn't thinking too clearly. I probably wouldn't have hurt anybody. I just knew I had to get away."

"Did you shoot Trudy?"

"No way! Like I said 'we' didn't intend to hurt her. I only shot holes in the cover so she could get air."

"What did you do to Trudy after you took her from her home?"

"I took her to the car, put her in the trunk and drove right up to Grahamsville. I didn't touch her sexually – if that is what you are inferring."

"Ron, after you tied Roger up, you showed him a typewritten note. What did the note say?"

"It just asked what time his wife got home from work."

"Did you type this note?"

"Yeah. I typed it out on our typewriter in the real estate office."

"If Roger was part of the plan to kidnap his wife, why was it necessary to show him a note asking what time his wife got home from work?"

"Ah, well, it was intended to add credibility to a stranger taking her."

"Why did you throw kitchen knifes at the cupboard doors before taking Trudy out of the house?"

"I wanted to scare her so she would know I meant business and wouldn't resist."

"How did you think that Trudy would survive any period of time in that dark, tiny hole?"

"Well, I went back the next day to check on her and tried to get her to eat a peanut butter sandwich and drink some milk, but she wouldn't take them. I didn't think she would be in there too long because Roger said that

Harry would pay the ransom without calling the police. If he had paid and not gotten the police involved, she would have been released."

"When did you return Roger's Firebird?"

"Late that night. After leaving Grahamsville, I drove up to Woodstock to swap cars back but John was out with my 'vette. I drove around for a while looking for him until I got tired; then I slept in the car for a little bit. Some cops checked me out while I was parked alongside the road, but they didn't give me a ticket or nothing, just told me that I couldn't sleep parked on the road. So I went over to John's place and parked in his driveway. He came home real late and we swapped cars back."

Having exhausted his list of questions, Chandler turned to Fuente and McGillicuddy and asked, "Do you have any questions you would like Ron to answer?"

Both men shook their heads in the negative and one responded, "No, not at the moment. If we think of anything else we will come back at him."

Giving his inquisitors a questioning look, Ron responded, "What happens now?"

Chandler fought the urge to smirk as he responded, "You have to be fingerprinted and photographed Ron. After that, you will be taken to court and charged with Kidnapping and Murder. The court may, or may not, set bail and will order your commitment to the Sullivan County Jail, pending a preliminary examination, and Grand Jury action. The court will also assign an attorney to represent you. District Attorney Gellman is out in Grahamsville at the moment, but when he returns, I will inform him that you were cooperative. His recommendation to the arraigning magistrate will be important to whether or not you receive bail. Any other questions?"

"I guess not at the moment. But remember to tell him that Roger was behind this whole thing. Could you get me another McDonald's sandwich and a soda or something?"

14

The police carefully avoided releasing any information to the media regarding the kidnapping for over two days fearing that such release would spook the kidnapper and result in Trudy's death. After finding her body and arresting Krom for Kidnapping and Murder, a detailed release was prepared and a press conference held, hosted by Sullivan County District Attorney Emmanuel Gellman. The horrific crime shocked residents of the Hudson Valley, most greatly impacting the communities of Ellenville, Monticello and Grahamsville. The victim was the well-known and respected daughter of millionaire industrialist Harry Resnick, niece of deceased former Congressman Joe Resnick and Lou Resnick a very popular, greatly admired member of the Ulster County Legislature. During her brief residency in Sullivan County, Trudy had endeared herself to her co-workers in Sullivan County Mental Health and all who knew and loved her felt pain and sadness. The sadistic manner in which she died heightened their grief.

The residents of Grahamsville were shocked and dismayed to learn that someone from their community – the son of a respected family, and graduate of the local high school, where he participated in track – had committed such a despicable crime. Many residents would later tell police, media, or most anyone who inquired, that Ron Krom had grandiose ideas, bizarre plans and acted strange at times, but they never thought him dangerous or capable of hurting anyone.

However, after reading newspaper accounts, one resident felt a chill run up her spine and was compelled to call the state police. Thirty-year old Marilyn Jennings told Investigators Robert King and John Gallagher about a conversation she had with Ron in May 1976. "I was moving to a trailer that I had rented through Krom Realty in Grahamsville. Ronnie and salesman Larry Johnson were helping me move my furniture into the trailer. We were inside the trailer taking a break, when Ronnie asked my sister and me if our parents had any money. We told him that if they did we would own a chalet and wouldn't be moving into a trailer. I then asked Ron what made him ask that question? He replied that my cute sister was the reason. That response didn't answer my question, so he explained, 'I could kidnap her, hold her for ransom, and we could all split the money.' At the time I thought he was just being funny, so we laughed, and no more was said about it. We just finished getting my furniture in and then he left. After reading today's newspaper, it frightened me to think he was probably giving serious thought to kidnapping my sister."

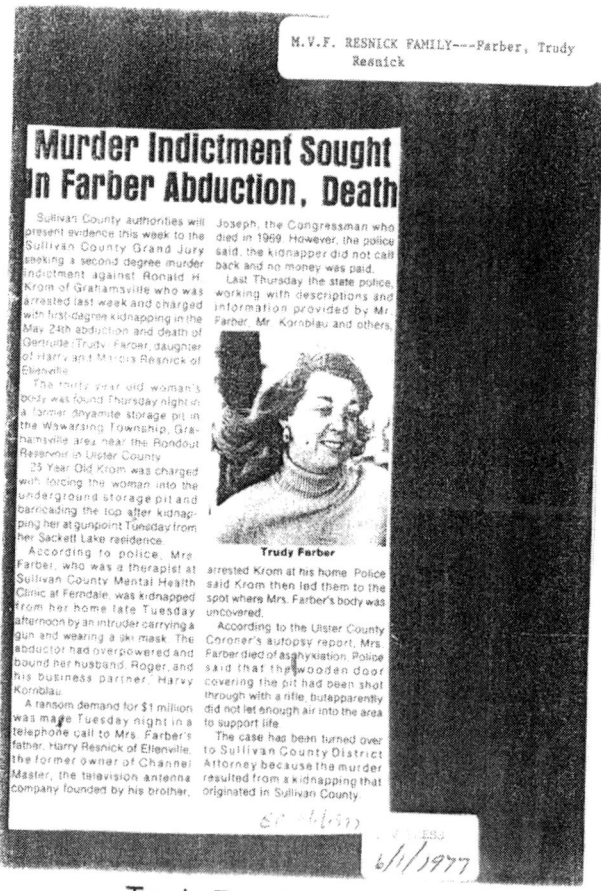

Trudy Resnick Farber

15

Every experienced police detective knows the importance of sealing off a crime scene so that crucial evidence is not contaminated or lost. Crime scene evidence often irrefutably connects a suspect to the commission of the crime and contributes to an ultimate conviction. Senior Investigator Wilfried Holik, supervisor of the troop "F" identification bureau, recognized the importance of his work as a forensic investigator and loved performing what many 'street detectives' considered tedious and boring work. In 1977, the New York State Police consisted of 9 troops, each having their own forensic crime scene unit, internally referred to as an identification bureau. Troop F's identification bureau supervisor was a man with superb intelligence and magnetic personality who more resembled a professor or medical doctor than a police officer and who was hailed by prosecutors, judges, defense attorneys, supervisors and peers as one of the best crime scene specialists in the state. Supervisors knew that when Holik responded to a crime scene no stone would be left unturned and every item of possible evidence would be photographed, measured and carefully preserved. When Willy, or Will, as he was affectionately referred to by fraternity brothers, responded to a crime scene he was fully prepared to set up camp and remain until certain that every possible item of evidence had been identified and secured, and his expertise didn't end there. His professional appearance and coolness on the witness stand, combined with a noticeable German accent, made defense attorneys look like buffoons and greatly influenced juries as to the defendant's guilt.

Holik arrived at the Farber residence approximately two hours after Trudy was dragged from her home. He would be at the residence for the remainder of the night taking photographs, drawing diagrams and meticulously gathering evidence. His report would reflect the finding and seizure of 15 items of evidence identified as:

Several pieces of bed sheet, a knife found on the master bedroom night stand, pieces of nylon string found in several locations throughout the house, two pieces of cloth found on the kitchen floor, newspaper used by perpetrator to write note, a knife found on the kitchen counter, a pillow case found on the kitchen floor, the victim's passport, plaster cast of suspect's footprint found alongside Sunset Drive and plaster cast of tire print left by suspect's car on shoulder of Sunset Drive.

Although John Rogers readily gave his permission for police to search his Firebird, because the car had been in possession of Ron Krom when Trudy was abducted, it was decided to obtain a search warrant to search the vehicle for the purpose of securing evidence. And as the Firebird was in Ulster County, the process for obtaining and executing the warrant was placed in the hands of State Police Investigator Carl VanWagenen, who having made an in-depth study of New York law concerning search warrants, was given the distinction by his peers in the police profession, and more importantly by prosecutors and defense attorneys alike as "The State Police Expert on Search Warrants." Carl was meticulous in laying out probable cause in his search warrant applications and, as a result, none of the evidence recovered pursuant to execution of a search warrant obtained by him had ever been suppressed. On May 27, 1977, Carl presented his application requesting "that a warrant be issued by the court authorizing the seizure and search of a 1976 Pontiac Firebird, color orange, owned by John F. Rogers, bearing New York registration JFR-2, for evidence pertaining to the abduction of Gertrude Farber, to Woodstock Town Justice Rudolf Baumgarten, who issued the order. The previous day, Investigators Robert Greaves and Lawrence Topping, had obtained a warrant in Sullivan County, authorizing the seizure and search of a 1976 Chevrolet Corvette, color orange, owned by Ronald H. Krom, bearing New York registration 978-FPR, for evidence pertaining to the abduction of Gertrude Farber. The execution of the search warrants was easy for the Investigators as their task was to simply take custody of the vehicles and preserve them for processing by Senior Investigator Wilfried Holik, supervisor of the Troop F Identification Bureau. The Corvette was taken to the Ferndale barracks and secured in the garage. The Firebird was taken to the Kingston barracks and secured in that garage. Taking only short rest breaks, the seemingly tireless forensics investigator had been working practically non-stop, processing first the Farber residence in Monticello, the burial site in Grahamsville, and now the vehicles associated with suspect Ronald Krom. No evidence of consequence was recovered from the Corvette;

however, fingerprints – later identified as belonging to Trudy Farber – were found on the inside lid of the Firebird's trunk.

State police examine the area where Trudy Farber of Sackett Lake was found dead Thursday night near Grahamsville. Her body was discovered in what is believed to be an unused dynamite magazine.

Crime Scene Inv.

Evidence Find

A milk box found by police at the scene of Trudy Farber's death contained a pair of sneakers, sunglasses, a peanut butter sandwich, an apple, ammunition and other items allegedly belonging to accused kidnaper-murderer Ronald Krom.

Milk Box at Burial Site

16

On May 28, 1977, a one and one-half inch headline on the cover of the New York Daily News proclaimed: "NAB EX-FRIEND IN HEIRESS KIDNAP – Victim Suffocated in Burial Pit." The accompanying article on page 3 under the headline "Childhood Friend Is Held In Kidnap of Slain Heiress" reported, "A childhood friend of Trudy Resnick Farber, 30-year old daughter of a Catskills millionaire, was jailed as her alleged kidnapper yesterday after leading authorities to a gravelike storage pit where she had been buried alive. The suspect, Ronald Harrison Krom, 25, took police to the dirt pit in a wooded area of upstate rural Grahamsville on Thursday night, two days after the kidnapping. After lifting a hatch cover from the shallow pit, police said, they found Mrs. Farber's fully clothed body. Her fingers and face were bloodied, apparently from a desperate attempt to free herself. An autopsy disclosed that Mrs. Farber had died of suffocation. "She did not survive very long after she was abducted," said Sullivan County Sheriff Robert Flynn. Authorities said that Krom, who reportedly had spent a month in a mental institution the last year, had called the Farber home in Monticello on Tuesday, the night of the abduction, and demanded a $1 million ransom." (As the call had actually been received at the Resnick home in Ellenville, this was technically incorrect) The article continued, "There were reports that a second call had been made detailing how the ransom drop would be made. But before any arrangements could be completed, Krom was picked up for questioning. State Police said that he was suspected because he had attempted recently to borrow money from Mrs. Farber's husband, Roger. "They had a scene over it," police said. The kidnap drama began at about 6 p.m. Tuesday when a man wearing a ski mask and carrying a .22 rifle entered the Farber home, an expensive split-level house on a gravel road over-looking Sackett Lake in Monticello. Police said the rifle had been found at the pit site. According to authorities, the kidnapper bound Mrs. Farber's husband and the husband's business partner, Harvey Kornblau, both 32, with cord and pulled a pillowcase over Kornblau's head. The kidnapper then waited for Mrs. Farber to return home from her job as a counselor at the Sullivan County Mental Health Center in Ferndale. When Mrs. Farber showed up at about 7 p.m., the kidnapper led her to his car and drove off with her. Authorities theorized that the suspect drove her directly to the storage pit, which is about 15 miles northeast of Monticello on the site of the New York City owned Rondout Reservoir. Mrs. Farber apparently was ordered into the pit, a former storage area for explosives." (The finding of a metal box containing evidence and secreted in the ground near the burial site may have triggered the erroneous report that Trudy was buried in a former magazine for explosives that were used in the construction of the reservoir. Most subsequent newspaper articles would also state she had been buried in a magazine intended for the storage of explosives) "The heavy wooden hatch cover was then put back on, locked with a padlock and weighted down with a large rock. Authorities said that Krom and Mrs. Farber had been friends as children and that their families had lived next door to each other in Ellenville. Krom now lives with his parents in Grahamsville, which abuts the Rondout Reservoir. Krom's name was found listed in Mrs. Farber's private phone book, police said, and he was picked up for questioning late Thursday afternoon. At 9:30 p.m. that night, police said, he led them to the pit. Krom was later arraigned on the kidnapping charge before Liberty Town Justice Richard Herring and ordered held without bail. Authorities said that Mrs. Farber's husband, who is co-owner with Kornblau of three Radio Shack stores in the Monticello area, had rounded up $1 million in case to make the ransom payment. According to state police, Krom, described as a part-time real estate salesman, had been committed for a month to the Middletown State Hospital after "flipping out." Mrs. Farber was the daughter of television antenna magnate Harry Resnick of Ellenville and the niece of the late millionaire Rep. Joseph Resnick, who represented New York's 25th Congressional District in Dutchess and Ulster Counties from 1965 through 1968."

Typical of most newspaper accounts, the article although not totally accurate, was technically correct. Trudy had been kidnapped at around 5:30 p.m. rather than 7 p.m. and the reporters were mislead in believing that Ron was picked up for questioning because his name appeared in Trudy's address book.

In the May 28th edition of the Middletown Times-Herald-Record, Sullivan Bureau Chief Jeffrey Page reported under the banner "Neighbors call

Krom wheeler-dealer, cut up," the following: "Neighbors of Ronald H. Krom reacted with shock and surprise as the news of this arrest for the kidnapping of Trudy Farber spread through this northern Sullivan County hamlet…One resident said Krom was in her daughter's high school graduating class, and had visited her home a number of times. 'He was always such a nice young man,' she said. 'I was simply horrified when I heard about this. He was always the kind of kid that you'd welcome into your home if he showed up.' Tri-Valley school was closed Friday, using an unused snow emergency day, and teachers were not readily available…One resident reported that Krom ran the Green Hills Realty Corp. on Rt. 55 here. Krom reportedly took over the business from his father, Harrison Krom, who is a retired New York Telephone Co. employee. 'I had heard that Ronnie was much of a cut-up when he was in school,' the man said.' 'But this! Whoever would have thought anyone could do something like this?' Yet another Grahamsville man described Krom as, 'something of a wheeler-dealer, who was always coming up with a new scheme. He was talking a while back about bringing a stock car track to Sullivan County,' he said. 'But nothing ever came of it. I think it was mostly talk, like some of the rest of his plans.' The man refused to elaborate. One source said that during his arraignment before Liberty Town Justice Richard Herring late Thursday night, Krom expressed astonishment when Herring ordered him jailed without bail, pending another hearing. But no justice can set bail in a felony arrest until a suspect's previous record, if one exists, is obtained. Sullivan County Dist. Atty. Emanuel Gellman declined comment Friday on whether Krom had a record. It was learned that Krom had been a patient in the Sullivan County unit of the Middletown Psychiatric Center some time during the past six months. Earlier Krom seemed calm and composed as he was led from a state police car to the Ferndale barracks for booking. Meanwhile, the calm in this valley hamlet was shattered Friday. This was attributed to both Krom's arrest and the location of Mrs. Farber's body about four miles past the Ulster County line. 'It's something you don'᾽t expect,' a woman said while wheeling a baby carriage near Route 55. 'It's something you always read about happening somewhere else and when it strikes close to home, you find yourself locking your door and beginning to look over your shoulder. And that's not what it's supposed to be about up here. It's different in the city, but you expect it to be different here."

In the same Middletown-Times-Herald edition of May 28, 1977, Staff Writer Charlie Crist wrote, "Trudy Farber of Sackett Lake suffocated while relatives worked to get the $1 million ransom money demanded by her kidnapper. According to a high police official, the ransom was prepared, but the kidnapper was apprehended before instructions could be made for its delivery. Mrs. Farber's body was found in rural Ulster County about 8 p.m. Thursday in a five-foot-deep pit believed once used to store dynamite. The pit's lid had been tightly closed and a stone rolled across it. Air holes apparently made with the rifle used in the kidnapping weren't enough to sustain life. Ronald Harrison Krom, 25, of Grahamsville, was first charged Thursday night with first-degree kidnapping and then, on Friday murder charges were lodged in connection with the case. He is being held in Sullivan County Jail without bail after his arraignment before Liberty Town Justice Richard Herring. Testimony seeking an indictment for second-degree murder will be presented to the grand jury next week, Sullivan County Dist. Atty. Emanual Gellman said Friday. Both first-degree kidnapping and second-degree murder are Class A felonies, punishable by up to 15 years to life in prison each. Mrs. Farber was the daughter of Harry Resnick of Ellenville, a founder of the Channel Master Corp., and a niece of former Congressman Joseph Y. Resnick. Krom and Mrs. Farber were once neighbors in Ellenville. He was arrested after his voice was recognized during a telephone call demanding ransom. Since the kidnapping took place in Sullivan County and the alleged murder was a result Gellman said the entire matter will be prosecuted in Sullivan County. Mrs. Farber was taken at gunpoint from her home late Tuesday. Police said her husband, Roger, and his business partner, Harvey Kornblau, of Ellenville were bound by their hands and feet. Krom allegedly accosted Mrs. Farber when she arrived home from work about 5:50 p.m. Tuesday. She was a therapist at the Sullivan County Mental Hygiene Clinic in Ferndale. Police were notified of the abduction when Farber and his partner freed themselves. Police believe Krom immediately drove Mrs. Farber to an isolated area off Rt. 55 near south Hill Road. At gunpoint he forced her to climb a steep wooded hillside, police speculate. Once up the hillside, near a recent lumbering operation parking lot, about 1000 yards off Rt. 55, Krom then forced Mrs. Farber into the dynamite magazine, police said. The earthen magazine is about five feet deep, four feet wide and five feet long. Heavy wood planks form a framework for a wood lid, with stones laid around the framework. The magazine was believed used during construction of the New York City Merriman Dam, also known as the Rondout reservoir. When Mrs. Farber was found, the lid of the wood framework and cover was tightly closed and locked. A large stone was on top of the lid. Her body, police said, was in a sitting position. She was fully clothed. Results of an autopsy ordered by Ulster County Coroner Steven Corcoran of Kerhonkson, have not been released. Gellman said they are confidential. But, he said it is believed Mrs. Farber suffocated. An autopsy was performed at the Kingston city laboratory located in Kingston City Hospital by Dr. Roberto Benitez.

Ulster County Chief Asst. Dist. Atty. Michael Kavanagh confirmed that Mrs. Farber died of asphyxiation. No time of death was listed on the autopsy report, and it apparently won't be known for several days. State Police maintained surveillance at the scene throughout the night. Early Friday, troopers and investigators searched the area where Mrs. Farber was found. Discovered near a log and covered with leaves and sticks was a metal milk container, the type used by homeowners to receive deliveries. Police said it had been imbedded in the ground for a long time. 'It may have been a magazine for blasting caps,' one officer said. In the metal box were about 500 rounds of .22 ammunition; a knife; a pair of sunglasses; two ski masks; a jump suit; sneakers; a peanut butter sandwich and an apple. A small caliber rifle believed used during the commission of the crime was also found in the same area. Police said the weapon used in the kidnapping was a rifle. The apple and sandwich, police said, may have been for Mrs. Farber. A police spokesman said it was believed the items inside the box, were placed there by Krom. They said the clothing matched a description of what the kidnapper was wearing given to them by Mrs. Farber's husband. Also found in the area were several spent .22-caliber shell casings, police said. There were several holes shot through the lid of the dynamite magazine, police said. The major break came when a second ransom telephone call was made to Mrs. Farber's father in Ellenville. The call was made Wednesday night, sources said. It could not be determined when Krom was picked up. Once Krom became a suspect, he was questioned by state police investigators and reportedly admitted to the kidnapping early in the probe. The Times Herald-Record learned that Mrs. Farber's father confronted Krom during the police interrogation. It is believed that the property where Mrs. Farber's body was found, was at one time owned by the suspect's mother, Mrs Harrison Krom of Moore Hill Road, Grahamsville and Mrs. Farber's mother-in-law, Mrs. Henry Farber of South Fallsburg. It was sold recently, Krom's brother, Wayne, told state police. The suspect, according to his brother, was well acquainted with the property, having hunted there and participated in the property sale."

Although poorly written and somewhat redundant to the article written by co-worker Page, most of the information reported by Crist was technically correct. In the same May 28th edition reporter Crist wrote a more poignant article titled, "Slaying cut short a 'beautiful' life." The article was apparently intended to pay tribute to Trudy Farber, and was a somewhat commendable presentation. Crist wrote, "People who knew Trudy Farber in her varied roles as family member and clinical therapist came together Friday in their assessments of their murdered friend. Relatives and clinic clients used similar words to describe the 31-year old Mrs. Farber. "Sterling, Good, beautiful and brilliant" were among the adjectives used. "She was down to visit us in New York last week," Mrs. Farber's cousin, Michele Cohen of New York, said at the Harry Resnick home here. "The news of her death is simply inconceivable." Mrs. Farber was Resnick's daughter. Mrs. Cohen said she and Mrs. Farber were not especially close when they were young, but that a deep relationship had developed in recent years. "We took trips together and she was just a wonderful person to be with," Mrs. Cohen said. "We would often just sit and talk about the past." Mrs. Farber attended the Ellenville school system and obtained a bachelor's degree from Rider College in Trenton, N.J., and a master's in psychology from New York University. She had been employed at the Sullivan County Mental Health Clinic in Ferndale for about the last three years. Mrs. Cohen said her cousin had recently expressed interest in going to graduate school to work for her doctorate. "She was at the point of investigating various schools," she said. Additionally, Mrs. Farber was about to open a part-time therapeutic practice in Ellenville. "The telephone wasn't installed yet, but she had her business cards and even had her first client," Mrs. Cohen said. One of Mrs. Farber's county clients, a resident of Loch Sheldrake said, "She was sympathetic, she was understated and she was understanding; while I never knew her outside the clinic, I always believed that she carried these attributes to her non-professional life." Another client, a Woodbourne man, seemed shocked when he discussed Mrs. Farber's death. "It's just unbelievable," he said. "She was just a beautiful person, a person who helped and was always there to talk and communicate with." Mrs. Farber's 33-year old brother, Justin Resnick, described his sister as "a fine daughter and a fine sister. She was a very, very brave person and an emotionally strong person. She was someone who was able to gather strength on her own over the years," he said. Resnick added, "Mrs. Farber was interested in the field of psychology for as long as he could remember. She was a strong believer in 'no waste,' he said. For this reason, she cultivated an unusually large vegetable garden and put up the produce after the fall harvest each year. "She believed in always remaining true and loyal to her friends," Resnick said. "We want to say that, as a family, we are extremely grateful to the FBI."

The same edition of the Middletown Times-Herald Record posted this short article under the banner "Resnicks: Family of Stature, Means" The reporter was not identified. The article described Harry Resnick "as one of Ulster County's leading citizens. Harry Resnick had the clout to raise a $1 million ransom quickly. But all of Resnick's stature in the community wasn't enough to save the life of his daughter, Trudy Farber, who died sometime between Tuesday and Thursday as the result of a kidnapping scheme."

The article continued by providing a biographical sketch of the Resnick family and pointing out that the Resnick family were respected philanthropists who contributed to many worthwhile causes. The article reported, "Harry Resnick was once quoted as saying, 'Ellenville is my home. I owe a lot to Ellenville and its people.' Friday Harry Resnick grieved quietly for his daughter at his Ellenville home. For a self-reliant man, it must have been hard. There was nothing to be done."

17

In a small sense of irony, at the same time hundreds of mourners began gathering to pay their respects to Trudy, Sheriffs' Deputies and members of the State Police were escorting Ron Krom to Liberty Town Justice Court. As Rabbi Herman Eisner intoned God to embrace Trudy in his kingdom, Town Justice Richard Herring was informing Ron Krom that as he had been charged with Second Degree Murder and First Degree Kidnapping. He was remanded to the Sullivan county Jail without bail, pending Grand Jury action.

Middletown Times-Herald Record Reporter Chris Farlekas attended the funeral for Trudy Farber, which was held at the Temple Ezrath Israel in Ellenville, on Monday, May 30, 1977, and would report, "To dwell on the evil deed is to defame the image of God." "With these words, Rabbi Herman Eisner tried to rub balm on the open wounds of family and friends mourning the murder of Trudy Farber, daughter of Harry Resnick, a founder of the Channel Master Corp. here…Hundreds attended the funeral for Mrs. Farber Monday…The immediate family huddled around the plain coffin made of beautifully polished wood. For rows behind, and overflowing into the outside, friends, co-workers and patients of the county Mental Health Clinic therapist gathered by the hundreds. They started coming an hour before the 2 p.m. service. Most greeted each other in whispers, quickly touching fingers, looking at the gaunt coffin. Tears streamed down almost every face during the 45-minute religious service. For many, the Hebrew words and chants gave a strange kind of comfort. In singing and speaking, the Rabbi had a rolling, poetic edge to his voice. 'Remember, we are but strangers on this earth…our flesh is like the grass or flower of the field. It withers and fades. But the word of God endures forever. A link is broken in the chain of love. We look for a word, a gesture to help ease the crush of pain of Trudy's death. She was a kind, sensitive soul who wasn't interested in diamonds and furs. Her sole interest was people. She planted her garden with love. Many of the people she moved are here today and they could all give eulogy to her.' Rabbi Eisner quoted what her husband told him the night before, that, 'the sunshine of her personality helped me to grow.' Then he added, 'Trudy helped us all grow.' Gently touching the coffin, he (Rabbi Eisner) said in a faltering voice: 'To you, dear Trudy, I say may God hold you up in His heavenly way.'"

Record photo by Chris Fariekas

Pallbearers carry out Trudy Farber's coffin Monday from Temple Ezrath Israel in Ellenville.

Funeral

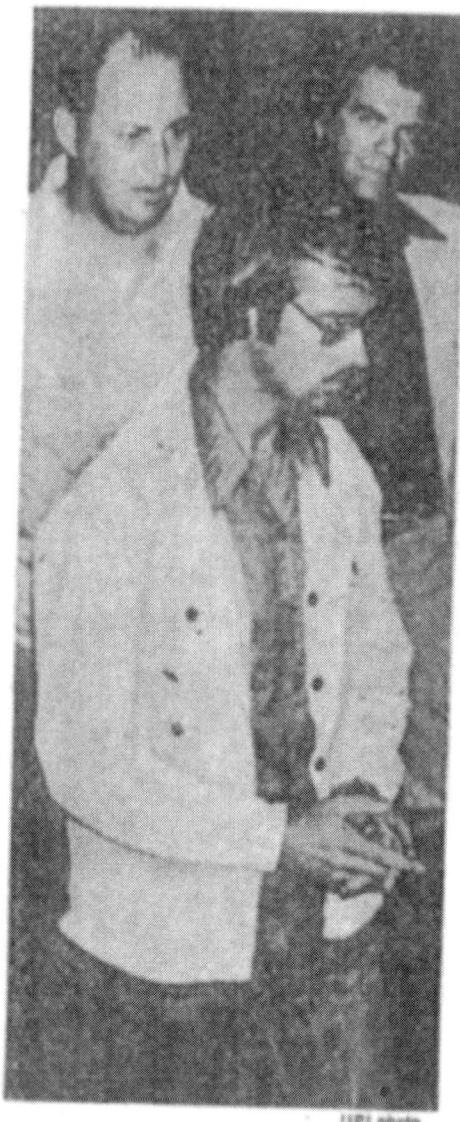

Ron Krom in Custody

18

In police jargon, the prosecution had Ronald Krom "by the short hairs." Establishing motive and opportunity to commit a kidnapping was a "grounder." Several witnesses could testify that Ron had told them of his plans to kidnap 'someone.' Ron had confessed to kidnapping Trudy, albeit in a convoluted fashion to shed blame on the victim's husband, and probably most damming of all, was his personally taking police to what would turn out to be Trudy's gravesite. His retrieval from under a rock of the key that opened the lock securing the cover over the grave would certainly strongly influence a jury toward guilt. However, investigative legwork was needed to establish that Krom acted alone in both planning and commission of the crimes. It also needed to be established that Ron's schizophrenia did not diminish his mental capacity to know and understand that his actions in taking Trudy and imprisoning her for ransom were wrong and criminal acts. Establishing ownership of the rifle used in the commission of the crime was an important piece of evidence toward proving guilt beyond a reasonable doubt. In discussion with investigators subsequent to the finding of Trudy's body, Krom related that he had purchased the .22 Winchester semi-automatic rifle; at the Woolworth store located in Orange Plaza, Middletown, New York.

On May 29, 1977, Middletown BCI Investigator Larry Grogan visited Woolworth's and spoke with sales clerk Susan Horton. Examination of the store's firearm transaction records indicated that Susan had sold a .22 rifle and 'brick' of 500 bullets to Ronald H. Krom on May 13, 1977 (11 days prior to the kidnapping). Log entry #829 reflected "Ronald H. Krom, date of birth July 9, 1951, residing at Moore Hill Road, Grahamsville, New York, purchased a model 190 .22 Winchester rifle bearing serial number 1956978" from the store. Krom had presented his driver's license as proof of identity, required for the purchase. Although acknowledging that she had transacted the sale of the rifle, Susan told Grogan that she did not remember the transaction or the customer. Even after examining a photograph of Krom she could not recall that he was the customer purchasing the rifle. Investigator Grogan seized the sale transaction record and provided Susan a receipt.

19

A kidnapping for ransom had been solved and the perpetrator arrested; however, there was no cause for celebration and exhausted police investigators felt only dejection, bitterness and sadness. Additionally, those who found Trudy's body and helped remove her from the hole that claimed her life would have the horrible, cruel manner of her death forever etched in their minds. Many would replay the investigation over and over in their minds second-guessing whether Trudy would have lived 'if only we had done this, or done that, and, would we have found her sooner and perhaps saved her life?' Under the circumstances, their self introspection was understandable; however, in truth, acting under the provisions of investigative jurisprudence they had done everything humanly possible and in fact, having very little to go on initially, had arrested Trudy's abductor and located her – albeit deceased – in slightly less than three days. Although the case had been solved, the investigation was far from over. Investigators would now have to interview dozens of people and develop evidence that would provide a prima facie case for prosecution and ensure that Trudy's killer would not go unpunished.

On May 31, 1977, a Sullivan County Grand Jury, indicted Ronald Harrison Krom for three counts of Murder in the 2nd Degree, Kidnapping in the 1st Degree and Burglary in the 2nd degree. Krom was ordered confined to the Sullivan County Jail, without bail, pending the outcome of continued legal proceedings against him. Monticello Legal Aid Attorney Edward Leopold was appointed to represent Krom, and numerous legal strategies would delay the charges against Krom from going to trial for two years. In February 1978, Leopold left his position as Executive Director of the Legal Aid Society, accepting position as Sullivan County Assistant District Attorney. Monticello Attorney Carl Silverstein replaced Leopold and inherited Ron Krom as his client.

Although readily admitting his role in the kidnapping for ransom plot, Krom insisted and maintained that the victim's husband Roger Farber, a friend for many years, had masterminded the crime because he needed money and was cheating on his wife. No physical evidence and no other witnesses had been found to support Ron's claim that Roger aided and abetted in having his own wife abducted for ransom. However, police and prosecutors were troubled as to how two reasonably powerful young men were overpowered and tied up by Krom, armed only with a twenty-two caliber rifle, because it seemed reasonable to believe that Krom could not have held the rifle pointed at them while tying them up. And, it troubled some as to why – after freeing himself from his bonds so quickly; Roger did not run to get his gun and chase after the man who was taking his wife. The District Attorney believed Krom was solely responsible for Trudy's abduction and murder, but he was concerned that during trial the defense would somehow succeed in planting suspicion in the minds of jurors that Roger was involved. Therefore, he insisted that police conduct an in-depth investigation into Roger Farber's life, identify any and all connections he had to Ron Krom and have Farber take a polygraph examination. As a result, Roger Farber was interviewed numerous times by State Police investigators, who would report to the District Attorney, that he remained cooperative, appeared to be truthful and was willing to aid the prosecution in any way that he could to have Krom convicted and punished. It was established that Roger, who was four years older than Ron became acquainted with him when his parents and Ron's parents partnered in real estate investments, while both were quite young. Roger characterized Ron at that age, as a dreamy teenager with a lot of grandiose ideas and plans, which he readily shared with Roger. However, Roger would tell police he never formed a close relationship with Ron, partly because of their age difference, but mostly because Ron frequently boasted that he was more intelligent than most people and he was destined to accomplish great things. When police pointed out that Ron apparently resented not being invited to Roger and Trudy's wedding, Roger said that he was unaware that Ron harbored those feelings. He pointed out that because Ron was not considered a close friend, he was not even given consideration for an invitation to their wedding. He had not realized that Ron would consider that lack of invitation a snub and certainly did not realize that resentment over a perceived snub may have been wholly or partly responsible for Trudy's abduction. Roger told investigators, "I had not seen or heard from Ron in a long time, and then suddenly several months ago, he appeared at my Radio Shack store in Monticello. When he appeared, I knew immediately that he was not making a social call and apparently wanted something from me. Turns out, he wanted me to partner with him to purchase a bar that was for sale in the Village of New Paltz. He said that all I needed to do was put up the money and he would operate the bar. All I would have to do is be his silent partner and make lots of money. I think that in his mind, my marriage to a member of the Resnick family had automatically made me a very wealthy man. The truth was, Trudy and I were working on our own to forge a living and my business was just starting to turn a profit. I did not have the money needed for the investment and more importantly, I had no interest what so ever of going into the bar business. Ron did not seem to believe me when I told him I did not have the money to either invest or loan him. When he left, he was obviously angry, although he didn't outwardly express his anger. I didn't give Ron's reaction to my turn down much thought until about a month later, when Trudy told me that she had received a telephone call from a Ron Krom of Grahamsville and his call made her uncomfortable. She said that Krom told her that I was working on something with him that required a large sum of money as an investment. Since her family was rich, she could get the money from them, and it would be in her best interest to cooperate. Trudy told me that the manner and tone of Krom's conversation seemed threatening. I told her that Ron was trying to get me to invest in the purchase of a bar in New Paltz and I had turned him down. I also told her that I would have a conversation with Krom and inform him not to call or bother her again. A few days later, I called Ron, told him that I was not interested in investing in any business enterprise with him and told him not to call my wife again because she did not want to be bothered. Ron spoke calmly during this call, and told me that he had found another source to get the money. I did not speak to him again until I heard his voice when I answered the phone at Harry's house."

On June 14, 1977, Roger Farber accompanied Investigator's Jim Chandler and Ralph Fuente to the Manhattan office of renowned polygraphist Richard Arthur, because he had agreed to take a polygraph examination. The main issue under consideration was to determine if Farber was telling the truth regarding having no prior knowledge of his wife's planned abduction and had not partnered with Ron Krom in any plot to abduct his wife for the purpose of obtaining ransom from Harry Resnick. At the conclusion of the examination, Arthur reported that Farber was truthful when he denied having prior knowledge of the crimes of abduction and murder of his wife. Also, that he was telling the truth when he denied partnering with Krom in any plot to obtain money from Harry Resnick.

The District Attorney breathed a small sigh of relief when he received the news that Farber had tested truthful in his polygraph examination. He was now confident that he could refute and overcome any defense strategy to portray Roger as an accomplice in the crimes.

Note: Former Sullivan County District Attorney Joseph Jaffe told this author that he never believed Roger Farber had anything to do with his wife's kidnapping. Defense Counsel Carl Silverstein told this author that he was certain Roger Farber had nothing to do with his wife's kidnapping.

20

A mental competency hearing was held on June 23, 1977. Judge Louis B. Scheinman – who would ultimately preside over every phase of the criminal actions against Krom - heard testimony from psychiatric professionals testifying for both prosecution and defense. The witnesses were in general agreement that Ron Krom suffered from schizophrenia and at times manifested delusional behavior; however, disagreed as to whether Krom understood the seriousness and nature of the crimes with which he was charged. At the conclusion of the hearing, Judge Scheinman deemed that Ron Krom was reasonably intelligent, understood the seriousness and nature of the crimes he was charged with and directed that prosecution could continue.

A second competency hearing was held on August 18, 1978, as to whether Krom (a diagnosed schizophrenic, frequently exhibiting delusional behavior) was mentally competent to assist in his defense. At the conclusion of this hearing, Judge Scheinman deemed that defendant Krom was mentally able to do so.

A third competency hearing was held on December 11, 1978, to again determine Krom's mental competency. Judge Scheinman determined that "the defendant is not an incapacitated person and the court hereby directs that the criminal action against him shall proceed."

A Suppression Hearing also referred to as a Huntley Hearing commenced on May 31, 1979 and would end June 20, 1979. The purpose of the hearing was to determine if the defendant had been properly advised of his "Right to Counsel and Right to Silence" as provided for in several United States

Supreme Court decisions – the most notable of which being the case of "Miranda v Arizona."

Investigators James Chandler, Ralph Fuente, John Bult of the New York State Police and SA Leo McGillicuddy of the FBI presented testimony as prosecution witnesses. Each would testify that Krom had been provided the Miranda Warning and that he had been provided the opportunity to invoke those rights. Also, that Krom had alternately exercised and waived his right to counsel, subsequently making admissions concerning the crimes under investigation. Former District Emmanuel Gellman would testify that he provided the defendant the right to counsel, the defendant waived that right and attempted to negotiate a contract to cause Mrs. Farber's release. Attorney Barry Martin would testify that he spoke with the defendant, who was described to him by police as a suspect at the time. He would testify that his conversation with the defendant took place in the Ferndale State Police station, and after speaking with Krom, he decided not to represent him. He also testified that he recommended that Krom contact the Legal Aid Attorney for representation. Liberty Town Justice Richard Herring would testify that when the defendant appeared before him for arraignment on charges of Kidnapping and Murder, he advised him of his right to counsel and Krom responded that he would represent himself.

Dorothy Krom and Harrison Krom would testify that when two state police Investigators first appeared at their home they did not hear them provide their son any sort of rights. Under cross-examination, both would admit that they were not with their son when he first met the police officers. Wayne Krom would testify that he drove Investigators to his parents home to meet with Ron and did not hear them advise his brother of any rights.

On day three of the hearing the young neatly groomed defendant who more resembled a docile, studious college student than a cold-blooded killer, arose from his seat at the defense table and walked confidently to the witness chair. It is quite possible that in the minds of those few persons present in the court room, upon visual study of the young defendant, wondered how it could be possible for him to commit such a heinous crime. After being sworn, Ron took his seat in the witness chair and as instructed by his attorney, gazed momentarily at Judge Scheinman, giving the Judge a smile intended to display honesty, sincerity and innocence.

Defense Counsel Silverstein flashed a confident smile at his client, and began his questioning. "Ronald, where are you presently residing?"

In his typical quiet voice, Ron answered, "Two Bushnell Avenue."

Silverstein continued, "And how long have you been there?"

Ron's answer would not answer the question, "I have been there – from there – Mid-Hudson back to Middletown and Mid-Hudson and back."

That was fine with Counsel, because he was intent to show that his client's confinement in mental facilities was proof that Ron was a victim of mental illness and this disability, may have prevented him from understanding his right to counsel and his right against self incrimination. He continued, "You have also been at Mid-Hudson?"

"Twice."

"The first time would have been June of 1977, April 1978?"

"I don't have the dates," Ron answered in his soft, boyish sounding voice, and continued, "I was there briefly. I am not sure – you have the records Mr. Silverstein."

"You were there on two different occasions, is that correct?"

"Correct."

"Now, you understand this hearing is only with regard to any statements you have made to police officers, not going into the whole case, just statements; you understand that?"

"Yes."

District Attorney Jaffe interrupted the questioning by objecting to the manner of questioning stating, "This is his witness."

Judge Scheinman immediately responded, "the objection is overruled," without providing clarification for his decision.

Silverstein continued, "Ron, when I ask a question, try to answer just that question. Don't go on about other things, okay?"

Ron responded, "No leading."

It could be surmised by the momentary look of dismay on Silverstein's face, he had come to the realization that his client had already forgotten the pre-testimony instructions he had given him. He continued, "I just don't want you to go all over the ball park."

"Okay," Ron answered.

"Did there come a time on May 26, 1977 when two investigators came to your home? It would have been a Thursday morning."

"Yes."

"Do you remember who they were?"

"Yes, I do."

"Who were they?"

"The officers who came to my house were Mr. Fuente and Mr. Chandler."

Judge Scheinman interrupted the questioning, asking, "Can you speak up, please?"

District Attorney Jaffe flashed the judge a smile and stated, "Thank you, Your Honor."

Silverstein continued, "Where were they when you first saw them?"

"They drove in the driveway with my brother Wayne."

"Did you see them drive in?"

"No, I was cooking breakfast for myself."

"When did you actually see them for the first time? Where were they?"

"I believe that they were in the driveway."

"And where did you come from to meet them?"

"I was at the stove and I went out into the driveway. Wayne came in and said he had people to see me. I thought it was people for a real estate deal."

"When you went out there and saw them, did you recognize them from any prior occasion?"

"I didn't know the officers personally, no."

As Ron whispered this answer, District Attorney Jaffe interrupted the questioning and addressed the court, "I am sorry, I cannot hear the witness."

Judge Scheinman responded, "He says he didn't know the officers personally." Turning attention toward Ron, he then added, "Try to speak a little louder, if you can."

Counsel Silverstein continued, "When you saw them, who started the conversation?"

"I believe they initiated it," Ron whispered in reply.

"Who was present at that time?

"I believe that Wayne was there initially and that Wayne went into the house and I spoke with the officers in the garage; my Dad came out – he was there briefly and then he went back in."

"When you say Wayne was there initially, for how long a period of time?"

"Not very long at all."

"Ten hours, ten minutes, ten seconds, how long - your best estimate?"

"About four minutes."

"Do you remember which one of the officers initiated the conversation?"

"I don't recall."

"What was said to you and what did you say to them?"

"I would just like to say that, you know, a lot of people don't seem to remember I have a couple of scars – drugs and drugs – it is a matter of record."

Judge Scheinman gave the witness an incredulous look and stated, "Ronald"-

Ron did not let the judge finish his statement and immediately upon hearing his name responded, "It is hard for me to recollect now. I don't really recall. I believe that it was Mr. Chandler. Mr. Fuente was there, too, and he asked some questions."

Silverstein continued, "What did they say to you and what did you say to them?"

"The substance of what was said was that Trudy Farber was missing and they wanted to know if I could help them find her, and I said I had some information about it. I believe the officers wanted her returned safely."

"Did they state that to you?"

"Yes."

"What did you say to them?"

"I said I had information about it but I didn't really give them very much information at that time."

Hearing this answer, D.A. Jaffe shook his head in the negative and responded, "I move to strike the answer, 'I didn't give them much information at that time.'"

Without providing explanation, Judge Scheinman responded, "Denied. Next question."

Silverstein continued, "Was there any other conversation that took place there?"

"We were in the garage and I wanted to see Mr. Resnick. I was upset about what happened."

"Did you say that to the officers, that you wanted to see Mr. Resnick?"

"I didn't state it. That's what I was thinking."

"Did you say anything to them about it – I mean –"

Before Counsel Silverstein finished his question, Ron responded, "I said I felt like taking a long walk."

"And then what did you do or say?"

"I don't recall specifically. I didn't really say very much. What happened was we spoke in the garage and I believe the car door on my car was opened and I might have sat down on a bucket seat but I believe that they had taken the keys out. I didn't get in the car and try to run out as they said."

"Did there come a time when you left the house and went to Ferndale?"

"Yes, but before that, we went into my room. I said come into my room, I have a very large room and I said if you want the answer, here it is. I have a safety deposit box with a two-digit combination."

"Go ahead."

"And that the answer is in this. And the answer was my courier card."

"What was your courier card?"

"It's a business card that I had I believe about seven years ago."

"Is that when you told them about the C.I.A.?"

"No."

District Attorney Jaffe, obviously disgusted by the line of questioning and confusing answers being provided by the defendant, interrupted, "Your Honor, I object. It's his witness."

This time, Judge Scheinman agreed, and responded, "Sustained."

Counsel Silverstein continued, "All right, Ronald, about how long were you at your house talking to the Investigators from the time they arrived until you left to go to Ferndale? How long a period of time?"

"Quite awhile – talked quite awhile. I don't mind if – I believe about forty-five minutes."

"Okay, and you have already told us some of the things said during the forty-five minutes. Can you think of anything else said during the forty-five minutes?"

"Not really. Not very much."

"Have you exhausted your recollection of the discussions in the driveway?"

"No."

"What else can you remember?"

"I really didn't know exactly what they were there for until they indicated Trudy was missing. You know, we just –" (Ron hesitated after the word just, apparently searching his brain for an appropriate continued response)

"Go ahead," Silverstein encouraged.

"Not a hell of a lot was said."

"Are you indicating then that was basically all of the discussion, was that Trudy Farber was missing and if you knew where the location was?"

(Author found the choice of "the location was," rather than "where she is" a poor choice of words, but apparently this seemed insignificant to both Judge and District Attorney)

Ron answered, "I never indicated that I knew where her location was. I knew that I was supposed to pick up the money and deliver it to the locker which had a padlock on it."

"Did you tell them that?"

"I never indicated that to them and I never really indicated that Trudy was overly involved. I just said that Gertrude was safe. This was after we got to the barracks."

"I am just talking about the house now. At the house now, I am just trying to get all of the conversations you can remember that took place while you were still at the house, whether in the bedroom or outside on the driveway."

"I wrote up quite a bit of it and forgot. I believe I made notes about this."

Judge Scheinman addressed Ron, "I don't know what those notes are, Ronald. You have to answer the question."

Ron responded, "It's hard for me to recollect."

Judge Scheinman took over questioning, asking, "You have the notes to refer to?"

"I believe I do."

"That I do?"

"Yes."

"Are those part of the letters you have been sending now?"

(Since his arrest Ron had become a prolific letter writer, sending letters to Judge, District Attorney, his assigned counsel, the Sullivan County Sheriff, various State Police personnel, and most troubling of all, to many Resnick family members. For the most part, Ron's letters were self-serving delusional ramblings proclaiming his innocence)

Ron responded to Judge Scheinman's last question, "I personally delivered them."

Upon hearing this, District Attorney Jaffe, arose from his seat at the prosecutorial bench and asked, "May I interrupt and personally approach the bench for a minute, Your Honor?"

(Court reporter notes that Jaffe approached the bench at 2:30 p.m.)

As Jaffe approached the bench, Ron blurted out, "One psychiatrist said I have three breasts. Do you know what three breasts is? It's a bullet hole."

The whispered bench discussion between Judge and the two attorneys is not known, but it is reasonable to assume that it pertained to the unwelcome plethora of letters that the Resnick family considered harassment.

Following the discussion, Counsel Silverstein resumed questioning his client. "Ronald, do you recollect anything else of what was said either - in the garage, the driveway, or in your bedroom - that you haven't told us about yet?"

Ron answered, "I can't recollect at all."

"At any time during the conversations with the officers, were you ever advised that you had a right to a lawyer?"

"I interrupted them. They started to read the Miranda's and I said I could have been a lawyer."

"On the driveway at the house?"

"At the corner of the house when we were going into my room, I have a private entrance."

"While Wayne was there?"

"Wayne was in the house, I believe."

Judge Scheinman interrupted, "Wayne was in the house, you believe? Is that what you said?"

Ron smiled at the Judge and answered, "Yes."

Silverstein resumed questioning, "You interrupted them and said you could have been a lawyer?"

"That's true. I was admitted to the University of Kentucky."

"Did he continue and say anything to you with regard to your right to a lawyer?"

"No."

"Did he tell you how you have the right to remain silent?"

"Yes."

"Did he tell you anything you said could be used against you in a court of law?"

"They got that far."

"Did he tell you that if you could not afford a lawyer that they would provide one for you?"

"No."

"Or one would be provided for you if you could not afford one?"

"They did say that, yes."

"Did they ask you if you wanted to have a lawyer?"

"I know my rights."

"Did they ask you if you understood your rights?"

"No. No legal discussion there."

"Did they ask you if you waived your rights?"

"No."

"Excuse me. What was your answer? I didn't hear you."

"What was the question?"

"Did they ask you if you waived your rights?"

"I said there was no legal discussion. They just said half of the rights."

By Counsel Silverstein's demeanor and the look of frustration on his face, it was obvious that he recognized that his client was not making a favorable impression on Judge Scheinman. He responded to Ron's last answer by snapping, "I can't hear you."

Judge Scheinman turned toward Ron and encouraged, "Would you repeat your answer? We couldn't hear you, Ronald."

Ron directed his attention to his lawyer and responded, "You asked me if they asked, 'Do I waive my rights?' I never waived my rights."

"Did they ask you that question? Silverstein immediately asked in reply.

"I would never waive my rights anyway."

Frustration mounting, Silverstein continued, "I know. Did they ask you the question? Do you remember?"

"The question was not asked, no."

"Okay. Now, did there come a time you got in Wayne's car and went down to Green Hills Realty?"

"Yes, there did. Actually, the automobile was in my name. So it's my car, really. I paid insurance on it."

Upon hearing this answer, Judge Scheinman asked Ron, "The one that has been referred to as Wayne's car actually was your car?"

Ron replied, "It was transferred to my name. I helped him out with some payments on it."

"And when you got down to Green Hills Realty, did you transfer to the State Police car?"

"We did."

"And were you transported up to Ferndale?"

"Yes."

"Did you have any conversation while you were in the car going either from – did you have any conversation at all while going from your house down to Green Hills Realty?"

"Nothing substantial. Waited until we got to the barracks."

"Any discussion in the car from Green Hills Realty up to Ferndale?"

Mind wandering or perhaps losing focus, Ron asked in return, "What was the question before that? Any discussion from my house to Ferndale or"-

Displaying a look of frustration, Silverstein did not let Ron finish, responding, "Your house to Green Hills Realty."

It was fairly certain that his frustration increased with his client's answer, "It's really hard for me to remember now."

"I am just asking for your best recollection."

Ron pondered for a moment and then replied, "As I remember, not very much was said at all."

Hearing this answer, Judge Scheinman interjected, "Gentlemen, it is now almost twenty of three and the Court Reporter has been here working on other matters before this. He has been working steadily since one-thirty. I think he should have a little break. We will take a ten minute recess."

During the break, District Attorney Jaffe conversed with Defense Counsel Silverstein and asked that Silverstein make available any notes or other evidence held by his client that pertained to the substance of the hearing. Silverstein stated that, in his opinion, prosecution was not entitled to this material, citing attorney/client privilege.

Court was called back to order at 2:52 p.m. and Ron Krom returned to the witness stand.

District Attorney Jaffe opened, "Your Honor, since I assume Mr. Krom will be finished with his direct sometime shortly, I cannot plan now that all notes about the matters he has testified about is either in his or his attorney's possession."

Judge Scheinman responded, "You agree it is always a good idea for opposing counsel to have Rozario material (notes, evidence, etc.) well in advance after the"-

Counsel Silverstein stood and interrupted, "I object and refuse to turn over the notes because of the attorney/client privilege and that is not waived and is not Rozario material according to the law."

Judge Scheinman responded, "I think Mr. Silverstein seems to be right. It sounds logical to me. I will reserve."

Jaffe responded, "I want it clear on the record in light of the conversation we had with Mr. Silverstein during the recess that it is, at this time, his position as counsel for the defendant, that the defendant has had fair and adequate time and he is prepared to go forward with his testimony."

Judge Scheinman gave Jaffe a critical look, while responding, "I don't think it is necessary for you to put it on the record."

Silverstein immediately argued, "I think it is unethical and I ask it be stricken."

Judge Scheinman nodded his head in agreement stating, "I will grant that motion."

Jaffe responded, "I am trying to protect myself from other claims, Your Honor."

Judge Scheinman replied, "I don't see how you are involved."

Jaffe took his seat, stating as he sat down, "Very well, Judge."

Judge Scheinman added to his last statement, "You have no control over what defense counsel does. Mr. Silverstein, please continue."

Defense Counsel Silverstein arose from his seat at the defense table, approached the witness stand, gave his client a now stay with me look and asked, "Ronald, do you remember approximately what time you arrived at Ferndale that Thursday?"

"My recollection, I believe, I would say ten forty-five."

"Did you have a watch on that day?"

"Yes."

"Were you looking at it from time to time?"

"Yes."

"When you got to Ferndale, where did you go?"

"We went into one of the rooms in the back."
"And was anybody in the room with you?"
"Mr. Chandler and Mr. Fuente."
"And was there a door to the room?"
"Yes."
"Was it closed?"
"I don't recall specifically if the door was open or closed when we went in. Went in to the room"-
"How about after that room, did they close the door after they entered?"
"I know what you are getting at. I believe that the door was closed."
"At any time from the time you reached Ferndale until Mr. Martin came up to see you, did you ever have to go to the bathroom?"
"I never went to the bathroom there, no."
"In all the time you were there?"
"I'm not sure if they have one. I don't have one in my office. My office is small."

(Silverstein may have rolled his eyes in amazement at Ron's answer which, in essence defended the police for not permitting him to use the rest room) He continued, "You actually were in Ferndale or with the police right through until about midnight that day, isn't that so?"

Jaffe stood and interjected, "I object to any leading questions and ask the lawyer pose non-leading questions to his witness."

Before the court ruled on this motion Ron continued, "Actually, we were there, I believe, until approximately eight o'clock – between eight and nine. I believe it was light when we got there. I saw the key on the stone, and the stone was near the locker"-

Silverstein interrupted Ron and asked, "I am asking about how long you were in Ferndale. Were you there until midnight except for this excursion?"

"In entirety, yes," Ron answered.
"Ever go to the bathroom the entire time?"
"No."
"Ever ask to go the bathroom?"
District Attorney Jaffe called out, "Objection to relevance."
Judge Scheinman immediately replied without explanation, "Overruled."
Ron continued, "I don't believe I did ask, no."
Silverstein continued, "All right. Now, after you went into this room about ten forty-five or whatever time it was in the morning, what happened or what took place in the room?"

"They wanted to know if I knew where Gertrude was."

"And what did you answer to that?"

"I really wasn't very specific. I requested to see Roger Farber."

"Anybody else?"

"I did request to see Harry Resnick, yes. I wanted to make arrangements to defend myself."

"And did you communicate to the investigators that you wanted to make arrangements to defend yourself?"

Jaffe again called out, "I object to leading."

Before Judge Scheinman responded, Ron, continued, "I just wanted" –

Judge Scheinman stopped Ron, stating, "Wait a minute. You have to wait until I rule on the objection. When an objection is made, wait until I rule on it. I sustain the objection. You have to ask another question, Mr. Silverstein."

Silverstein continued, "Just keep telling us what was being said during this period of time. We were talking basically up until approximately two o'clock in the afternoon. Do you remember a time that you said you wanted an attorney? Do you remember that? I am doing this as a preliminary question."

Judge Scheinman interceded, responding to Silverstein, "Why don't you let him do that?"

Silverstein nodded his head in understanding and asked Ron, "Do you remember a time coming when you asked to see a lawyer about two o'clock?"

Ron answered, "I believe I did request a lawyer. I requested Mr. Martin, and I believe that I called Mr. Martin and he was out having lunch."

"That was at two o'clock approximately?"

"This was several years ago. I don't recall exactly what time. I believe it was in the afternoon, yes."

"Do you know what it was that caused you to ask for Mr. Martin?"

District Attorney Jaffe immediately railed, "Can we have no leading?"

Silverstein responded, "I don't see where it is leading at all. It doesn't tell him what he is to answer." Turning his attention once again to his client, he asked, "Would you tell us what it was, if anything, that caused you to ask for Mr. Martin?"

Ron answered, "My family had done business with Mr. Martin before."

"Had something been said to you that made you ask for a lawyer?"

Jaffe again railed, "Your Honor, that's absolutely suggestive. The witness seems to have no trouble when he is asked a question to tell a whole story."

Judge Scheinman responded, "Sustained." Then turned his attention to Ron and asked, "Something happened in the barracks to make you feel you wanted to talk to a lawyer?"

Ron looked up at the kindly-appearing Judge and replied, "I felt that I could see that I might be charged with a crime and I would like to say that I was supposed to pick up the money, you know, and I wrote Mr. Jaffe a letter and said I would confess to the charges that haven't been brought."

Shaking his head in frustration, Scheinman beckoned to Silverstein to continue.

Counsel Silverstein continued questioning Ron, "At any time that you were in the Ferndale barracks, did you ever say to somebody that you were going to pick up the money, ever state that to anybody or only in your mind?"

"I never really told them very much about it," Ron replied.

"Tell everything you can remember, what they said to you, what you said to them between the time you got to the barracks and the time you asked for Mr. Martin."

"Everything that was said?" Ron asked in response.

"Everything that you can remember?" Silverstein explained.

"Yes." Ron answered.

"Starting from the beginning and going right down the line," Silverstein encouraged.

"You want to know what was said while Mr. Martin was there?"

Silverstein was losing patience with his client but he held his feelings in check and responded, "No, no. When you first got to the barracks."

Judge Scheinman recognized Counsel's frustration and encouraged Ron, "From that point when you first got to barracks until Mr. Martin came."

While the exchange was occurring between Silverstein and his client, District Attorney Jaffe displayed his frustration by lowering his head to the prosecution table giving the appearance he was tired and falling asleep.

Recognizing Jaffe's display of frustration, Counsel Silverstein addressed Judge Scheinman, stating angrily, "Your Honor, if Your Honor please, Mr. Jaffe is doing things I think is completely improper and unprofessional. It is concerning both myself and I think the witness. When you are putting your head on the table, it is indicating some sort of despair. I think it is improper."

Ron immediately responded to this accusation by his counsel, "Mr. Jaffe is allowed to think in this court."

Judge Scheinman revealed the trace of a smile as he responded, "Mr. Krom, would you tell us what happened, what took place, what was said, and anything that happened that you can remember between the time you got there in the morning and the time Martin got there?"

Ron spoke directly to Judge Scheinman as he answered, "Okay. They wanted to know if I knew the location of Gertrude. I said I was under the impression that she was in a motel in the County somewhere. I really did not know. I was kept in the dark about everything that happened. There were different plans that took about – I don't know - Six or seven years to plan this and I really didn't know specifically what Roger Farber wanted to do."

Judge Scheinman continued questioning, "This is what you told the police?"

"I indicated to the police and I said that I thought she was – what I actually thought was she was in the County when they came to my house and then I knew something was wrong so I figured that she probably was in Carolina."

Upon hearing this answer District Attorney Jaffe interceded, "I object and ask to strike what he thought."

Nodding his head in agreement, Judge Scheinman responded, "Okay."

Ron immediately responded without being questioned, "What I said was she was in Carolina watching a color T.V., eating Kentucky Fried Chicken and drinking Cool Aid and that she was okay. I never really indicated to the officers or never said that she was abducted or never implicated her in the crime, but in fact was extortion, and she was suppose to be abducted."

While listening to the exchange between Ron and Judge Scheinman, Counsel Silverstein gave the appearance that he would rather be any other place in the world at the moment than seated in this courtroom listening to his client who appeared to be running mentally amok.

Judge Scheinman continued, "You told them that?"

"I never did. I never made it clear to them."

"What else was said during that period of time? Do you know what period of time, just talking about your statement and their questions."

Ron was confused by this more statement of fact than question, and responded, "You were talking about the period of time at the State Police barracks, right?"

Scheinman explained, "From the morning until Mr. Martin was called. I am talking about from approximately ten forty-five or eleven o'clock until two p.m. A period of three hours going through the lunch."

"Repeating this same thing," Ron answered, "My words were repetitious and consistent and I thought basically what he said was according to plan. I said that she was in Carolina, having Kentucky Fried Chicken, watching color T.V., and the room was air-conditioned."

Counsel Silverstein resumed questioning his client, "And is there anything else said during that three hour period?"

"I didn't really give the officers much information on it."

"Can you think of anything else? Did they ask you about the phone call to Mr. Resnick?"

Ron immediately answered, "No, I don't recall," and then explained, "Not during the three hour period. Nothing was mentioned at all. I mean – I didn't know anything about the phone call. They never mentioned anything about it. Nothing was said about it."

"During the three hour period, were you ever placed under arrest?"

"I believe Mr. Gellman (Assistant D.A. Emmanuel Gellman) read me my rights and I was under the impression I was arrested then and at the sight, at the property, Mr. Fuente said I was being arrested for murder."

"Do you ever remember being told by Mr. – Investigator Fuente you were being arrested for kidnapping?"

"No, he said murder."

"I mean earlier in the day. Do you remember any time of the day that you were told you were being arrested for kidnapping?"

"If he said this to me, I won't call him a liar. But I wouldn't remember."

"You asked for Mr. Martin, is that correct?"

"Yes, I did."

"Mr. Martin came and saw you?"

"Yes."

"And you had a discussion and he left."

"Correct."

"What happened right after he left?"

"I was attempting to get another lawyer. I wrote up some papers but I don't believe the papers I have seen are my writing, only they are a reasonable facsimile."

Silverstein walked to the defense table, picked up some papers, returned to the witness stand and stated, "And let me show you Exhibit Three" –

Ron interrupted his counsel, blurting out, "I know how a computer can do that because" –

Shaking his head in the negative indicating that he wanted Ron to listen instead of talk, Silverstein interrupted his client and continued, "Showing you Exhibit Three, do you need to hold it or can I hold it?"

Ron responded, "I can hold both."

Silverstein pointed to the papers and asked, "Have you seen that document before, not a copy of that, but that particular piece of paper?"

Ron responded, "I really don't remember this. I think I've seen – I don't believe that this – it says in addition to cash already paid. I believe that Mr. Resnick had the one with Mr. Chandler."

"Any further conversation had at that time?"

"Yes, Mr. Chandler was concerned about her safety and I wasn't really sure if time was of the essence at that point."

"What was said between you and Mr. Chandler – Investigator Chandler?"

"I think he was very angry with me. He thought I was misleading him but I really didn't know. I was under the impression she was probably in the County and two hotels were mentioned."

"Who mentioned them?"

"I mentioned them to you much later."

Shaking his head in the negative, Silverstein continued, "We are talking about between Chandler and yourself after Martin just left. Isn't it a fact that after Martin left, Chandler was there for a short period of time and District Attorney Gellman came in?"

"I seem to remember Gellman. I don't know if Gellman – I am not exactly sure at what point in time he came."

"Do you remember his coming?"

"He arrived, yes."

"Do you remember having a conversation with him?"

"I don't really recall."

Silverstein did his best to mask the frustration he was feeling with his client, however, his next question was asked in a louder voice than his previous, "I am just asking if you remember having a conversation. I am not asking what it was."

Ron pondered this question for a moment and then responded, "I believe – I definitely remember having a conversation with him, yes."

"Do you remember any part of the conversation?"

Ron gave Silverstein a quizzical look and responded, "Specifically?"

"In substance," Silverstein replied, "You don't have to have the exact words."

"I don't. It's hard for me to reconstruct specifically what was said. There was a point in time after I was arrested where I was placed on drugs and went to a complete stop and they brought me back."

"When was it you say you were put under drugs?"

"I was on medication," Ron explained.

Upon hearing this answer, District Attorney Jaffe called out, "I object. We are talking about the events surrounding May 26, not after" –

Judge Scheinman cut Jaffe short responding, "I presume that's what he is talking about, too."

Counsel Silverstein addressed the court, "That's why I am trying to find out the date."

Ron immediately responded, "Specifically what was said, it's hard."

Judge Scheinman gestured to the attorneys to remain silent, turned his attention toward Ron and asked, "The question about drugs; did you receive drugs or medication on May 26th when you were in the barracks?"

The confused, incredulous look on Judge and both attorneys, faces upon hearing Ron's answer portrayed an appropriate summary for the entire hearing.

Having raised the issue of being medicated, Ron now answered, "No, I never used drugs in my life. I don't smoke, don't drink very much, I don't even have coffee."

Regaining his composure, Silverstein asked, "At the barracks, you were not given anything other than food, water and things of that sort?"

"I was given French fries, but I am not sure if I had a hamburger, which I believe came from McDonalds. I believe a milkshake. I usually drink milkshakes and milk."

"Anything else besides those three items?"

"No."

"Didn't on that day?"

"I am not sure if I had a hamburger. I believe it was French fries and a milkshake."

"Did you have any other food that day?"

"I hadn't eaten breakfast."

"Any food in the evening?"

"No."

"Now, did there come a time when you spoke to Mr. Gellman?"

"I said I don't really recall specifically what was said. It seems to me – I am not sure if it was – I don't really remember that much about it."

"After Mr. Gellman, did somebody else come into the room? Do you remember Investigator Magilligutti?" (Spelling in actual transcript)

"Oh, yes, I recollect Magilligutti."

"You remember him coming to the room?"

"He came in and in essence, he was a negotiator from New York and he said that you would do the right thing and he kept repeating that and" – Ron stopped speaking before concluding his answer.

"Go ahead, what else did he say or did you say to him?"

"I said to him that I thought she was in Carolina and she was safe. I never really implicated her at all. You know, I never said she was involved. But she was involved, but I didn't say it."

"What did you actually say to Magilligutti?"

"I told Mr. Magilligutti substantially the same thing that I told Mr. Chandler."

"And what was that?"

"That she was safe and I really didn't know, I wanted to speak with Roger Farber. That's another part that I was told; he was in Middletown State Police barracks there."

"Anything else you can remember that you said to McGillicutti or he said to you?"

"No."

"Did there come a time that Mr. Resnick came into the room?"

"Yes."

"Mr. Resnick came later and Mr. Resnick came to the room, Investigator McGillicutti and Fuente and Chandler were still there?"

"Just specifically who was there at that point, I believe that – it seems to me there were three officers there. I believe that other officers might have come in to the room and they left."

"Did you have a conversation with Mr. Resnick? Directly to you and you to him?"

"Yes."

"What did you say to him and what did he say to you to the best of your recollection?"

"He said to me, 'Gertrude can help you,' and he is right."

"What?"

"He was right."

"Go ahead. Then what? Did you say anything to him?"

"I didn't really say that much to him."

"Say anything to you?"

"I can't recall the whole context of the situation. I can't recall specifically what he said. I recall he said, I recall he said that Gertrude could help me and eventually I said 'let's go.' I knew a tentative place where she might be and there was a property that our parents had previously owned together - Roger's family, my mother and a third party."

"When you say, 'let's go,' did you say anything just before that?"

"I am not really sure."

"Did you ever indicate you knew where Trudy was?"

"Not specifically. I never indicated that I knew where she was. I had been asking to see Roger Farber. I think basically you should write one paragraph and give you what information I gave all of the officers which was she was in the County and that then when I realized – you know that things hadn't gone according to plan and the reason was as I wrote you in the letters I refused to pick up the money and believe this – I had received – you wanted the whole story and I don't mind narrating. Two calls on the 26th and in the evening and the first one was and she said this is Wednesday, she said could we have a date tonight, would you like to see me and it was during that week and I said well – I said okay. I said I will come over and pick you up and I had always gone to the trailer and she was living in Swan Lake and I would pick her up and we would go out or usually I would bring her back and we would watch television."

Ron's rambling, confusing answer appeared to be either an intentional avoidance of answering the question directly, or a manifestation of panic triggered schizophrenia. Judge Scheinman, Jaffe and Silverstein exchanged looks of confusion and for a few moments, there was silence in the courtroom as they tried to make sense out of what amounted to a rambling dissertation rather than an answer. Neither, judge or attorneys, cautioned the defendant not to ramble incoherently when answering questions. Why, remains unknown; however, one could speculate that they decided it would be unproductive.

After the brief silence, Silverstein resumed questioning asking Ron, "What was the second call?"

"The second call was this character named Tony and I believed he called – I am not sure exactly which one. I believe he called subsequent to her call. I have a phone in my room and I said "no" because I was indicating all along, I admit and agreed to which I helped promote this and I wouldn't say he was participating."

Upon hearing this confusing answer, Silverstein fully expected an objection from Jaffe and/or some sort of chastisement from Judge Scheinman. However, Jaffe remained silent and sat smiling at the prosecution table. Judge Scheinman just nodded to Silverstein with an indication to move on.

Silverstein continued, "Did you ever tell this to Investigator Chandler or Fuente?"

"No, I didn't tell them."

"You didn't tell them?"

"No."

"Now, we are talking about when you said, 'let's go.' Did you ever tell them you knew the location of Trudy?"

"I never did. You see, I was – I believe that is where they might have been because Roger and Gertrude came in, I believe there was a lean to or shack or something like that on the property. I thought that" –

District Attorney Jaffe interrupted the completion of Ron's answer calling out, "Objection! It is not responsive and I move to strike. He is saying he thought or believed. And he said he didn't communicate this to the officers. I move to strike."

Judge Scheinman responded, "The question was, did you know whether"

Jaffe interrupted Scheinman stating, "The question was what did he say to the officer and he is now telling us what he thought and believed about her."

Judge Scheinman directed his attention to the witness and asked, "Is that so?"

Ron answered, "I didn't tell the officers very much."

Judge Scheinman responded, "Wait a minute. If that's so and Mr. Silverstein is indicating it is, then the testimony of the witness in respect to the question will be stricken. What did you tell the officers when you said, 'let's go?"

Ron answered, "I didn't tell the officers anything.

Silverstein resumed questioning of his client. "Now, you then went to someplace outside Grahamsville on Route 55?"

Ron nodded his head in the affirmative and replied, "Correct, yes."

"And went up some dirt road. Did you get out of the car?"

Ron did not answer the question and instead stated, "Here is something I think is important. I said to slow down; this road is a little shale road. It goes up the incline and I said slow down. We drove past it and went in the left side by the reservoir and turned around and came back and we made the road. I believe that is about fifty yards, maybe between the cul-de-sac and the incline."

Silverstein reformed his previous question asking, "Did you take the officers somewhere?"

"We went up to the top and I wouldn't call it a road up there but the road was up and we parked the car there and I didn't see anything. We just went up the small grade. It's about – it's a ways up."

"What were the light conditions at that time?"

"I believe it was about dusk."

"Did you have flashlights or anything with you?"

"I believe that the officers went down to the car after I had opened the thing up. The key was on the rock there. The rock was very near to the locker. The key was silver, and I saw the key on the rock and I opened the padlock. It's a bullet-proof lock."

"What happened next?"

"I looked in. She was apparently deceased."

"Then what happened?"

"I didn't feel very well, emotionally, mentally and otherwise."

"Then what happened?"

"One of the officers helped me over to a log there and I sat down and I saw the cardboard box and the gun, the .22 caliber gun. I grabbed the gun and I tried to shoot myself. I couldn't get the safety off anyway. I got the gun up and I was subdued."

"Is that when Fuente placed you under arrest for murder?"

"I was placed for arrest – under arrest I believe when we went back down near the car."

"Did you go back to Ferndale?"

"Yes, we did."

"And during the trip back to Ferndale, was there any conversation in the car?"

"I think the officers were concerned that there were other people involved in this instant case and they wanted to know who."

"Did you tell them?"

"I said that Roger was involved and that it was clear to me it would be probably – Roger and I – Roger went to law school and I worked for a law firm in Ellenville."

"Are you telling the police this?"

"No, I am telling you now."

Ron's answer to the question somehow met without objection or chastisement from the court.

Silverstein restated the question, "Was this in the car?"

Ron answered, "It was clear to me it was going to be damn hard to prove what happened."

"What did you say? What did they say? What came out of their mouths? What came out of your mouth?"

"I didn't really say very much, no. I was thinking about" –

Silverstein did not let Ron finish answering, and broke in, "When you got back to the barracks, you went back into one of the rooms?"

"I believe we did, yes."

"Were there some additional questions asked of you when you got back to the barracks?"

"I was photographed and I was fingerprinted. Really not much was asked."

"Do you remember any discussions with the officers before you were fingerprinted and photographed?"

"Discussions, no. I wasn't orally fluid and I didn't really say very much."

"Go ahead. Did you tell them you put Trudy in the box?"

"No, I didn't."

"Did you tell them you had kidnapped Trudy?"

"No, I didn't."

"Did you tell them you had been the masked person over at the house?"

"No."

"Do you remember Investigator Chandler testifying here a few days ago?"

"Yes, I do."

"Do you remember him testifying that you became orally fluid in everything you told him?"

"He said that but it might not be true."

"Was it true or not?"

"It wasn't true. I just picked the words out of their notes."

"Was there anything that he testified to from the time you came back from the scene that they found Trudy Farber until you were fingerprinted, anything that Investigator Chandler said about that, true?"

Ron had difficulty thinking of an appropriate non-incriminating answer to this question and responded, "What are you saying?"

"You don't remember?"

Ron fidgeted nervously in the witness box and replied, "I don't understand the question."

"Did you hear Investigator Chandler testify two days ago?"

"Yes, I did."

"Do you remember what he testified, that you said after you came back from where Trudy Farber was found?"

Ron was struggling to devise an appropriate non-incriminating answer and unable to do so immediately; he responded with an answer he commonly used throughout this hearing. "I don't recall specifically what he said – that I said after we came back. I really didn't say very much."

His own attorney was not letting him off the hook this easily. Silverstein pressed, "What did you say after you came back that you can recollect?"

"I said that – I remember specifically that I said Roger was involved and I believe the officer thought that he must have been a pretty lousy bastard to do what he did to his wife. I think he felt that there was another girl involved. He had a girl on the side. I think otherwise" –

Silverstein cut him off and asked, "Do you remember being taken down to Judge Herring?"

"Yes, I do."

"Do you remember what you said to Judge Herring?"

"I didn't really" –

"What?" Silverstein asked interrupting his answer.

"Not specifically."

"Do you know what you said to him, if anything?"

"I recall his testimony here the other day."

Judge Scheinman broke in and admonished Ron, stating, "You were asked what you said to Judge Herring and whether you were in his court. Not what he said here the other day."

Ron stared at the Judge, pondering how to answer the question.

Silverstein interrupted the silence by asking, "Do you remember?"

Judge Scheinman again addressed Ron's failure to answer the question, sternly asking, "Do you remember what happened in his court?"

Ron responded, "Sub-consciously, I am sure I do."

Judge Scheinman gave Ron a stern look and admonished, "Well, tell us, if you can remember."

Subconsciously, something in Ron's brain was telling him to be careful in answering this question. He responded, "Thirteen trillion brain cells – I believe I said that I wanted the bail to be low because Mr. Harry Resnick was going to pay my bail and he said he would pay my bail and that's the impression I was under."

Silverstein resumed, "And do you remember anything else you said to Judge Herring, just yes or no?"

"I don't recall specifically, no."

"Do you remember being transported" –

Ron interrupted his counsel in mid question, blurting out, "He talked. I met with Mr. Herring on another occasion."

Silverstein ignored this statement and asked, "Do you remember being transferred by a police vehicle to the County jail?"

"Yes."

"Was Investigator Bult in the car?"

"I believe Mr. Bult was in the car, yes."

"And also Investigator Ruth?"

"There were two officers. I believe it was Mr. Ruth."

"What did they say to you, and what did you say to them in the car ride, if anything?"

"I don't recall. Again, this is a few years ago. I read Mr. Bult's notes and found about forty-eight mistakes."

Judge Scheinman responded, "Tell us whether you remember what was said in the car?"

Ron responded without looking at the Judge, "No, I don't."

Silverstein then asked Ron, "And who said it?"

Ron's failure to immediately answer the question resulted in Judge Scheinman asking, "You don't remember?"

Ron stated blankly at the Judge and his attorney, remaining silent.

"Do you remember being asked any questions by either of the investigators in the car?" Silverstein again asked.

"No, they didn't say anything. They didn't ask me anything. I might have just said that I wasn't guilty of the charges."

"Did you volunteer any information as to what you had done?"

Before Ron answered this question, District Attorney Jaffe called out, "Objection. That is a conclusion."

Judge Scheinman responded, "Overruled," with no explanation provided.

Ron answered, "I never volunteered, never volunteered information. If I wanted to give information to somebody I would give it to them."

Silverstein continued, "Did you give Investigator Bult or Investigator Ruth information during that car ride?"

"As I recall, I was very upset about the whole thing and I didn't say very much."

Jaffe immediately responded, "I ask that that be stricken as not being responsive."

Ron responded to the District Attorney, before Judge Scheinman rendered a decision on the request to strike testimony stating, "I didn't really say very much. I am a quiet person."

Jaffe waved his hand in a gesture of disgust, but remained silent.

Counsel continued, "Did you tell them anything about the Trudy Farber incident at all?"

Evoking the evasive answer that seemed to carry him through the proceeding, Ron responded, "I didn't really say very much, no."

Silverstein did not let this answer pass and probed, "When you say you really didn't say very much, it means you did say something?"

Jaffe arose from the prosecution table and stated in a voice expressing disgust, "Asked and answered five times."

Ron immediately fired back, "Again, this is over two years ago."

Judge Scheinman gently chastised Ron by turning toward him and instructing, "If you don't remember, say you don't remember."

Ron faced the judge and responded, "I don't remember, but I know specifically that the entirety of the information I gave, they gave out because I was under the impression until I saw her dead in the box that she was probably out of the county. I was under the impression she was in the county until I was questioned about the situation."

Upon hearing this answer, Judge, defense Counsel and Prosecutor exchanged looks that could be translated to "What did he just say?" All three had already come to the conclusion that while Ron continually used the word 'specifically' when answering questions, he was seldom specific about anything.

Ron's confusing response to the Judge was allowed to go unchallenged and Silverstein continued questioning asking, "Is that the little or not very much you said to Bult and Ruth?"

"That's about it, yes."

His next question of the witness caused Jaffe to immediately jump to his feet voicing a loud "Objection!"

The question Silverstein asked was, "Ronald, why did you try to shoot yourself with the gun?"

Judge Scheinman immediately ruled "Sustained," without explanation.

Silverstein went in a different direction, asking, "Ronald how did you feel after the investigators came to the house?"

Jaffe again called out, "Objection!"

Judge Scheinman waved his hand at Jaffe and responded, "Overruled."

Ron responded, "I will tell you the truth. I didn't really know what was going on. You know, they said that Gertrude was missing, that I felt that something had gone wrong because I have written about fifteen to sixteen hundred pages" –

Judge Scheinman turned to Ron and interrupted his answer, stating, "The question is how you felt."

Ron answered, "I was under the impression somebody was supposed to pick up the money because that was in the" –

Upon hearing Ron's response both Judge and District Attorney, shook their heads negatively reflecting their frustration.

Counsel Silverstein cut Ron's answer short, asking him, "How was your health and mind?"

"I was not in a very good mood."

"Okay. After you found out that she was missing, were you still in a good mood?"

"I was concerned, very concerned."

"Were you still in a good mood?"

"No, I was calm then."

Frustrated and fully believing that this line of questioning was leading no where, District Attorney Jaffe called out, "Objection."

Judge Scheinman overruled the motion without explanation and motioned to Counsel to continue questioning the witness.

Silverstein asked Ron, "Did your mood change in any way in Ferndale and up there (?) in the morning?"

"I believe that it was pensive all the way," Ron quietly answered.

"You had complete control of your faculties, right?"

"Sure."

"In good health?"

"Yes."

"Nothing was bothering you?"

"That's right."

"For the whole time you were with the police?"

"I wouldn't say for the whole time I was with the police. I wouldn't say" –

Silverstein cut his witness's answer short and asked, "When did it change if it ever did change?"

"When it was apparent to me that she might be in danger. I never really believed she was in danger until I saw her dead. I didn't really know what was going to be in the locker. I thought the money might have been discovered there for all I know."

DA Jaffe immediately responded, "I move to strike that out."

Judge Scheinman agreed, ruling, "Motion is granted." He then asked Counsel, "Do you have any other questions?"

Silverstein responded, "One second." Again directing his attention to Ron he asked, "Did you ever waive your rights to have a lawyer?"

Displaying that he was growing tired of what he considered to be repetition and a waste of time, Judge Scheinman admonished Silverstein stating, "He said he never waived any of his rights."

Silverstein responded, "That was up at the house."

Ron injected himself into the debate between his attorney and the judge, blurting out, "No, I didn't."

Realizing that Judge Scheinman's patience was wearing out, Counsel Silverstein stated, "No further questions."

21

District Attorney Jaffe arose from the prosecution table and addressed the court, asking, "May I have a few minutes to organize? I believe it will save us quite a bit of time."

Judge Scheinman responded, "All right."

The record of the hearing would reflect that the court recessed at three forty-three p.m. and reconvened at three fifty-three p.m. Ron was directed to return to the witness stand and District Attorney Jaffe was directed to commence cross-examination.

"Mr. Krom," Jaffe asked, "you sat through a number of hearings in this courthouse, have you not?"

"True." Ron responded.

"And would you try to keep your voice up so I can hear you and you can hear me?"

"You mean louder?" Ron asked in reply.

"Louder."

"Okay." Ron quietly responded.

"Sir, you understand what I am saying to you now, you can hear me?"

"I can hear you, yes."

"You understand what I am saying to you, you hear the words and understand the words?"

Perhaps under the impression that the District Attorney was toying with him or wishing to demonstrate his superb intelligence, Ron smirked at Jaffe and responded, "Je pouvais entendre et je crois que je peux parler."

Upon hearing the answer, Judge Scheinman interceded, stating, "Let the record indicate the defendant says in French, what would be translated as being, 'I could hear and I think I can speak.' Go ahead, Mr. Jaffe, and Mr. Krom, please answer in English."

Ron evinced a look of surprise when Judge Scheinman so easily understood French. His respect for the distinguished looking magistrate increased dramatically.

Jaffe gazed intently into Ron's brown eyes and asked, "You are a person of more than average intelligence, are you not, sir?"

Ron smiled at Jaffe in return and answered, "I am a genius."

"You have heard and read the various reports of the psychiatrists and psychologists on the prior hearings we have had; is that correct?"

"Yes."

"Now, sir, directing your attention to 1977, specifically May of 1977, according to your testimony on direct-examination, you were part of a plan to commit an extortion; is that correct?"

"I was involved."

"Yes or no. Were you part of a plan?"

"Part of a plan. I was a participant."

"You participated in an extortion scheme, correct?"

"You might say that."

"And you, as part of that scheme, hoped to get some money from Harry Resnick?"

"My fee was not discussed, I was doing it for Gertrude and" –

Judge Scheinman cut Ron short asking him, "Were you supposed to get money from Harry Resnick?"

Evincing a look of surprise that Judge Scheinman had asked this question, Ron hesitated for a moment before answering; then stated, "I was supposed to pick up the money from Roger and deliver it to the locker on the property on Route 55."

Jaffe resumed questioning asking, "The money was supposed to come from Harry Resnick, is that correct?"

"Yes."

"And did there come a time in May of 1977 that you were at your house in Grahamsville and you saw Investigators Chandler and Fuente?"

Either Ron's mind wandered, or he did not like the question as he responded, "What was the question?"

Jaffe gave the witness a probing look and slowly reiterated his previous question. "There came a time on May 26, 1977 that you saw Chandler and Fuente?"

"Yes, there did."

"And there came a time Fuente, as you testified on direct, started to give you your rights and you interrupted him; is that correct?"

"That's correct."

"Now, sir, you do know what the Miranda rights are, isn't that right?"

"That's right."

"And you know them today and you knew them in May of 1977, is that correct?"

"Yes, I do." Ron answered, then started to elaborate, "Miranda against Arizona. About a Spanish guy" –

Jaffe broke in to the witness's dissertation on the Miranda Supreme Court decision, firing this question at Ron, "You didn't need a police officer to tell a person of your intelligence what your rights were, correct?"

Ron again smirked at Jaffe and responded, "Nevertheless, it's the law, correct?"

Jaffe glared at Ron and responded, "Mr. Krom, answer my question. You knew the rights without regard to what anybody said to you?"

"I knew the rights, yes." Ron answered.

"Now, there came a time after you interrupted Fuente giving you your rights that Fuente and Chandler had a discussion; right?"

Ron quietly responded, "Yes, there was a time we had a discussion."

Not sure that he had heard the answer correctly, Jaffe gave Ron an inquisitive look and stated, "I can't hear your answer. Did you have a discussion?"

Ron remained silent and Judge Scheinman responded, "He says yes, there was a discussion."

Jaffe continued, "Isn't it a fact either Fuente, Chandler or both of them in the vicinity of your home or your parents home where you were staying on May 26, 1977, told you there had been a kidnapping?"

Ron quietly responded with the one word answer, "No."

"They never said that?"

"No, Gertrude was missing."

"Isn't it a fact, sir, they asked you and you in fact told them you could help find her?"

"I said that I had information about it."

"You also said, did you not, you could help them find her?"

"Well, I could"-

Judge Scheinman broke in, gave Ron an inquisitive look and asked, "Did you say you could help find her?"

Ron looked up at the Judge and replied, "I don't know if I used those very words."

"In substance?" Scheinman shot back.

Ron answered, "That I might have information which would lead to her ultimate location, yes."

Judge Scheinman gave Jaffe a nod, indicating he could resume questioning the witness and Jaffe asked, "There came a time shortly after that, did there not, you also told Fuente and Chandler that you wanted money from Resnick for information for Trudy to go free?"

"That's not true."

"Never said that?"

"No. I said for my legal defense that I wanted to be supplied with a lawyer. I mean they – they had no idea that I was involved and I made no admissions."

"Isn't it a fact, sir, you told Chandler and Fuente you wanted money from Resnick and that you also told them you had called Resnick and told him you wanted a million dollars in fifties and hundreds?"

"I don't recall that and it is not true."

"You don't recall it or you never said it?"

"I don't recall it, I never said it, and it is not true."

"Isn't it a fact that you told Fuente and Chandler that you knew the Resnicks and his brothers and that, if they were to liquidate, they would be able to get the money?"

Instead of answering the question, Ron once again put his superior knowledge on display by responding, "Liquidate is an economic term and it is the ability to move to cash."

Looking up and rolling his eyes, District Attorney Jaffe responded, "I move to strike."

Judge Scheinman responded, "Motion is granted."

Jaffe resumed, "Now, sir, isn't it a fact that shortly after eleven thirty a.m., the morning of May 26th, you told Fuente and Chandler that you knew where Trudy was?"

"No." Ron answered.

"Isn't it a fact, sir, you were asked to tell Fuente and Chandler where she was, and you said if you did that you would give up a good hand of cards and you would get nothing?"

"I never said that at all. I don't play cards."

"Isn't it a fact, sir, that you told Fuente and Chandler that Harry Resnick was going to pay for your five years of suffering?"

Jaffe looked surprised when Ron answered, "I said something like that, yes."

Concerning motive Ron had opened the door a crack and Jaffe intended to force the door fully open. He probed, "As a matter of fact, sir, you were kind of angry at the Resnicks because you weren't invited to a wedding."

There was a hint of bitterness in Ron's quiet voice as he responded, "Personally, it didn't bother me in the least bit but I was dating a girl and she was – she says to me I thought you were a good friend with them and I said, 'well, my parents are going and it doesn't matter to me. I could probably buttonhole them and we could go. I personally rather not do it and"-

Jaffe interrupted by asking, "Did you not tell all that to Chandler and Fuente?"

"Not in those words, no. But I indicated that and I said that I wasn't invited to the wedding and that"-

"The wedding was five years before May of 1977, is that correct?"

"I believe. I don't recall the specific date."

"Isn't it a fact you told Fuente and Chandler for those five years, 'I have been planning to get even with Resnick'."

"Me get even with Resnick? It would all even out in the end. That's a true statement."

"Isn't it a fact you told Chandler and Fuente you and Roger Farber were planning this scheme for five years and that you were going to get a least three hundred thousand out of it?"

"I never really knew what Roger was going to give me and I"-

Jaffe interrupted Ron's response and asked the court, "I move to strike and ask the witness to respond."

Judge Scheinman turned toward Ron and asked, "Did you tell the police you and Roger had been planning this for five years and you hoped to get three hundred thousand dollars out of it? Did you tell that to the police or not?"

Ron responded without looking at the judge, "I don't recall saying that, no."

Jaffe continued, "Isn't it a fact you also told Fuente and Chandler that that night before sometime between eleven and midnight, you yourself made a telephone call to Resnick's house?"

"I believe I was on a date, if you remember my testimony about fifteen minutes prior – I was on a date with Cynthia Black."

"I will renew the question. Isn't it a fact you told Chandler and Fuente you called the Resnick's residence between eleven p.m., and midnight?"

"I never said that."

"Isn't it a fact you told them you had heard Roger Farber answer the telephone, so you hung up?"

Ron responded to Jaffe's question with a question. "Why would I hang up on him if he allegedly did this and its true?"

Judge Scheinman interceded, asking Ron, "Did you tell the police that you heard Roger Farber"-

Ron responded before the Judge finished his question, "No, I never did. I think some of questions aren't exactly coherent. You have to get into the casual ideology in order to understand."

Judge and District Attorney exchanged looks of bewilderment at Ron's response. Judge Scheinman considered responding, thought it would serve no purpose and so motioned to Jaffe to continue his questioning of the witness.

Jaffe asked Ron, "Now, sir, isn't it a fact that after you gave quite a statement or quite a deal of conversation with Fuente and Chandler at the New York State Police barracks in Ferndale, you wanted to leave?"

"I believe that I indicated that I wanted to go, yes." Ron answered.

"And there came a time Fuente told you that you couldn't go; isn't that right?"

"I think he said, 'why don't you stay and help us;' I said, 'okay.' I just thought, you know, how about going for lunch and I would come back and see him. I never really said anything. I indicated I was going to walk out."

"There came a time you said you wanted to talk to a lawyer?"

"That's right."

"And somewhere around two o'clock on May 26, 1977?"

"Approximately."

"There is no question, is there, that in fact Fuente and Chandler stopped talking to you and gave you a telephone and you called Martin; is that correct?"

"I believe that they did stop talking and that I made the phone call to Mr. Martin and I believe he was out to lunch and subsequently he came."

"And he talked to you, is that correct?"

"Yes, he did."

"And afterwards, he left, right?"

"I believe that he" –

Jaffe interrupted Ron demanding, "Yes or no, did he leave?"

"I believe he went back to his office, yes."

"And subsequently, you talked to Mr. Gellman and to Fuente and Chandler, is that correct?"

As Ron did not immediately answer, Judge Scheinman turned to him and said, "Can't you answer that yes or no?"

Ron gave Jaffe a blank look and responded, "Correct."

Jaffe continued, "Mr. Gellman told you all your rights, did he not?"

Nodding his head in the affirmative Ron responded, "Mr. Gellman did, yes."

"And you understood them, did you not?"

"Yes, I did."

"You didn't need him to tell you your rights, did you?"

Giving the District Attorney a smug look, Ron answered, "No, I studied the case, Joe; I went through constitutional law in Vassar College."

Ignoring that the witness had just referred to him by the shortened version of his first name, Jaffe asked, "Thereafter, you talked to Fuente and Chandler, did you not?"

"Correct."

"And you also spoke to McGillicutti, did you not?"

"That's true."

"You heard Fuente, Chandler and McGillicutti all testify in this courtroom, did you not?"

"Yes, I did."

"Were you able to hear their testimony?"

"Yes, I heard it."

"Did you understand their testimony?"

"Yes, I did."

"You heard each of them in substance describe various statements made by you, is that correct?"

Ron's failure to immediately respond resulted in Judge Scheinman asking, "Did you hear them?"

"I heard them," Ron replied, and added, "I also heard quite a few inconsistencies, too."

Judge Scheinman repeated, "Did you hear them?"

"I heard them, yes."

Jaffe continued, "In substance, isn't it correct you told Fuente and Chandler and McGillicutti, in substance, in fact that you were involved, that you knew where Trudy Farber was; isn't that a fact?"

Counsel Silverstein, who had remained silent throughout Jaffe's cross examination of his client thus far, called out, "Objection."

Before the court had a chance to rule on the objection Ron blurted out, "I never said I knew where she was."

Counsel added, "We don't know what he said to all four."

At this Ron looked at the District Attorney and blurted out, "You are being redundant anyway."

The look on Judge Scheinman's face revealed that he did not like this uncontrolled exchange between Counsel and client. His "Overruled," was expressed in a louder voice than normal. Then he turned toward the witness and asked, "Can you answer that question?"

Ron responded, "If I knew where she was? No."

Judge Scheinman motioned to Jaffe to continue.

"There came a time," the District Attorney asked, "did there not, when you took McGillicutti, Chandler and Fuente to Grahamsville?"

"Well, I don't know if I would say that I took them," Ron answered. "We went. I was in the backseat of the car, not the front."

"You gave them instructions to drive, did you not?"

"I said proceed to Grahamsville and they went to Woodbourne" –

"You told them to go to Woodbourne?"

"No."

"Did you tell them to take 52 to 42 and take a left on 42 and go to Grahamsville?"

"That's correct. I don't recall if I gave them specific directions. They just went the long way."

"There came a time that you came into Grahamsville that evening of May 26?"

"That's right."

"Did you give instructions to where Trudy Farber's body was ultimately found?"

"I didn't give directions to where the body was found. I mean we went there, I said proceed across the reservoir and said turn up this road and I never told them who owned the property. I never" –

Normally a very patient man, the look on Judge Scheinman's face indicated he was losing patience with the witness's attempts to avoid answering questions in a direct manner. He interrupted Ron and asked, "Did you tell them to turn right in Grahamsville, go past the reservoir?"

Ron answered, "Yes, I did."

Judge Scheinman continued, "When you got past South Hills Road, did you tell them to turn right up a dirt road?"

Ron responded, "It's not a right, it's an oblique turn. It goes" –

Scheinman cut him off and in an unfriendly tone of voice asked, "Towards the right, up a hill?"

"In the direction right." Ron answered.

Judge Scheinman continued questioning, asking, "Up in that property it later turned out that Trudy's body was found on that property, is that right?"

Ron started to answer by stating, "I believe that;" however, the glower on the Judge's face caused him to hesitate and reconsider his answer. "Yes that's true," he then said.

"All right." Judge Scheinman responded. "Mr. Jaffe you may continue."

Jaffe asked, "They didn't give instructions on how to get there, you gave the instructions, right?"

"That's true," Ron answered.

"You had been there before, had you not?"

"With Roger. I believe Roger gave directions, too."

Shaking his head in the negative, Jaffe addressed the court, "Your Honor, objection, I move to strike."

In response, Judge Scheinman gazed sternly at Ron and asked, "Had you been there before that day, yes or no?"

Ron meekly responded, "Yes."

Jaffe continued, "You had built that particular – whatever you want to describe it - the box in the ground, had you not? Yes or no."

Ron did not immediately answer and when he did, said, "I was thinking of an answer in French. Let me see. Roger had built it, Roger had a" –

Judge Scheinman again cut Ron short and snapped, "Did you build it, yes or no?"

Ron responded, "No, I didn't"

Jaffe resumed questioning asking, "Did you plant the ammunition box next to it?"

"No."

"You knew it was there?"

"Yes, I did."

"You had, in fact, spent sometime in that area, had you not?"

"Our parents own the property. Obviously I sold the property."

Judge Scheinman responded in an angry tone of voice, "The answer is yes."

Ron looked up at the Judge and stated, "He knows the answer, why is he asking the question?"

"Because I don't know the answer," Judge Scheinman replied.

Ron gave the Judge a confused look and stated, "All right."

Jaffe took charge of questioning the witness again, asking, "Isn't it a fact, sir, you knew the area, you knew the box, you knew the ammunition box, you had been to the area in the recent days before May 26, 1977. Yes or no?"

Not liking that question, Ron responded, "Recent days preceding? I had lent a car which I borrowed"-

Jaffe tilted his head upward in an act of frustration, and stated, "I move to strike."

Judge Scheinman again glared at Ron and asked, "Had you been recently there before May 26?"

"On the 24th I was there," Ron replied.

Jaffe resumed, "Now, sir, there was a rifle which you tried to use that you testified about on direct-examination, a .22 rifle; is that correct?"

"Correct."

"It was there, at the scene, where you took Fuente and Chandler and McGillicutti; is that correct?"

"It was there, yes."

"And you knew it was there because you left it there, did you not? Yes or no."

"I had given them a gun, yes."

"I asked whether you left the rifle there, yes or no?"

"I bought the rifle two weeks before. I happen to have a gun collection and"-

Judge Scheinman again cut Ron short and asked, "Had you placed it there?"

"Yes." Ron quietly responded.

Jaffe continued, "Not only had you placed it there, you, in fact, shot holes in the box in the ground; had you not?"

Ron's self-described genius mind was going into overload as it searched for some sort of non-incriminating answer. He sputtered, "I was perturbed"-

Giving the witness a hard look, Jaffe cut Ron off and in a loud voice asked, "Did you shoot holes in the ground; yes or no?"

Feeling Jaffe misspoke when he said 'ground,' Judge Scheinman interceded, amending the question to, "To the box cover. Did you shoot the holes in the box cover with that rifle?"

Ron's genius mind was definitely in overload, and it did not want him to answer that question in a forthright manner. He blurted in response, "They thought I was going to come with a Cadillac at the start and they wanted to see the gun work and I demonstrated the gun"-

"You demonstrated the gun to whom?" Scheinman interrupted.

"Tony." Ron answered.

(Ah, a schizophrenic's mind can be so creative)

Judge Scheinman gave Ron an incredulous look and asked, "You don't recall the name?"

"I was never given the name," Ron answered.

Judge and District Attorney shook their heads in frustrated disbelief and Jaffe resumed questioning. "Isn't it a fact, sir, just the way you told Fuente and Chandler, that you had gone up with Trudy Farber put her into that box in the ground and before you put her in the box, you shot holes in it so she could breathe?"

"That's not true," Ron fired in reply.

"You made up the story for Chandler?"

"I never said"-

"You didn't make any statements to which they testified?"

"Some of what they said is true. But I am specifically denying that particular statement."

Jaffe walked to the prosecution table, selected some photos from a file and then returned to question the witness. He laid the photos on the desk in front of Ron, stating as he did so, "Pictures marked people's exhibit fourteen through twenty for identification."

Then he asked, "Do you deny telling Chandler and Fuente you had abducted Trudy Farber and put her into a car that you borrowed from the fellow real estate person?"

"I never said I abducted anyone."

"Did you tell them that Trudy Farber wound up in the trunk of a car that you drove to a certain area?"

"No."

"You never said that?"

"No."

Jaffe gave Ron a look of disbelief and stated, "I said at the hearing the other day if they say fingerprints were in the trunk, that might be true. I show you Exhibit nineteen for identification and ask if you recognize that vehicle?"

Before Ron could answer Judge Scheinman interceded and asked, "What number?"

"Nineteen for identification," Jaffe responded.

Judge Scheinman handed the photo to Ron and asked, "Do you recognize it?"

Ron glanced at the photo and quietly responded, "Yes."

Jaffe continued, "Isn't that the vehicle a fellow real estate broker owns?"

"I believe it's his wife's car. I don't know whose name it's in."

"You have driven that vehicle before, isn't that right?"

"That's true."

"Isn't it a fact that on May 24, 1977, you borrowed that vehicle from that real estate dealer?"

"He left me the car."

"And you had it in your possession, isn't that correct?"

"That is correct."

"Isn't it a fact you went to the Farber residence and that shortly after Trudy Farber was in the trunk of the vehicle, you were at the seat of the vehicle driving from the Farber residence to Grahamsville?"

"No, I was in New Paltz and made a long distance call to my house."

"The answer is no, you did not make that statement?"

"That's right."

"You were never stopped by a police officer in Woodstock who told you you can't sleep in that vehicle?"

"I wasn't intending to sleep in the car. I was waiting for Mr. Shander to come home."

"In fact, you were in Woodstock, is that correct?"

"I had gone from New Paltz to Saratoga and back to Woodstock via Woodstock and I was in Woodstock, yes."

"Did you not tell that to Chandler and Fuente?"

"I did tell them that."

"And, at the same time, you told them that, that was the vehicle you used to get Trudy Farber from the house up to the box?"

"No."

"Now, you say Roger Farber built the box?"

"Or had it done. It was there."

"Not you?"

"No."

"You never had seen the box open?"

"I have looked inside it, yes."

"Did you look in it prior to May 24, 1977?"

"I had seen it, yes."

"You spent a night in it, didn't you?"

"I never really slept in it, no."

Upon hearing this answer, Judge Scheinman interceded and expanded on the previous question, asking, "When you spent the night?"

Avoiding providing a direct answer, Ron responded, "To tell you the truth, I don't think a person"-

Shaking his head no, Scheinman stopped Ron in mid answer and asked, "Had you spent a night in it?"

"No," Ron softly replied.

Judge Scheinman motioned to District Attorney Jaffe to continue cross of the witness. Jaffe presented another photo to Ron and stated, "I show you Exhibit Fourteen for identification and ask if it looks like the top of the box in that area?"

"This is it," Ron answered.

Jaffe presented another photo to Ron and asked, "I show you Exhibit Seventeen and ask if it looks like the box open?"

It was long apparent that whenever Ron's – self-described – genius mind did not like the question being asked it would not permit a direct answer and sought to frustrate the questioner. "It seems to me it was painted" Ron replied. He then asked, "This is the box open, correct?"

Jaffe ignored the witness's return question to him, holding another photo in front of Ron's face he asked, "And I show you fifteen for identification and ask if that's the box with the lid on it with the bar and lock in place?"

"I don't know who arranged this," Ron answered, "but this is a picture of what you described. I don't know who did this."

Judge Scheinman immediately responded with the admonishment, "He didn't ask you that. He just asked if it's a picture of the top of the box with the bar in place."

Not looking at the Judge, Ron answered, "Yes, it is. I think they were in a hurry."

Jaffe continued, "Now, sir, next to the box there was an ammunition box also buried, correct?"

"Some type of tin-box in the ground. I don't know what it was," Ron answered.

"Like a milk case or ammunition box, either one?"

"One or the other, yes."

"You know that it was up there on May 24, 1977?"

"I knew it was there, yes."

"And on May 26, 1977, didn't you?"

Giving his questioner a sarcastic look Ron replied, "Of course I did."

"As a matter of fact, prior to May 26, 1977 you had gone up there and left some food in there because Trudy Farber refused to eat it; isn't that correct?"

"That's not true."

Jaffe presented Ron another photograph and stated, "I show you eighteen for identification and ask if you recognize the contents of that smaller buried box?"

Ron immediately responded, "No, I don't."

"You didn't put that in there?"

"No."

"And you didn't tell Chandler or Fuente you put it in there?"

"No."

"So, any testimony or notes to that effect is false?"

"That would be true."

"The weapon that you described before, is that the weapon in Exhibit twenty?"

"Well, I will tell you this"-

Having had his fill of the witness's rambling answers, obviously intended to confuse his questioner and avoid incrimination, Judge Scheinman quickly cut Ron off and snapped at Ron, "Is that the weapon?"

Ron responded, "It looks similar. I don't see the serial number on it."

Jaffe immediately fired another question at Ron. "Isn't it a fact you knew that weapon was where it was on the evening of the 26th when you went to grab it?"

Judge Scheinman raised a hand in Ron's direction indicating he did not have to answer and responded to the District Attorney, "He already said he did. The question was already answered."

Jaffe responded to the Judge, "He said he purchased it."

Apparently the length of the hearing and frustration were telling on the Judge for he responded to the District Attorney, "He said he placed it there."

Jaffe may have considered having the court reporter read back testimony to prove that in fact the witness had not testified that he placed the gun, but thought better of it because he did not wish to further frustrate or anger the Judge. In any event, it had been established that Ron purchased the gun and the gun he purchased was the same weapon he picked up at Trudy's gravesite, so there was no need to belabor the issue.

Ron took it on his own to interject himself into the brief exchange between Judge and District Attorney, stating, "I am not sure. I had demonstrated the gun as I said."

Jaffe emitted a sigh, took a deep breath and asked, "Let me direct your attention back to the afternoon of May 26th. Isn't it a fact you were trying to work out an agreement with Harry Resnick and a separate agreement with either the State Police or Mr. Gellman, the then District Attorney?"

Ron answered this question with a question. "To work out a separate agreement, what do you mean? Two different agreements?"

Jaffe rolled his eyes, looked toward the ceiling and in a voice reflecting frustration responded, "I withdraw the question."

Ron responded in kind, "I understand what you meant."

Jaffe then asked, "Isn't it a fact you tried to reach an agreement with Mr. Resnick?"

"For my bail, for my legal fees," Ron answered.

"Isn't it a fact you had at first wanted to get one million dollars from Mr. Resnick?"

Judge Scheinman raised his hand, turned toward the witness and asked, "Can you answer that?"

Ron responded, "Isn't it a fact I tried to?"

Jaffe shot back, "That's correct, sir."

"No, it is not a fact," Ron argued.

Jaffe presented Ron a document and asked, "I show you 'three' in evidence. Isn't that your handwriting?"

Ron glanced briefly at the signed, written statement and replied, "I already said before it is a reasonable facsimile. It's pretty sloppy."

Upon hearing this answer, Jaffe turned his attention to Judge Scheinman, stating, "I ask that Your Honor decide at this point for this witness to be compelled to give a handwriting exemplar at the conclusion of today's proceedings or sometime in the near future."

Judge Scheinman nodded his head in the affirmative and responded, "All right. It will be ordered."

Jaffe returned attention to the witness, "It is a fact, is it not, you read this Exhibit - Exhibit Three?"

"You read it," Ron responded, "I didn't read it just now, no."

Jaffe read aloud to the witness, "It says, 'Harry Resnick agrees to pay Ronald Krom the balance in addition to the cash already paid, the sum total of one million dollars within five days or as soon as possible to cover legal and other expenses. If bail is more than this amount, the balance, therefore, is to be paid; in addition and in consideration of this money, the services of Mr. Krom will be employed on my behalf.' That's the agreement you wanted, is it not?"

Ron smiled and played cutesy with his questioner replying, "Which Ronald Krom. There is the one in Ellenville or the one that was a police officer."

Judge Scheinman immediately chastised Ron stating, "Just answer the question. You know we are talking about you. Is that the agreement which you wanted from Mr. Resnick?"

"No," Ron answered, "I had requested four hundred thousand dollars as Mr. McGillicutti said and I don't know anything about that agreement and somebody is trying to – who was the guy arrested for impersonation" –

Jaffe interrupted Ron's question back to the court by presenting Ron another paper statement, stating as he handed it over for perusal, "Mr. Krom, I show you Exhibit Four in evidence and ask you to look at that."

Ron studied the document briefly then responded, "This is the context of what was said but I can't be sure it is my writing. I tend to write small."

Jaffe continued, "I take it, it is your testimony this document and your reading of it refreshes your recollection, you had a discussion with Chandler and Fuente on the afternoon of the 26th and this is the agreement you wanted to reach; is that correct?"

In responding, Ron called upon a word that he had frequently used in his responses throughout the hearing whenever he decided to avoid giving a direct response. His genius mind thought it was a cool legalistic way to confuse the issue at hand without lying or telling the truth. He responded, "I am not sure specifically. I don't think it's the document, to tell you the truth."

Upon hearing this answer, Judge Scheinman chastised the witness again stating, "He is asking you whether it is the agreement. The agreement mentioned in the document that you tried to reach."

Ron responded, "I believe that's accurate with what I wanted. I wrote"-

Counsel Silverstein arose from the defense table and interrupted his client, stating, "You knew at that time"-

Judge Scheinman cut Silverstein off stating, "Mr. Silverstein, let him finish his answer."

Silverstein shook his head, yes, in understanding and sat down.

Ron continued, "I wanted three hundred thousand for myself and one hundred thousand for Roger who wasn't arrested, and I don't think F. Lee Bailey, the lawyer I wanted, would have taken it for three hundred thousand."

Responding, "This document reads as follows:" Jaffe commenced reading the hand scrawled document aloud. "We agree to get Ronald H. Krom special consideration of the District Attorney for assisting us in solving a complex crime in which he is involved." Lowering the document, Jaffe stared into Ron's brown eyes and asked, "You wanted special consideration, did you not?"

"Yes, I did," Ron quietly replied.

"You wanted special consideration because you had been told you were charged with kidnapping; is that correct?"

"That's true," Ron softly answered.

"And the trooper told you that the B.C.I. men, Chandler and Fuente, wouldn't sign the agreement; is that not correct?"

"No," Ron responded in a louder tone of voice. "They did sign it and your own thing which I read said terminate statements. Somebody handed them, clipped off at the bottom"-

Jaffe shook his head in frustration and interrupted Ron in mid answer by stating, "Mr. Krom, yes or no to my last question."

"I know I am right," Ron argued in reply.

Once again Jaffe waggled his head in a back and forth motion in a visible display of frustration, and loudly addressed the court, "Your Honor, would you direct the witness to answer?"

Judge Scheinman nodded his head in the affirmative and responded, "Maybe this would help"-

Ron interrupted the Judge, stating, "I am right."

Judge Scheinman had had about enough of Krom's stonewalling the proceeding and he decided it was time to humble the witness who had earlier proclaimed himself a genius. He fixed Ron in a stern look and firmly stated, "Bright people are able to understand questions when the questions call for a yes or no answer. And sometimes when people repeat questions and keep repeating and suggest things that are not precisely responsive to questions shows they are not too bright. I suggest that you listen to the questions and if they can be answered yes or no, just answer them yes or no."

Ron recognized that Judge Scheinman was telling him that the manner in which he was responding in court indicated he was not too bright and he did not like that at all. Giving the Judge a haughty look in return he responded, "I suggest the following"-

Judge Scheinman immediately cut him off and told him that there was no need for a response because, "There is no question before you."

Ron immediately replied, "I had in my possession"-

"MR. KROM," judge Scheinman called out, cutting Ron off, but before he finished his chastisement, he was rudely interrupted by the witness again,

In the loudest tone of voice he had used throughout the hearing Ron responded, "I AGREE! I AM MR. RON KROM!"

Judge Scheinman pointed at Ron and in a brusque tone commanded, "Just be quiet when I tell you to be quiet. Now, go ahead."

Ron evinced a wry smile and replied, "Between us, we know I am right."

Judge Scheinman let this pass and nodded to District Attorney Jaffe to resume his questioning of the witness.

"Mr. Krom, isn't it a fact, sir, you had been told you were under arrest for kidnapping, yes or no?"

Completely ignoring the direction he had just been given by the Judge, Krom responded, "I have told you, you see this theory about arrest"-

Cutting Ron short, Jaffe fired back, "Were you told you were under arrest, did somebody tell you?"

Ron glared at his questioner and responded, "I was told I was under arrest for murder at the property."

Jaffe's head again moved back and forth in a display of frustration and he raised both hands toward Judge Scheinman indicating the witness was being stubborn and uncooperative

Scheinman turned toward Ron and asked sternly, "Were you told at the barracks that you were under arrest for kidnapping?"

"I think Mr. Gellman said I was under arrest," Ron answered.

Jaffe resumed, "Isn't it a fact you knew you were under arrest and as a bright person you tried to make a deal so you could get some help from the District Attorney?"

"I don't feel I was guilty of the charge. I don't feel – I was a participant. I did try to get special consideration."

"And ultimately you did get a signed document, didn't you?"

"Yes, I got a signed document."

Judge Scheinman turned toward Ron and sternly asked, "Yes or no?"

Ron meekly answered, "Yes."

The Judge's statement in reply was apparently a manifestation of the frustration he was feeling and an intended dig at the witness. "Maybe you couldn't understand the question," he stated, adding, "maybe you are not bright enough."

Upon hearing the Judge, Jaffe smiled, cleared his throat to stifle the laugh that rose in his throat and asked Ron another question. "Now, sir, isn't it a fact that on May 26th, that when you said to McGillicutti, Chandler and Fuente, 'let's go,' you knew very well you were taking them up to Trudy Farber?"

"That's not true," Ron responded. "I said I was taking them – I didn't say, in my mind"-

Judge Scheinman interrupted, "The answer is no! Anything else Mr. Jaffe?"

Jaffe nodded yes and asked, "You said it was in your mind you were taking them to her?"

"I didn't say," Ron answered. "I was interrupted. It was in my mind we were going to a tentative place where she might be alive."

"These statements you made subsequent to what each of the witnesses testified about, about how you had taken food and put her in the box, you deny those statements now?"

"I never made the statements."

"Isn't it a fact that on May 26th, when you left the barracks having said, 'let's go,' you knew very well you were taking them to see the person who appears here in Exhibit Sixteen because you put her there?"

"As I remember, the face was whiter – I didn't put her there."

It was apparent that he was not going to get the defendant to answer any questions in a forthright manner, Jaffe decided to end the frustration. Glancing at Judge Scheinman, he stated, "I have no further questions."

Judge Scheinman looked toward the defense table and asked, "Any questions, Mr. Silverstein?"

Counsel Silverstein arose from his seat and responded, "The only thing was there was an application for an order and I was not heard on the application. As far as the handwriting exemplars are to be taken, I want them done in the presence of one or more of the people in my office."

Jaffe immediately responded, "No objection to that."

It is probable that Judge, District Attorney and Counsel were more relieved than the witness when Judge Scheinman stated, "All right, Mr. Krom, you can step down." He then added, "Mr. Silverstein, do you expect to call any more witnesses?"

Silverstein answered, "I cannot answer that for you now, Your Honor. As I indicated to you this morning, I have a question as to whether or not I will call Mr. Resnick and I have a question as to whether or not I will call a psychiatrist."

Judge Scheinman concluded the hearing after a brief discussion as to when, and, or if the murder victim's father would be called to testify in the hearing.

The defense would subsequently call highly regarded psychiatrist Dr. B. Thomas Houghton who had examined the defendant and previously testified during a mental competency hearing. Dr. Houghton testified, "…Based on my research I am of the opinion that Ronald Krom was not capable of making a knowledgeable determination as to the waiver of rights…"

The prosecution countered with Dr. Daniel Schwartz, a New York City psychiatrist of renown. Dr. Schwartz testified, "…At the time of his (Ronald Krom's) statements to the police, he did not, as a result of mental disease or defect, lack substantial capacity to know or appreciate that he was waiving his rights to counsel and incriminating himself…"

It did not take long for Judge Scheinman to render his decision. He ruled that the defendant had been provided the appropriate warnings against self-incrimination and the right to counsel and that the admissions he had made to the police could be used against him. On Friday, he notified defense and prosecution of his findings and at the same time advised them that trial would commence at 9:00 a.m. the following Monday.

Prosecution psychiatrist Daniel Schwartz, right, discusses testimony with Sullivan DA Joseph Jaffe.
Record photo by Ken Farber

DA Jaffe / Dr. Schwartz

22

District Attorney Emmanuel Gellman would not get to present the 'State's' case against Ronald Krom at hearing or trial.

A young attorney and Sullivan County native by the name of Joseph Jaffe who had earned the respect of the general public - first as a police officer in the Town of Fallsburgh and later as a federal prosecutor - entered the political arena and announced his candidacy for Sullivan County District Attorney. Jaffe possessed the perfect credentials for a politician. He was tall, dark, handsome, intelligent, articulate, and possessed a charismatic personality. He could turn on a smile that would melt ice and, at the appropriate moment, display boyish charm. In addition, Joe was respected by his peers in the legal community and by members of law enforcement. All of these attributes resulted in his winning the office of Sullivan County District Attorney in 1978. In winning the election, he inherited the case of "The People of the State of New York v. Ronald Harrison Krom."

Although young (winning election at the age of 33) Joe Jaffe was an experienced prosecutor, and like most prosecutors, wanted an airtight case if at all possible. As the newly elected District Attorney, Jaffe recognized the importance of winning a conviction in a case of such magnitude. Trudy Resnick Farber's kidnapping and death had shocked and outraged residents of the county and the fact that a member of the wealthy and well-known Resnick family had suffered a horrific death captured national media attention as well. Jaffe also knew that the Resnick family had the power to either make or break a political career, so he decided to personally prosecute the case and would use every means at his disposal to convict Krom and achieve the maximum sentence provided under New York State law.

Joe was pleased to learn that the defendant had confessed to the crimes with which he was charged, and had directed police to the victim's location. There also was a wealth of witnesses and evidence that connected the defendant to the crimes. He was also pleased that Roger Farber had passed a polygraph examination, which refuted the defendant's claim that Farber was a co-conspirator in the plot. Of course, as polygraph examinations were not admissible evidence of either guilt or innocence, he would not be able to introduce that fact at trial, but it did ease the concern as to how Farber would react under cross-examination.

Joe cupped his chin in one hand and listened intently as his predecessor, Manny Gellman summed up the case against Krom. When Manny had concluded, he smiled and nodded his head in the affirmative. Then his brow displayed wrinkles of concern as he responded, "I agree we have a strong case for prosecution Manny. The only issue left for the defense to hang their hat on is Krom's mental competency. Carl will play on the fact that his client is a certified schizophrenic, will try to convince the court and jury that he is mentally incompetent and put a couple of shrinks on the stand who will attest to that fact. Although Carl is also convinced that his client acted alone, he may try to point out that – because of mental illness – Krom actually believed the story he concocted about Roger Farber. We know it's the hallucination of a certified nut case, but we don't want to plant any seeds in the minds of the jury."

Nodding his head in agreement, Manny responded, "That bothered me, too. How do you intend to deal with this issue?"

"We will use Doc Schwartz," Jaffe replied. "He examined Krom, testified in the competency hearing, is an excellent psychiatrist and very convincing on the witness stand."

Again nodding in agreement, Gellman responded, "I agree. Schwartz will be an excellent counter to the defense psychs."

"But, I am not going to rush to prove Krom is competent," Jaffe responded. "He (Krom) has been indicted by the Grand Jury and is secure in the county slammer. I will wait for Carl to reveal whatever mental deficiency strategy he intends to take and then hit him with Doc Schwartz. Schwartz is expensive, but he is worth every cent because he will make monkeys out of any psychiatric experts used by the defense."

Gellman smiled at the man who had beaten him for District Attorney and complimented, "Very astute strategy, Joe. I would have handled the prosecution in the same manner."

Jaffe smiled at Gellman in return and responded, "Thanks, Manny. Your handling of the case thus far has been excellent. I will do my best to ensure a conviction."

Continuing to smile, Gellman winked as he replied, "I'm sure you will and the fact that every citizen in the county wants Krom to burn will give you a totally unbiased jury."

"Yes," Joe replied, "I just hope there is no change of venue for the trial. However, if the defense does move for change of venue and wins, my strategy will remain the same and I am confident of conviction. Besides, this is a must win case Manny. I cannot let down the Resnicks."

Fully aware of the political clout wielded by the victim's family, Manny displayed a knowing smile as he responded, "I know, this case could very well determine your tenure as District Attorney. As I recently learned, there will always be some hotshot young attorney eager to take the job away from you. A prosecution victory in this case is almost certain and you can rest assured that everyone in this office will bust his butt for you."

Jaffe exhibited a broad smile in return as he responded, "Politics is a tough business, Manny, but I am appreciative that you left this office and this case in such great shape."

23

In October 1979, both prosecution and defense advised Judge Scheinman that they were ready for trial. Then without warning, schizophrenic Ron, dropped a small bomb, announcing to Judge Scheinman, "Your Honor, I am dismissing Mr. Silverstein as counsel and exercising my right to go pro se. I will be representing myself during the trial against me."

Jaffe and Silverstein exchanged looks that translated, "Oh, no, here we go again," then took turns expressing to Scheinman why the defendant should not be permitted to represent himself.

Silverstein was first to respond, "Your Honor, I do not believe that my client has an adequate grasp or understanding of criminal law or jurisprudence and should not be representing himself."

Giving Silverstein an angry look, Krom retorted, "I know my Constitutional Rights and that I have the right to represent myself!"

"Your Honor," Jaffe intoned, while displaying a smile of bemusement, "I concur with Mr. Silverstein. It is a certainty that if the court permits the defendant to represent himself this trial will be turned into a circus."

Judge Scheinman had not seemed surprised by the defendant's request, likely as a result of expecting unexpected behavior at any moment from a schizophrenic mind. Ron was correct that the Constitution provided for self-representation; however, that right could be revoked. Choosing not to respond to either attorney, he gave the defendant a serious look and advised, "Mr. Krom, proceeding pro se may be your right, but representing yourself would be a serious mistake. You do not have a good grasp of jurisprudence, you have a propensity for interrupting witnesses at will and self-representation will have a negative effect on the jury. Are you dissatisfied with Mr. Silverstein's representation?"

Ron flashed the hint of a smile at Silverstein, then, focusing on Judge Scheinman, responded, "I find no fault with Mr. Silverstein; however, I have a tactical strategy and I can appeal to the jurors on a more personal level by representing myself."

As a seasoned member of the bench, it is likely to presume that Judge Scheinman, who had already presided over several hearings to determine Ron's competency, and knew Ron was capable of acting in a bizarre manner and making nonsensical statements, was reluctant to grant the defendant's request. However, he astutely realized that arbitrarily denying the right to self-representation, without just cause, could result in an overturn on appeal. To prevent such an occurrence, he immediately commenced - what the New York State Court of Appeals would later report in a ruling on September 16, 1983 – "a searching inquiry" to determine if the defendant was capable of proceeding pro se. He asked, "Mr. Krom do you fully understand the seriousness of the crimes with which you are charged?"

Looking quite knowledgeable and astute, Ron stared at his questioner through his horn-rimmed glasses and responded in words that he envisioned a Lawyer would use, "I realize the gravity of the situation. I know what I am facing and I am prepared to deal with those issues."

Scheinman continued probing, "What is your level of education?"

Displaying an egotistical look of disdain, Ron answered, "I am a graduate of Tri-Valley High School, attended law school for a time and my attainment of a college degree from New Paltz State University was prevented by my unlawful arrest. I am quite intelligent and capable of representing myself."

Scheinman studied Ron and asked, "Do you understand that self-representation will put you fully on display before the jury. Your words, your body language, your treatment of witnesses, your errors and omissions will be scrutinized and analyzed as if you were a bug under a microscope. In essence, Mr. Krom, you must be made aware that self-representation paints a very bleak picture for the outcome you desire."

Giving the Judge his very best impersonation of what he believed a lawyer looked and sounded like, Ron answered, "I would really prefer to represent myself. I feel I could be more specific as to actual relevant facts, vis-a-vis, the case and I have my papers here to submit."

"There are rules regarding the submission of evidence," Scheinman admonished. "Any evidence introduced must be admissible, applicable to the matter at hand and approved for admission by the court. Your lack of expertise in this regard could have a dilatory effect on these proceedings."

"I am quite familiar with the rules and procedures for introducing evidence," Ron responded, "and with your permission, I would keep Mr. Silverstein as my advisor to ensure that any evidence the defense introduces is handled properly."

"Never-the-less Mr. Krom," Scheinman again admonished, "it is my duty to see that every defendant going to trial gets a fair hearing. It seems to me you would be depriving yourself by what you are doing."

Ron immediately responded, "I think I would get a fair trial if I represented myself and it seems to myself that a lot of this would be suppressed if the law was followed. The affirmative – there was no affirmative – waiver of Mr. Martin who waived me instead, means I can best represent myself."

Judge, prosecutor and counsel, momentarily exchanged a confused, incredulous look, before Scheinman responded, "Mr. Krom, the issue which you have raised and which is under consideration, is self-representation. What are the dangers of your proceeding without having your attorney represent you?"

Ron stared at the Judge and answered, "The dangers of proceeding without counsel are possible admissibility of items that otherwise wouldn't be submitted. I feel there are other advantages and"-

Lifting his hand to silence the defendant, Scheinman interrupted by admonishing, "I didn't ask you anything else. I asked about the dangers. Don't tell me about the advantages. Do you know any of the other dangers?"

Ron immediately responded, "The dangers are very clearly that I am not privy to a legal education."

Judge Scheinman warned, "I must caution you sir, that the appellate courts have ruled that 'ignorance of the law does not vitiate a waiver as appellant must bear the personal consequences of his decision.' Having been made aware of this, is it still your wish to proceed pro se?"

"As I said," Ron answered, "I have a plan and feel I can carry it out better than Mr. Silverstein. It is my definite wish and desire to proceed as my own counsel."

Displaying a look of consternation, Judge Scheinman – before responding – spoke directly to the court reporter. "Let the record show that the defendant has requested to represent himself in these proceedings and that the court has conducted an inquiry to determine whether the defendant's wish to proceed pro se should be granted." Then focusing on the defendant he stated, "Mr. Krom, I will agree to your request under the condition that Mr. Silverstein remain at the defense table and assist you. Be advised sir, that if you do not conduct yourself appropriately, become disruptive or abusive toward the bench, the prosecutor, any witness, or member of the jury, this privilege shall be immediately revoked. Do I make myself clear?"

Ron exhibited a brief smile of victory and answered, "I understand and you don't have to worry. I have a plan and can carry it out."

Ron's diabolical smile while stating that he had a 'plan' evoked exchanged looks of consternation between Judge, prosecutor and defense counsel. Having experienced the defendant's proclivity to provide bizarre answers to questions and interrupt the proceedings, they feared the 'plan' might lead to a mistrial. In chambers the three discussed this possibility and Judge Scheinman advised that at the first sign of outburst or disruptive behavior, he would revoke the defendant's right to pro se.

In November 1979, almost two and one-half years after Trudy Farber was laid to rest, two Sheriff deputies escorted Ronald Harrison Krom into the dated Sullivan County courtroom and he joined Legal Aid Attorney Carl Silverstein at the defense table. District Attorney Joseph Jaffe stood at the prosecution table and stared menacingly at Krom, who seemed not to notice. A Sergeant-At-Arms called the court to order, announcing that the case of The People of The State of New York against Ronald Harrison Krom had commenced and that the Honorable Louis Scheinman would be presiding. Judge Scheinman entered the courtroom, and after he was seated on the bench, all participants in the drama took their seats. Judge Scheinman had closed the court to spectators and the media during the jury selection phase of the proceedings.

Scheinman glanced at Jaffe and asked, "Are the People ready to proceed?"

Jaffe stood and responded, "Yes, Your Honor."

Turning his attention to the defendant, he asked, "Mr. Krom are you ready to proceed?"

Looking quite scholarly in a dark suit and white shirt open at the collar, Ron peered at the Judge through horn-rimmed glasses and responded, "Yes, the defense is ready."

"All right, gentlemen," Scheinman intoned, "we will commence selection of a jury shortly. Mr. Krom, you are entitled to peremptorily challenge a prospective juror, or challenge a prospective juror for cause. I would caution you that peremptory dismissal of a potential juror is limited, whereas removal for cause – if the cause is valid – is not. Is the jury selection process clear in your mind?"

Displaying a look of self-assuredness Ron responded, "I am quite familiar with the voir dire process. As I have told the court many times, I studied law and could have been a lawyer."

Jaffe flashed Ron a bemused smile in response to his answer; then, he turned his attention on Judge Scheinman to see how he would respond.

Scheinman focused on the defendant with a sober look and admonished, "Mr. Krom, the fact is you are not a lawyer and you are engaged in a very serious process. Do you fully understand that the panel of jurors that you and Mr. Jaffe agree upon will ultimate decide your fate?"

"I know what I am doing," Ron replied in a flippant manner, adding, "there is no need for you to treat me in a condescending manner. I am quite capable of managing my own defense."

Giving Ron a stern look, Judge Scheinman admonished, "Sir, you will not respond to me again in that manner. Do I make myself clear?"

"Well, you shouldn't have asked the question if you didn't want the answer," Ron snapped in reply.

Looking disgusted and shaking his head in the negative, Scheinman responded, "Let's get on with it. Bailiff, call the first person on the panel of prospective jurors."

To the amazement and consternation of the Judge and the advisor to the defendant, the first juror seated was a retired FBI agent, who in retirement owned a well-known tavern; the second juror selected had retired from the New York State Police. Ron had not opted to use a peremptory challenge for either, had not requested dismissal for cause and in fact, approved both and seemed quite pleased that the two former police officers were seated.

Jaffe was both surprised and pleased when Ron approved of their selection but he astutely recognized that the Court of Appeals might consider placement of former police officers on the jury as prejudicial to the defense. He argued, "Your Honor, although the prosecution is pleased at having the defense select former police officers to sit on the jury, I would believe their placement would not be in the best interest of the defendant or the court. I therefore"-

Interrupting, Ron jumped to his feet, glared at the prosecutor and screamed, "You have no right to decide what my best interests are! You represent the Gestapo that caused my unlawful arrest and I have the right to select a jury that will act in my best interest!"

For the first time in the proceedings, Scheinman used the gavel that had remained ignored on his desk. "Mr. Krom," he called out, "you are out of order and are directed to sit down and remain silent until called upon to respond. Do I make"-

Ron did not sit down, instead interrupting. He challenged, "You have no right to order me to sit down. I am on trial here for crimes another person is responsible for and I have the right to select a jury that will act in my best interest."

Appearing to close his eyes and count to ten before responding, Judge Scheinman rebuked, "Mr. Krom, you were previously warned that disruptive behavior would result in your losing the privilege of per se. If you do not sit down and conduct yourself in an appropriate manner, I will revoke that privilege and reassign counsel."

Continuing to alternately scowl at Judge and prosecutor, Ron took his seat and folded his arms across his chest.

Silverstein had watched the selection of the jurors and the subsequent exchange of vitriol in disbelief and decided it was time to settle Ron down and get him on track. He addressed the court from his chair, "Your Honor, before continuing, may I have a moment to confer with the defendant?"

Ron gave Carl a puzzled look, but did not verbally respond.

Judge Scheinman glanced at the clock on the rear wall of the courtroom, then focused on Silverstein and replied, "We will take a ten minute recess."

Silverstein and Krom remained seated and sat in silence staring at each other until Judge, prosecutor, the two seated jurors and potential jurors had left the courtroom.

After they were alone, except for the presence of two armed sheriff's deputies assigned to watch over the defendant, Carl asked, "Ron, you just selected two retired police officers to be members of the jury. It is a certainty that both – because of their former careers – are prejudiced in favor of the prosecution. They both could have easily been rejected by peremptory challenge or for cause. Why in the world did you consent and agree to place them on the jury?"

Looking directly into his questioner's eyes, Ron answered in all seriousness, "They are part of the plan. As I told you, I was in the CIA. After I was arrested, I spoke with Brennan in the Agency's office and he told me the Agency would put two CIA plants in the jury pool and that they were former police officers. They will make certain that I am acquitted."

Rolling his eyes and nodding his head in disbelief at what he had just heard, Carl responded, "Excuse me Ron. I am going to the men's room."

Upon leaving the courtroom, Carl bypassed the men's room and went directly to Judge Scheinman's chambers, where he found His Honor and the District Attorney engaged in conversation. Both men greeted him with a smile and both recognized that the look of amazement on Silverstein's face meant he had an issue that needed to be addressed.

Jaffe was first to speak, "Are we ready to continue jury selection Carl?"

Silverstein shook his head in the negative as he replied, "I am sure you will agree that my client is not capable of conducting his own defense. If he is allowed to continue, in all likelihood, he will cause a mistrial."

By the look on their faces, it appeared Scheinman and Jaffe had been engaged in a similar discussion before Silverstein entered the judge's chambers.

Giving Judge and Prosecutor alternating looks of consternation, Carl stated,

"He cannot be permitted to continue self representation. If he does, we are definitely headed for mistrial, and we don't want that to happen."

"You are right, Carl," Scheinman replied. "He has already demonstrated that he will be disruptive during trial and I am revoking pro se for that reason. When we resume, I am re-assigning you as Counsel."

"Oh, gee," Jaffe responded, displaying a broad smile, "I was just starting to really enjoy the defendant's wonderful cooperative attitude." Turning serious, he added, "You're right. I don't want this case to turn in to a circus and I certainly don't want that fact reported by the media. And, I don't want to have to prosecute this loony tunes twice."

Calling court back in session, Judge Scheinman focused on the defendant and admonished, "Mr. Krom, I am revoking self representation and Mr. Silverstein is hereby directed to continue as defense counsel. You"-

Krom interrupted, "You cannot deny me my right to represent myself. I was a federal agent and almost a lawyer and I know my"-

Judge Scheinman cut him off with the admonishment, "Mr. Krom, you were previously warned that your right to self representation would be revoked if you violated the rules of jurisprudence or created an atmosphere for mistrial. You have started down the path toward mistrial and I am not going to permit it. You are directed to remain silent and Mr. Silverstein will take over and resume selection of the jury. Is that clear?"

Displaying alternating looks of confusion, anger and resentment, Ron did not verbally respond; instead he picked up the law book on the table in front of him and pretended to absorb himself in reading it.

The two retired police officers seated on the panel were allowed to remain after assuring the court that they could render a fair and impartial verdict. Jaffe and Silverstein filled the remainder of the panel. The retired FBI agent would be selected as Foreman of the Jury.

24

On November 11, 1979, two-years, five-months and 18 days after Trudy was taken from her home and buried alive, 9 examinations of the defendant by psychiatric specialists, 3 mental competency hearings in court and one suppression hearing, the jury took their seats in the court room and Judge Scheinman opened the trial of The People of the State of New York vs. Ronald Harrison Krom. A gaggle of reporters, members of the legal community, members of the victim's family, members of the defendant's family and curious members of the community filled the courtroom to capacity.

Authors Note: The following trial testimony is neither meant nor intended as a facsimile of the testimony or behavior exhibited by witnesses, judge, prosecutor, defense counsel or defendant in the matter of the People of the State of New York against Ronald Krom. However, the trial - as envisioned by the author – is a reasonable portrayal of the actions and testimony that took place, as related by witnesses who participated, jurors recollections of the proceedings, police reports and documentation provided by the Sullivan County District Attorney's office. The names of some witnesses and participants have been changed to protect their identity.

Horn rimmed glasses perched on his nose and neatly dressed in a white shirt - open at the neck - and dark blue blazer, Ron Krom more resembled a scholarly choir boy, seated at the defendant's table than a calculating, hardhearted, cold blooded killer. In fact, apart from the fact that Defense Counsel Silverstein wore a necktie, whereas Ron did not, anyone who did not know either defendant or counsel, might have mistakenly presumed that the scholarly looking young man with the open law book in front of him was the attorney and Silverstein the defendant. The identity of each would become perfectly clear when the handsome, dark-haired gentleman dressed in a dark suit and red necktie stood and advised the court that the Defense was ready to proceed. Having previously observed his client's attempts to avoid answering questions directly and trying to display intellectual superiority while testifying during the Huntley hearing, Silverstein decided to keep Ron off the witness stand during trial - if at all possible.

At the prosecution table District Attorney Joseph Jaffe, attired in a dark power suit, his dark, curly hair freshly trimmed and combed to emphasize waviness and curl, looked especially handsome and confident. He flashed a warm smile in the direction of the jury, then to the Judge, and advised that the prosecution was ready. In fact, Joe was confident that his line-up of prosecution witness's would present a wealth of testimony and evidence indicating that the defendant was guilty beyond any reasonable doubt. He was also confident that – barring any surprise - he could establish that the defendant acted alone in the planning and commission of the crimes with which he was charged. In his opening remarks, he portrayed the defendant as an intelligent young man harboring a strong dislike for the Resnick and Farber families for perceived slights. The defendant's anger fueled a diabolical mind to devise a plan that would get even with the Resnick's and Farber's and make him wealthy at the same time. "Ladies and gentlemen," he intoned, "the witness's testimony that you will soon hear and evidence shown will convince you beyond a reasonable doubt that Ronald Krom acted alone in both planning and commission of the crimes he is on trial for. It will be shown that the defendant planned the abduction over a long period of time and believed that Harry Resnick was a weak personality who would quickly pay a large sum of money – in fact, a million dollars, to obtain his daughter's release. The defense will attempt to convince you that the defendant has a mental disability which confused rational thought and that he was only a confused participant in a plot devised and designed by the victim's husband. The truth is quite different. The testimony you are about to hear, as well as the evidence you will be shown, will clearly reveal that the defendant harbored a grudge against the Resnick family, was angry when Roger Farber would not provide him money to invest in a business enterprise and resented Trudy Farber for treating him condescendingly. He hatched a diabolical plan that would allow him to get even with the sources of his aggravation, while at the same time increasing his personal wealth. His plan involved force, fear, threat, intimidation, personal assault, kidnapping and entombment. You will also hear the defense claim that the defendant never intended that anyone would die as the result of his actions. The fact is that an intelligent young woman, in the prime of her life, did die a horrible death as a result of the defendant's actions. The law is clear and specifically provides that when death results during the commission of a felony – in this case, the multiple felonies of assault, abduction and imprisonment - the perpetrator is just as guilty of murder as a person who intended taking life. Ladies and gentlemen of the jury, after hearing all the testimony and viewing all the evidence, you will be convinced that the only way a minimum of justice can be served is by finding the defendant guilty as charged."

Knowing that he could not convincingly rebut the mountain of evidence against his client, Defense Attorney Carl Silverstein intended to convince jurors that Ron Krom had no previous criminal record, was not a bad individual motivated by anger and greed, but a victim himself. The result of a mental illness referred to as schizophrenia, which triggered delusional behavior and caused Ron to commit acts that he was not responsible for due to extreme emotional disturbance. Silverstein pointed out to the jurors that during the trial they would hear testimony from experts in psychiatry who would provide convincing evidence that this horrible mental illness known as schizophrenia had seized control of the defendant's mind, caused irrational thought, delusional behavior and was the demon that forced him to commit the acts for which he was on trial. "Ladies and gentlemen," he intoned, "schizophrenia should be on trial for these crimes and not the defendant. A just finding would be to find the defendant not guilty, with the recommendation that he receive psychiatric treatment and care."

Opening statements concluded, the prosecution began calling its witnesses to the stand.

Some members of the jury would note that Roger Farber seemed nervous but did not appear as grief stricken and traumatized as expected by the ordeal which had resulted in the death of his spouse. They also noted his failure to display the angry emotion expected by one facing the man who had kidnapped and murdered his wife. But then, 2 ½ years had elapsed since that horrific moment in his life and it also seemed feasible that the District Attorney had carefully prepared Roger for testimony. He had emphasized that while the display of sadness and grief was acceptable during his appearance on the stand, it would be wise to keep angry emotion in check.

After establishing Roger's relationship to the murder victim and the Resnick family, Jaffe asked Roger to reflect on May 24th, 1977, and explain what happened on that fateful day.

Roger related, "We – my business partner Harvey Kornblau and I – left the Radio Shack store in Monticello at around 5:15 in the afternoon. I drove Harv' to a local garage to pick up our business van which had been in for repairs. Harvey drove the van and followed me to my home. My home is a short distance from Monticello and we arrived there at around five-twenty or thereabouts. We loaded some display cases that were stored in my garage into the van. This only took a couple of minutes. It was a very warm afternoon and I invited Harv' in for a drink to cool him down. I went to my mailbox, got our mail and then Harv' and I went inside. I invited Harv' to wash his hands in our garage level bathroom and while he was doing so, I went to my bedroom." His face revealed a look of fear and revulsion, as he - for the first time – displayed emotion. He stammered, "and, and, then I saw it."

"Please continue," Jaffe encouraged, "you saw what?"

"I saw, I saw, the condition of our bed," he responded in a strained whisper, "and realized that someone had broken into our home."

A juror would later relate that from his perspective, Roger's sudden display of trauma seemed a scripted performance rather than a display of true emotional trauma.

Roger went on to testify as to how he and Harvey were confronted by the silent, identity-concealed by ski mask, rifle-toting individual, who forced them to lie on the kitchen floor and then bound their hands and feet with cord.

"When you first faced this masked, silent intruder who was pointing a rifle at you, what did you think his intentions were?" Jaffe asked.

"I was shocked and confused," Roger replied. "Until he took Trudy, I guess I thought he intended to rob me and Harvey."

"Please explain what happened when the masked intruder ordered you to enter the kitchen."

"He ordered me to lie face down on the kitchen floor and then he tied my hands behind my back."

"Did the intruder speak when ordering you to lie on the floor?"

"No, he just pointed at the floor and directed me to get down."

"Please explain what happened after you were bound and lying on the kitchen floor."

"He took a piece of paper out of his pocket and showed it to me. It was a note asking, 'What time, does your wife arrive home from work?'"

"Are you certain that this note asked the time you expected Trudy to arrive home from work?"

"Well, I was very confused and frightened at the time – and it has been more than two years – but, the note was typewritten – clearly readable – and to the best of my memory, it was a question asking me what time my wife arrived home, or what time I expected her to arrive home from work."

"When you read the note, did it change your mind as to what the intruder's intent was?"

"No, my immediate thought was that he wanted to be gone before Trudy arrived home, so that he wouldn't be seen by her."

"What did the intruder do with the rifle while he was tying you up?"

"I don't know. He had me lying on my stomach, facing the floor and I couldn't see how he was holding, or what he was doing with the rifle because he put a pillow case over my head."

Jaffe walked to the prosecution table, picked up the twenty-two-rifle that was lying there, and carried it to the witness stand. He extended the gun toward Roger and asked, "Sir, I show you People's exhibit ten. Does this gun look familiar?"

After taking a moment to study the rifle, Roger responded, "Yes, it looks exactly like the rifle that Ron - I mean the intruder - threatened us with."

Jaffe lifted the rifle in the air and stated, "Let the record show that the witness has identified this twenty-two caliber, semi-automatic rifle, that was wrested from the defendant by police at the time of his arrest as looking exactly like the rifle that the intruder was armed with on the afternoon of May 24, 1977."

"Now sir, you have testified that the intruder produced a typewritten note and you read that note. What did you tell him, how did you respond, after you read that note?"

"I told him that she – Trudy – usually arrives home between 5 – 5:30 p.m."

"And what time was it when you told him this?"

"It was around five-thirty."

"When you told him Trudy's expected arrival time, what did he do?"

"I thought he would leave, but he didn't. I heard the sound of writing and then he showed me a piece of newspaper on which he had written,' 'Don't call the police or F.B.I., you will be released in one hour.' "He had also written, 'Call Harry Resnick,' or, 'Harry Resnick will call you.'"

"You indicated that a pillow case was placed over your head. If that was the case, how were you able to read this note?"

"He pulled the pillow case up and held the piece of newspaper - with the writing on it - in front of my eyes."

"Please continue. What happened next?"

"I couldn't understand why he didn't go, and I began to dread the thought that he was waiting for Trudy to arrive and was concerned as to what he intended to do to her."

"Please continue. What happened next?"

"I heard a car come up the driveway and then Trudy came into the house. I – I, heard her call out, 'Hello! Where are you?' Then, I heard her scream out – more like choked out because she was so scared, 'Oh no!'"

Reflection on that moment caused Roger to hesitate. He studied his hands that were clasped on the witness desk in front of him; his face portrayed a look that some witnesses would interpret as sadness, while others interpreted as a look of guilt or betrayal for not having done something to prevent his wife's abduction. Introspection would have some on the jury panel come to the conclusion that perhaps fear would have caused them to react in much the same manner.

Jaffe allowed the witness a moment of self-evaluation and then in a quiet tone encouraged, "Please continue. What happened after you heard your wife scream?"

Still studying his hands, Roger answered, "I told her not to resist or do anything – just to do what he told her to do."

"Please continue," Jaffe directed. "What transpired next?"

"Well, Trudy started crying and he (the intruder) started acting crazy. He removed knives that were in a holder on the kitchen counter and started throwing them at our kitchen cabinets. One of the knives bounced off the cabinet and fell on the floor within my reach. After that I heard him with Trudy leaving out the back door. I managed to get the knife and used it to cut the rope he tied me up with. When I was free, I went to the kitchen window and saw 'him' pulling Trudy into the woods behind our house. I knew he (the abductor) must have a vehicle parked close by and was taking Trudy to it. I untied Harvey and told him to go down to the end of our driveway and write down the license plate numbers of cars passing. Then I called Harry, and told him what had happened and that Trudy had been kidnapped. Harry told me to call the F.B.I. and I did."

"You called the F.B.I. from your home phone?"

"Yes, immediately after hanging up from talking with Harry, I called the operator and asked for the F.B.I. I told them what happened and they asked me if a local police agency was involved and whether there was a police officer at my home. I told them that my father-in-law was calling the local police and he had told me to call the F.B.I. – which I did."

"You refer to the F.B.I. person or persons that you spoke with as them and they. Do you know who the agent was whom you spoke to?"

"No, my mind was racing at the time and I don't recall anyone identifying himself to me by name."

"What did the F.B.I representative tell you to do?"

"They – I don't even remember whether it was a man or a woman, but I do recall that they were in New York City – instructed me to wait for the police to arrive and not to disturb anything. I was told that agents would be in contact with the local police and would do everything in their power to find Trudy."

"What did you do after speaking with the F.B.I.?"

"The state police and sheriff's deputies arrived shortly after. They asked me a lot of questions and I showed them what 'he' (pointing at the defendant) did to the house, then I went to the state police building in Liberty."

"What did you do at the state police station?"

"A BCI detective spoke with me and typed my statement as to what happened."

To deflate an expected defense attack on Roger intending to plant seeds in the juror's minds that Roger was the mastermind of his wife's kidnapping, Jaffe gave Roger a hard look and asked, "Were you involved in any way, shape or form in the plot to take your wife and secure a ransom from your father-in-law, Harry Resnick?"

Portraying a look of sincerity and without hesitation, Roger responded, "No, sir! I loved my wife and had absolutely no reason to want to frighten or harm her! Trudy and I were doing well financially and there was absolutely no reason for me to want to take money from my father-in-law, for whom I have great admiration and respect."

"Did there come a time when the defendant approached you for the purpose of having you either loan him money or invest in some sort of business enterprise with him?"

"Yes, Ron both called and personally visited me to ask that I either loan him money or invest in business with him."

"What sort of business did he want you to join him in?"

"He wanted me to partner with him in some sort of bill board advertising business and most recently, he wanted me to either loan him money to purchase a bar in New Paltz, or invest as a partner with him in the bar business."

"When did he approach you with that proposal?"

"Several months before he took Trudy. He called me several times and stopped by my business unannounced a couple of times. He also stopped in at least once when I wasn't at the Monticello store and he spoke with Harvey. Harvey told me that Ron Krom had come in looking for me."

"And what was the result of all these requests for money and business investment proposals?"

"I told him that I did not have the money to loan him, that my Radio Shack investments were keeping me quite busy and that I was not interested in expanding into any other business."

"How did the defendant react when you repeatedly turned him down? Was he upset and did he display anger?"

"Well, by the way he presented himself, I was under the impression that he thought I owed him some sort of loyalty and I sensed that he was angry and not pleased; however, our conversations were polite enough and there was no open display of anger or resentment."

"Did there come a time when your wife told you she had received a telephone call from Ron?"

"Yes, a few months before Trudy was abducted - shortly after I had turned him down on his proposal to invest in the bar business - Trudy received a call from Ron. She told me that he wanted her to influence me to invest with him. When she informed him that she had nothing to do with my business and would not support his request, he got irritated, angry, became irrational and told her something to the effect that she was a spoiled rich snob and would regret treating him like a second-class citizen. As you know, Trudy worked in psychotherapy and was skilled in recognizing troubling behavior. She"-

Silverstein arose from the defense table and interrupted the witness, calling out, "Objection, Your Honor. The witness can only surmise as to his wife's skill in psychoanalysis, he was not a party to the call, and is not qualified to attest as to the emotional stability of my client."

Jaffe immediately countered, "Your Honor, the witness can surely attest as to his wife's profession and he can surely attest as to the emotions she was experiencing when she told him about the content of the call she received from the defendant."

"Stick to the substance of the conversation the witness had with his wife concerning the call, Mr. Jaffe," Judge Scheinman admonished. "Mrs. Farber's skill as a psychotherapist shall remain open to conjecture."

Silverstein retook his seat at the defense table.

Jaffe did not verbally respond to the bench, instead turning his attention to the witness and asking, "What did your wife tell you about her telephone conversation with the defendant?"

"She told me that when she informed him (Ron) that she did not interfere or participate in my business dealings, he became angry and threatening. She told me that he sounded irrational, and his conversation worried and frightened her. She asked me to see Ron and try to reason with him."

"And how did Trudy appear – what was her demeanor, when she told you this?"

"She appeared to me to be greatly concerned and worried. She told me that she wanted me to resolve the issue with Ron and inform him that he was not to call, or contact her again."

"And did you have a conversation with the defendant subsequent to this conversation with your wife?"

"Yes, I figured Ron would stop in to see me again, and he did. He"-

Jaffe interrupted, "How long was it after Trudy asked you to speak with him?"

"About a month."

"What was the purpose of his visit and did you inform him of your wife's concern about him?"

"He renewed his request that I partner with him in business and tried to convince me that by doing so, I would make a great deal of money. I told him that I was not interested and then I told him that he had upset my wife when he called her. I asked him not to call Trudy again."

"That's it? You didn't threaten any action against him if he called her again?"

"No, I figured that to do so would aggravate and anger him and possibly cause him to react in some bizarre manner." Having answered the question, Roger added, "In retrospect, Trudy had to be more frightened of him than I imagined. That morning – the day she was taken – when we were both departing for work, she mentioned to me that she was still concerned about him."

Jaffe flashed a sardonic smile in the direction of the defendant as he responded, "And she had just cause to be, didn't she?"

"Objection!" Silverstein immediately responded. "Mr. Jaffe is out of line, Your Honor!"

"Mr. Jaffe," Judge Scheinman admonished, "keep your personal feelings and thoughts to yourself." Then he turned his gaze upon the jury and instructed, "Ladies and gentlemen of the jury, please give no consideration or regard to Mr. Jaffe's statement." Then giving the prosecutor a look resembling that which a scolding parent would give a misbehaving child, he quietly intoned, "Please continue, Mr. Jaffe, and check any personal emotions that you might be feeling."

Jaffe fully expected that he would be chastised for his statement when he uttered it. He also knew that it would have a desired effect on the jury, which – despite the Judge's instructions - would connect the dots that connected the defendant's resentment of the victim to her abduction. He smiled at Judge Scheinman and responded, "Yes, Your Honor."

Once again, focusing his attention on the witness, Jaffe asked, "Mr. Farber, when did you surmise that you knew the identity of the individual who did all of these horrible things to you and your wife?"

"Well, I initially suspected it was Ron when"-

Jaffe interrupted, "Ron who?"

Roger gave his questioner a quizzical look and answered, "Ron Krom."

"Is Mr. Krom – Ron Krom – present in the court room?"

Roger focused on the defense table and replied, "Yes, sir, he is seated right over there."

"Is he the young man with dark hair wearing horn-rim glasses?"

"Yes, sir."

Jaffe turned toward the jury and stated, "Let the record show that the witness has identified the defendant as the individual who assaulted him on the afternoon of May 24, 1977. Please continue, Mr. Farber."

Silverstein started to rise from his seat to object but resumed his seat. He remained silent in response to Judge Scheinman's negative head and hand motions indicating that he did not want to hear such objection and would rule against him.

Momentarily confused by the legal shenanigans that had interrupted his train of thought, Roger looked at Jaffe and asked, "When did I first think that Ron – Ron Krom – was the one who did this to Trudy?"

"When did you first suspect, realize or know, that Ron Krom was the person who assaulted you on that afternoon and took your wife?"

Roger nodded his head in understanding and responded, "I immediately thought the man who confronted me with the rifle in my home was Ron Krom – even though he had a ski mask covering his head because he was about the same size and height as Ron and because I could see that the man was wearing glasses under the ski mask."

"Did you tell the F.B.I. – when you called them – of your suspicion?"

"No, I didn't."

"Why not?"

"I guess it was because of the note that he showed me that said not to call the police and, at that moment, I wasn't sure that it was Ron; if it wasn't, I would be sending the police after the wrong person."

"When were you absolutely certain in your mind that Ron Krom was the person who broke into your home, assaulted you and took your wife?"

"When I answered the telephone at my father-in-law's house and I heard him ask if I was Harry Resnick. I recognized the voice as belonging to Ron Krom."

"Was it then that you told the police that you suspected the caller was Ronald Krom?"

"Yes, I told them that I believed the voice that asked for Harry belonged to Ron Krom."

"What did you say to the caller who you suspected to be Ron Krom when he asked if he was speaking to Harry Resnick?"

"I told him that, no, he wasn't speaking to Harry and told him who I was."

"What happened when you told the caller that he was speaking to Roger Farber?"

"He hung up."

"Did you hear from Ron Krom, speak with him, or see him subsequent to answering the Resnick telephone on the evening of May 25, 1977?"

"No, the next time I saw him was in court after he was arrested."

"What convinced you that the voice you heard on the telephone asking if you were Harry Resnick, belonged to Ronald Krom?"

"Well, I had conversed with Ron many times and his voice had become very recognizable to me."

"After you were certain that your wife's abductor was Ron Krom, what did you do?"

"Well, I told the police why I thought the voice I heard belonged to Ron and then I told them how I knew Ron, how he had been trying to get money from me and about his telephone call to Trudy."

"During your acquaintance with Ron Krom, did you give him any reason to want to force his way into your home, assault you at gunpoint, abduct your wife and hold her for ransom?"

"No. I am a little bit older than Ron and although we knew each other, I did not consider him a close friend. During the time that I knew him, Ron troubled me because he frequently exhibited strange behavior and had grandiose plans and ideas. I was also aware that he had spent some time under psychiatric care, but I never knew him to be an aggressive sort of person."

"Why do you believe – no, let me reword that – in your opinion, what inspired or motivated Ron Krom to attack you, steal your wife and seek ransom for her release?"

"Well, I believe he was angry because I wouldn't invest in him, he did not like Trudy for some sort of perceived slight, and he didn't like Trudy's parents because they had money. He thought by kidnapping Trudy and obtaining money from her family, he was getting even with all of us."

Upon hearing this answer, Counsel Silverstein called out, "Objection! Prosecution is trying to establish motive by supposition and conjecture before any evidence has been introduced to support this conclusion."

"Certainly it is reasonable to conclude," Jaffe fired back, "that the traumatized victim of a horrible crime would opine as to what inspired the crime and why he and his family were targeted."

"Question asked, question answered," Judge Scheinman responded in a display of Solomon like wisdom. "What the jury has heard cannot be removed from their minds. However, I would caution that minus supporting evidence and/or testimony that establishes the motive suggested by this witness, what he suggests is merely speculation on his part. Please continue, Mr. Jaffe."

Jaffe flashed a smile in the direction of the bench, then turned toward the defense table and stated, "Your witness, Mr. Silverstein."

If given his druthers, Carl Silverstein, who was trying to establish a thriving law practice in Sullivan County, would not be representing a man who had already been found guilty in the hearts and minds of most Sullivan

County residents. Carl knew the prosecution would introduce a wealth of evidence and it would be impossible to diminish the fact that his client had taken the police to the site of Trudy's entombment and admissions made to police by his client would be heard by the jury. The fickle finger of fate had pointed at Carl to represent Ron Krom because he was the legal aid attorney for Sullivan County; this meant that his client was indigent and therefore entitled to free counsel. It also meant that Carl would be dedicating a considerable amount of time trying to defend the indefensible and would only be entitled to receive the hourly fee established by state law. Carl decided the best defense strategy would be to play on his client's insistence throughout the investigation that the victim's husband was involved with his client and that as a diagnosed schizophrenic, his client believed this bizarre plot was true. How well Roger Farber stood up under cross-examination, could very well decide the success or failure of his strategy. As he arose from the defense table and approached the witness stand, he noted that the witness displayed a look of apprehension and his hands, which were clenched together in front of him, trembled slightly. Silverstein gazed upon the witness in a look of sternness as he began his cross but he did not rush a verbal attack. "Mr. Farber," he asked in a calm voice, "how long have you known my client, Ronald Krom?"

"For quite some time," Roger answered in a quiet tone of voice. "Our parents were involved in the real estate business and I met Ron when our parents worked together in some sort of realty enterprise."

"Please speak up, Mr. Farber." Silverstein encouraged him with a stern tone of voice. "I can hear you fine; however, you need to speak up so that the jury can hear you."

Farber twisted nervously in his seat as he responded, "Yes, sir. Sorry."

"Would it be correct to say that after you met Ronald Krom, you became good friends?"

"Well, ah, it would be more accurate to say that we were friendly. I am three or four years older than he is. I believe he was just out of high school and I had started college when we met, and we did not attend the same schools. We never really became close friends, just knew each other because of our parents and we were friendly."

"Isn't it true that you played together and shared secret hopes and aspirations for the future?"

"No, that is not totally correct. We may have been alone together a couple of times, but as I said, he was younger than I and we were never close friends."

"Mr. Farber, you went hunting with Ron Krom, didn't you?"

"Not really. As I recall, we took twenty-two rifles out into the woods for target practice. I don't recall looking for, or shooting at any animals."

"You have testified that your parents and Ron's parents were involved in the real estate business together. Is that correct?"

"Yes, for a time they were, but that relationship dissolved."

"Mr. Farber, isn't it a fact that your parents and Ronald Krom's parents mutually owned a wooded parcel of land located on the south side of Rondout Reservoir, near the Ulster-Sullivan County line?"

"They may have, but I am not positive that they did. If they did, they no longer own that parcel of land and their partnership dissolved quite some time ago."

"You are aware, Mr. Farber, that the place in the woods where the police found your wife on the evening of May 26, 1977, was the same property formally owned by your parents and the parents of the defendant?"

Roger's face revealed the discomfort and stress he was experiencing from surmising the direction counsel was headed in. District Attorney Jaffe had prepared him to anticipate an attack by the defense counsel intended to implicate him in the plot to abduct his wife; however, he had relived the horrible events of Trudy's abduction over and over, resulting in a personal guilt feeling for allowing his wife to be taken without putting up a fight. However, he could not change or amend the circumstances of the fateful day and was now faced with keeping uncomfortable emotions in check. This was a formidable task when sitting on the hot seat in a court of law and having your words and actions closely scrutinized by Judge, jury, family members, media representatives and concerned citizens. "Yes sir, I was told by the police that was where she was found," he responded in a strained voice.

"Isn't it a fact, sir, that you went hunting on that same property with the defendant, Mr. Krom?"

"I don't believe hunting is correct, Mr. Silverstein." Roger responded. "As I recall, Ron and I went there to shoot our twenty-two rifles and we weren't hunting anything."

"When did you, and how many times did you, and Ron Krom go into these woods to – as you say – shoot rifles?"

"Only once that I recall."

"That you recall? Do you recall when you went to that patch of woods to shoot your rifles?"

"It was some time ago. It was before Trudy and I married, and we were married four years."

"When did you last visit the patch of woods where your wife was found?"

"That was the last time, sometime before 1973."

"Isn't it a fact that you were in that patch of woods with the defendant after you married?"

"No, sir, that is not correct."

"Isn't it a fact that while you were in that patch of woods with the defendant that you saw a hole in the ground that may have previously been used to store dynamite?"

"No, sir."

Silverstein moved in close to the witness gave him a stern, accusing look and asked, "You had seen that hole in the woods before your wife was taken and knew it would serve as a means to secrete your wife while extorting money from your father-in-law, didn't you, sir?"

"No!" Roger responded angrily, "That is not true! I loved my wife, I respect my father-in-law and I could never do such a thing!"

Prosecutor Jaffe watched and listened intently from his seat at the prosecution table. He was satisfied that Roger Farber was holding up as well as could be expected and he would not object to the defense attack upon the witness since he felt to do so, would have a negative effect upon the jury. It was reasonable to presume members of the jury would opine as to how they would have reacted if their spouse were being abducted in the same way Trudy was abducted. They may also wonder why her husband offered virtually no resistance. He had explained to Roger that he could expect to come under attack on the witness stand. The best way to handle the attack was to keep personal emotions in check and answer all questions truthfully. He had admonished Roger, "You cannot undo or change how you reacted that day. People will believe what they want to believe. During cross, you can expect Counsel to go on the attack because his client insists you were involved in your wife's abduction. He will try to show that your failure to put up any resistance lends credence to that claim. Just tell the truth, and let the chips fall where they may."

Staying on the attack, Silverstein fired, "Isn't it true that you told Ron which window you would leave open so he could gain easy access to your home?"

Soaked with perspiration and appearing to have just been squeezed by the rollers of a washing machine wringer, Roger responded shakily, "No, sir, that is not true. If a window was open, and, and apparently it was, it may have been opened by Trudy as she liked the fresh air. If that is how he, Ron, (giving a quick glance at the defendant) came into our home, it is because he found the window open."

Upon hearing this answer, Silverstein flashed a look of disbelief at the jury then refocused his attention on the witness. "Mr. Farber, I would remind you that you are under oath to tell the truth. Let's take it in smaller steps. Did you open that window?"

His face displaying confusion, uncertainty and angst, Roger took a drink of water from the glass in front of him, then took a deep breath and responded, "No, at least I don't remember opening the window. Trudy was the one who enjoyed letting fresh air into the house."

"You did open that window, didn't you, sir? And you opened it for the purpose of permitting Ronald Krom to get into your home without having to break anything?"

"No! That doesn't even make sense!" Roger nervously responded. "Ron made up these allegations against me because I refused to lend him money or get financially involved with him, and that made him mad at me."

"Mr. Farber, the intruder confronted both you and Mr. Kornblau. Is that correct?"

"Yes, sir, that is correct."

"What sort of weapon or weapons did this intruder display that placed you in fear?"

"He, ah, it was, he was holding and pointing a twenty-two rifle at us."

"Did the intruder display any weapon other than the .22 rifle?"

"No, none that we saw."

"Mr. Farber, you were tied up in some fashion by the intruder. Is that correct?"

"Yes, he first tied my hands behind my back."

"Please explain how this occurred. Explain how you were tied up."

"Well, ah, he had me lie down on the kitchen floor and he tied my hands behind my back."

"What did the intruder say to you? Did he tell you that if you didn't do as ordered, he would shoot you or, injure you in some way?"

Fully realizing that the seeds of negativity were being planted in the jury's minds, Roger fidgeted nervously with his hands and answered, "No, ah, he didn't say anything. He threatened with the rifle and pointed at the floor."

Silverstein again displayed a look of disbelief at the jury, then turned his attention back to the witness and asked, "What, if anything, did the intruder say to you during the entire time he was in your home?"

Roger stared at his hands as he answered in a strained voice, "He didn't say anything."

Silverstein again turned toward the jury and displayed a look that portrayed, "You've got to be kidding."

Jaffe could no longer let this tactic go unchallenged. Rising from his seat he called out, "Your, Honor, please direct Mr. Silverstein to refrain from trying to influence the jury with theatrics!"

Nodding his head in the affirmative, Judge Scheinman chastised, "Mr. Silverstein, save your theatre for your closing remarks. Confine yourself to questioning the witness minus personal display intended to influence the jury."

Silverstein accepted his chastisement without responding to either Judge or prosecutor. He instead refocused on the witness and asked, "Mr. Farber, are you attesting that the intruder never spoke, never uttered any words all the time he was holding you in your home and stealing your wife?"

"He showed me written threats. The notes said…"

Silverstein interrupted, "Sir, the question was, and is, did the intruder, who eventually took your wife, speak to you, or say anything during the entire time he was in your home?"

"No," Roger responded in a strained whisper.

"Please speak up, Sir. I believe I was the only one in this courtroom who heard your answer."

Just for a moment Roger studied the audience nervously, then looked down at his hands and responded, "No, sir, he did not speak."

"Mr. Farber, if the intruder did not speak, how did you know what he wanted you to do? What he intended to do?"

"He showed me a note he had written. A typewritten note."

"Did you just say that he presented you with a typewritten note?"

"Yes, sir," Roger quietly intoned.

"And what did this note say? What was the typewritten message?"

"It was a question that asked what time my wife arrived home from work."

"How did you respond to this note?"

"I told him she usually arrived home around five or five-thirty, and it was already that time."

"Was the intruder asking you this question for Harvey's benefit?"

Roger momentarily focused on his questioner with a confused look and responded, "What do you mean?"

"Because he already knew what time your wife would arrive home, because you had previously told him. Isn't it true that he asked you that question to make it appear to Harvey that you were not involved?"

Although Jaffe had previously decided to give Silverstein latitude with Roger, this was over the top. His loud "objection," as he arose from his seat, echoed through the courtroom. "Your Honor, Counsel's supposition is just that, and totally out of line!"

"Your absolutely right, Mr. Jaffe," Judge Scheinman answered, "and if you had not objected as quickly as you did, I would have informed Mr. Silverstein that his statement was uncalled for and given him a verbal slap." Turning his attention to the panel of jurors, he intoned, "Ladies and gentlemen of the jury, you are directed to disregard Counsel's suggestion. There has been no evidence or testimony introduced to support his allegation and Mr. Silverstein, as Mr. Jaffe succinctly stated, was out of line." Turning his attention to Silverstein, he gave him a stern look and spoke in a stern voice. "Mr. Silverstein, you will conduct your cross of this witness in an appropriate manner. I may have a reputation for leniency with counsel, but I caution you not to try my patience. Now proceed with a question of this witness or sit down."

Silverstein fully expected to be chastised for his suggestion, but he knew the jury would hear it and might be influenced. He gave Judge Scheinman an, 'I know I am a naughty boy look' and in a meek voice said, "Yes, Your Honor." Once again turning his attention to the witness, he asked, "Mr. Farber, what happened after you informed the intruder of your wife's expected arrival time?"

"He showed me another note that was written on a piece of newspaper."

"Was this also a typewritten note?"

"No, I heard him write it."

"What do you mean by 'heard' him write it?"

"I heard the rustle of papers and the sound that is made when someone is writing."

"What did this note say?"

"I remember that it was written on a piece of Times-Herald Record newspaper. It said, "Don't call the police or F.B.I.; you will be released in one hour. Call Harry Resnick, or Harry Resnick will call you."

"Were you concerned when you read this note?"

"I was frightened and confused. At first I wasn't sure what the meaning was, but when I thought about what the first note said, I was concerned that he intended to take Trudy."

"And Mr. Farber, is it your testimony, that all the while the intruder was in your presence, he did not utter a word to you?"

"He never spoke a word to me."

"What happened after you read this second note?"

"He tied my legs together."

"For clarification sir – is it your testimony that upon first being confronted by the intruder, he tied your arms or wrists together?"

"Yes, that is correct."

"What sort of knot did he tie in the bindings that secured your arms?"

Roger seemed to study his forearms and hands as he responded, "I don't know."

"Mr. Farber, I have personally tied many knots in my lifetime and I have never been able to tie any of them with just one hand. What did the intruder do with the rifle he was holding while he tied your arms or wrists together?"

Roger twisted uncomfortably in his seat and nervously answered, "I, well I couldn't see him when he did it because he made me lie face down on the floor while he was tying me up."

"While he was tying you up, did you give any thought or consideration that the intruder was using both hands and therefore had placed the rifle down?"

"No, ah, I could not see what he did with the rifle and I was confused and frightened."

"Now sir, you and the intruder were not alone at the moment he was securing your arms. Is that correct?"

"No, sir, Harvey was there too."

"By Harvey, you are referring to your business partner, Harvey Kornblau?"

"Yes, sir."

"Did Harvey say or do anything to prevent the intruder from tying you up?"

"Not that I recall. No, sir, I believe he was as confused and frightened as I was."

"Now let me get this straight; two young, healthy, adult men are confronted by a slightly built intruder holding a twenty-two rifle, and neither of you took any action to prevent the abduction of your wife?"

"Objection!" Rang out from the prosecution table. "Jaffe arose and argued, "Your Honor, the fact that the witness did not take any action to prevent the kidnap of his wife has no bearing on the fact that she was abducted. The witness has testified that he was confused and frightened. There is no reason to believe that an act of bravado would have prevented Mrs. Farber's abduction."

"Sit down, Mr. Jaffe." Judge Scheinman mildly rebuked, "I will give counsel some latitude here, as I would like to hear – and I am sure the jury would like to hear - this witness's answer to the question. Please answer the question, Mr. Farber."

Roger glanced nervously around the courtroom, then focused attention on his hands as he answered, "I don't know why I didn't do anything to stop 'him.' I have relived what happened many times during the past two years and I regret my failure to resist, but I didn't and, and, I have come to the conclusion that when we – Harvey and I - first confronted the intruder, I was under the impression he wanted to rob us and then would leave. By the time I realized he intended to abduct my wife, I was already bound and unable to stop him."

Silverstein had widened the space between the witness and himself, while Roger was offering this explanation. Maintaining that distance he responded, "All well and good, sir. Now, as I recall during direct, you testified that when the assailant exited your home with your wife, you were able to secure a knife and cut your bonds. Is that correct, sir?"

"Yes, one of the knives that 'he' had thrown had bounced off a cabinet and fell within my reach."

"And, I believe that you also testified that upon releasing yourself, you immediately looked out your kitchen window and saw your wife and her abductor outside. Is that correct, sir?"

"Yes," Roger responded in a raspy whisper, adding, "he was pulling her by the arm and I figured he had a car parked nearby."

"At that time, sir, did you own or have access to a firearm?"

"Yes," came a whispered reply.

"Excuse me, sir. Was your response 'yes?'"

"Yes, sir," Roger responded in a slightly louder strained voice.

"And where was this firearm at the time?"

"It was in a drawer in my bedroom nightstand."

"Did it occur to you to retrieve this weapon from the nightstand and pursue the man who was stealing your wife?"

"I ah, I ah, well, I was afraid that if I did, he would hurt Trudy."

"As it was, sir, your wife was much more than hurt. Wasn't she?"

"Yes," Roger responded in a sort of hissed, terse reply.

Jaffe started to arise and object, but did not because of Defense Counsel's next move.

Upon hearing Roger's answer, Silverstein turned his attention toward Jaffe and stated, "Your witness."

Jaffe briefly gave consideration to rehashing with Roger the circumstances of Trudy's abduction, but decided against doing so because Roger Farber looked like a whipped puppy. Instead, he arose from his seat, faced Judge Scheinman and stated, "I have no more questions for this witness at this time, Your Honor."

Judge Scheinman responded, "Very well," then glanced at the witness and stated, "Mr. Farber, you are excused."

Uttering a sigh of relief, Roger arose from the witness chair and headed for the exit doors. Having been wrung through the wringer on the witness stand, he was relieved to escape; however, relief would be short lived, as several reporters followed him out of the courtroom, eagerly seeking some sort of response from him that would lend sensationalism to the ongoing Sullivan Court drama. Still dazed from his ordeal on the witness stand, Roger kept responding, "No comment," as he sought refuge in his car.

Most of the reporters had returned to the courtroom by the time Jaffe had called his next witness.

"The prosecution calls Mr. Harvey Kornblau to the stand," Jaffe stated.

A bailiff opened a door in the rear of the courtroom and a dark-haired heavy-set young man who had been observed sitting on a bench in the hall outside, entered the courtroom. He was directed to the witness stand and instructed to raise his right hand.

"Mr. Kornblau," the court clerk intoned, "you have been called upon to give testimony in the matter of the People of the State of New York against Ronald Harrison Krom. Do you swear to tell the truth and nothing but the truth?"

Staring straight ahead and trying to ignore the buzz in his ears caused by tension and too much caffeine, Harvey answered, "I do."

Jaffe left the prosecution table, approached the witness stand, flashed a brief smile at the witness and encouraged, "Mr. Kornblau, I know it must be difficult to rehash the trauma that you experienced some two years ago. However, your appearance here is absolutely necessary. Think about each and every question carefully before you answer and let your answer be the best reflection on what you experienced on May 24, 1977."

Jaffe's words of encouragement did not call for an answer; however, Harvey nodded his head up and down in response and stated, "Yes, sir."

Jaffe continued by asking a series of questions that established Kornblau's identity, his age, residency and educational background. Having covered this ground, he asked, "Mr. Kornblau, what is your relationship to Roger Farber?"

Although visibly nervous and tense, Kornblau responded in a clear voice, "I have known Roger for several years and we became business partners about four years ago."

"What is the name of your and Roger's business, sir?"

"Catskill Electonics."

"And what sort of business is Catskill Electonics?"

"Roger and I operated Radio Shack stores in Monticello, Ellenville and Monroe. As I live in Loch Sheldrake and Roger lives – lived - just outside Monticello, we spent most of our time in the Monticello store."

"Mr. Kornblau, how successful was Catskill Electronics during the early part of 1977?"

Harvey momentarily focused on the ceiling of the courtroom while contemplating his answer. After this moment of silent reflection, he returned focus on his questioner and answered, "Well, I would say that we were just starting to take off then. I would say that we – Roger and I – were doing okay."

Jaffe fixed the witness with a serious look and slowly asked, "Mr. Kornblau, sir, I will cut right to the chase as to the events leading to why we are in this courtroom today. Please relate the circumstances that caused you to be at the Farber residence on May 24, 1977"

Harvey glanced briefly in the direction of the defendant who appeared to be engrossed in reading a law book, as he thought about his answer. Then he focused his attention on Jaffe and answered, "We had taken our business van to the garage that morning for repairs. That afternoon, Roger drove me to the garage and we picked up the van. We then went up to Roger's house to get some display cases that he had in his garage."

"What time did you arrive at the Farber residence?"

Unconsciously rubbing his chin, Kornblau answered, "Around five – maybe five-fifteen."

"Upon arrival at the Farber residence, what did you do?"

"We took the display cases out of his garage and loaded them in the van. It only took a couple of minutes."

"Please continue, sir; what happened then?"

"Roger invited me in for a drink."

"When you and Roger arrived at his home, were there any vehicles in his driveway or, did you see any vehicles parked in the vicinity of his driveway?"

"No, I do not recall seeing any vehicles in the vicinity."

"Upon entering the Farber residence, what did you see – do?"

"Well, it was warm that afternoon and I was a little sweaty. I asked Roger to use the bathroom and he told me to use the one just in from the garage. Roger went to use the bathroom off his bedroom. As I was coming out of the bathroom, Roger called to me. He said that someone had been in the house and he asked me to come to his bedroom to see the damage they had done. I went to his bedroom and saw that the sheets on his bed and been torn or cut. It appeared that the sheets had been torn or cut into strips and strips were missing. We"-

Interrupting the witness, Jaffe asked, "Could you be more specific sir? Were the sheets – and were they white cotton sheets – torn, or had they been cut with some object?"

After taking a moment to ponder the question, Harvey answered, "I remember they were white cotton sheets and they were in shreds. It was obvious that pieces of sheet were missing. I am not positive whether they were torn apart or cut with something."

"What did you think when you saw this?"

"I didn't know what to make of it at first. I believe I asked Roger if he had looked around to see if anything appeared to have been stolen."

"What was Roger's response?"

"I think he said that nothing else in the room seemed to be disturbed. Then we heard someone moving about in his kitchen."

"Where was the kitchen located in relation to the – was it the master bedroom?"

"Yes, the kitchen was on a lower level at the end of the hall – not too far, the house is, was, small – from the bedroom."

"When you heard this noise, what did you do?"

"We – Roger and I – went into the hallway and looked in that direction. That's"-

Jaffe interrupted, "You looked in the direction of the kitchen?"

"Yes."

"What, if anything, did you see?"

"A man dressed really weird and holding a rifle in his hands was standing on the stairs that went to the kitchen."

"At the time, you were certain the individual you saw was a male?"

"Yes."

"Please describe this individual whom you saw, who you say was dressed weirdly?"

Harvey looked over at the defense table as he answered, "He was slender, about six-feet tall. He had his head covered with what looked like an ace bandage and he had on plastic rimmed sunglasses. He was wearing a light brown waist length jacket and his pants were the same color."

"What was your initial impression upon seeing this individual?"

"Confused and scared! Dressed the way he was – hiding his identity – and having that rifle, made me believe he intended to hurt or kill us."

"If you recall, sir what was Roger's reaction when he saw the intruder?"

"He seemed calm, but I knew he was scared because when he spoke his voice was strained and a lot higher than normal."

"Okay, you and Roger had observed the condition of the bed and were confronted by the disguised intruder. What happened next?"

"I forgot to mention that he was also wearing gloves. He motioned to us that we were to come towards him. We were taken into the kitchen and forced to lie on the kitchen floor."

"How were you forced to lie down on the floor? Did the intruder speak to you – say anything to the effect that you were to get down?"

"No, he didn't say anything. Didn't speak. He pointed at us and then pointed down at the floor. We knew what he wanted us to do."

"After you and Roger were on the floor, what happened next?"

"He tied Roger's hands behind his back and put a pillowcase over his -Roger's – head."

"What did he use to bind – tie – Roger with?"

"It may have been strips of sheet from the bed. I'm not sure."

"What did the intruder do with the rifle while he was tying Roger's hands?"

Like Roger, Harvey had relived the events of May 24, 1977, over-and-over in his mind during the past two-plus years and recognized that his failure to resist, or put up a fight, would cause many people to judge him a coward. Subsequent to the public outrage over Trudy's horrible demise, the explanation that he was confused, frightened and had no way of knowing that Trudy would be abducted and killed seemed indefensible. Harvey now wished that he had tried to stop her abduction and save her life, but he had not, and now he was burdened with guilt. Before answering the question, Harvey glanced quickly about the courtroom, seemingly searching for either understanding or escape. The sea of faces focused directly upon him, waiting for his answer did not portray understanding. Even his questioner, who already knew the answer to the question, gave him a steely stare. Taking a deep breath, Harvey looked down at his hands and whispered in a hoarse voice, "He placed the rifle on the kitchen counter."

Knowing that in cross-examination the defense would make an issue out of Roger and Harvey's impotence at a moment that called for bravado, could be portrayed as circumstantial evidence that the victim's husband, and/or his business partner were somehow involved in the plot to abduct Trudy – as Ron had alleged to police. Jaffe decided to clear that hurdle first so as to lessen the damage. Holding the witness in that same steely stare, he asked, "Were you bound or restrained in any fashion when the intruder placed the rifle on the kitchen counter?"

Avoiding his questioner's stare, Harvey continued the study of his clenched hands and quietly replied, "No, sir."

"Please speak up, sir," Jaffe continued. "Did you make any move to thwart the intruder when he placed the rifle on the countertop?"

Glancing ashamedly at his questioner, then returning focus to his hands, Harvey responded, "No, sir."

"Did you give any thought – any consideration – to jumping the intruder when he laid the rifle down?"

Searching his questioner's face for understanding, Harvey responded, "Yes, I did consider it."

In an understanding tone, Jaffe probed, "Mr. Kornblau, sir, why didn't you – while the intruder was temporarily unarmed – do anything to stop his crimes?"

Harvey glanced briefly at the defendant who gave the appearance that he was engrossed in a law book and mentally disconnected from the proceedings, then returned his gaze on Jaffe. In an unsteady voice he answered, "I thought I knew who 'he' was. My mind was full of confusion and I was very afraid."

"At the moment the intruder placed the rifle on the countertop, you suddenly knew who he was?"

"Well, I, even before that, I thought it – 'he' – was Ron Krom."

"What made you believe your assailant was Ron Krom?"

"Well, it was the glasses for one thing. Ron cannot see well without glasses; also, his height and build and because he didn't say anything. He knew we would recognize his voice. And I also knew that Ron wasn't too happy with Roger because he wouldn't loan him money or go into business with him."

"Why didn't you tell the intruder that you knew his identity to get his reaction and try to reason with him?"

Before answering, Harvey glanced once more toward the defendant; then he returned focus on his questioner and replied, "I knew Ron was mentally unstable and there was no reasoning with him. Also, at first I wasn't sure of his intentions and figured he just wanted to rob Roger. I figured that if I let on that I knew him, he would shoot me."

Giving the witness a puzzled look, Jaffe asked, "But sir, why - if you recognized the intruder as Ron Krom – didn't you jump him when he put the rifle down?"

Harvey searched Jaffe's face for understanding as he responded, "I did give it consideration, but I also knew that although slender, Ron was strong and that mental instability could add to his strength. I was aware that if I jumped him and failed to overpower him, that he would kill us both. I, I guess you could describe that as fear. I was afraid." Not wanting to end on that note, Harvey added, "Also, it was Roger's house and Roger didn't put up any resistance."

"How well did you know Ron Krom?"

"Well, but not too well. He had come into the store to see Roger several times and I got to know him. Roger told me that his parents and Ron's parents had been in the real estate business together at one time. He told me that Ron had grandiose ideas and plans and he wanted Roger to partner with him and finance some of his business ideas, which he was reluctant to do. I knew that Trudy did not like Ron, because he had done something, or said something, that upset her. A couple of times Ron came in to the store looking for Roger and Roger wasn't in. Ron told me that he and Roger were good friends and he was trying to get Roger to invest with him in the purchase of a bar in New Paltz. He told me that the bar was very popular with the college kids and would make a lot of money. When Roger kept turning him down, he tried to get me to partner with him. I told him that first of all, I didn't have the money and second of all, I wasn't interested."

"How did you know that Trudy Farber did not like Ron Krom?"

"Roger told me that Ron had called Trudy to try and convince her to encourage Roger to go into business with him. When Trudy refused, 'he' said Ron went off the deep-end; called Trudy a spoiled rich snob and during his rant inferred that she would be knocked off her high perch, high horse, or something to that effect. Trudy called Roger at the store – very upset. She told Roger about Ron's call to her and said that his incoherent rant to her on the phone was threatening and frightened her. I was with Roger when she told him this and Roger assured her that he would have a talk with Ron and inform Ron that he was not to call, or bother her again. I was also present when Roger told Ron that he had upset Trudy – which Ron denied – and that he did not want Ron to contact his wife again."

"Do you recall when that conversation between Roger and Ron Krom occurred?"

Harvey again glanced at the defendant before answering, "To the best of my memory, it was shortly before 'he' came to Roger's house and took her."

Jaffe studied the witness intently as he asked, "Mr. Kornblau, you have testified that Ronald Krom was mentally unstable. What made you believe, or how did you arrive at that conclusion?"

Upon hearing the question, Silverstein gave brief thought to objecting, but then realized that the witness's answer might aid his plan to prove his client was unaware of the criminal nature of his conduct due to mental illness. He remained silent and listened intently for the answer.

Before answering, Harvey glanced at the defense table with an expectant look that defense counsel, who had started to rise, then sat back down, was going to object. When that did not happen, he refocused on Jaffe and answered, "Well, Roger told me that Ron had a strong imagination, crazy ideas and claimed to be many things he wasn't, and accomplished things that he hadn't. He – Roger – also told me that Ron had been put in a mental hospital - I think he said Middletown State - while he was in high school because he busted up his parents home. Also, Ron often didn't make a lot of sense when talking to me. He boasted about having been in the CIA, having participated in assassinations and that he had graduated from law school."

"Now, sir, you watched as Roger Farber was tied up by the intruder. Is that correct?"

"Yes, sir."

"Were you – did he – tie or restrain you in any fashion?"

"Yes, sir. After tying up Roger, he tied my hands and legs together."

Giving the witness a hard stare, Jaffe asked, "Where was the rifle when he was tying you up?"

Harvey lowered his head and softly answered, "It was on the kitchen counter."

"How would you describe the rifle that the intruder was armed with?"

Harvey was able to now look at Jaffe and he answered, "I knew it was a twenty-two - a semi-automatic as I recall."

Walking to the prosecution table, Jaffe picked up the .22 rifle that had been taken from the defendant at the time Trudy's body was found, carried it to the witness stand and held it for examination by the witness. "Mr. Kornblau, I show you People's exhibit ten. Do you recognize this weapon?"

After studying the rifle for a moment, Harvey answered, "This looks like the gun – the rifle – that (looking and nodding toward the defendant) 'he' had at Roger's house."

Holding the rifle in one hand and lifting it aloft so that it was clearly visible, Jaffe stated, "Let the record show that this rifle that the witness has identified, is the same twenty-two caliber rifle that the police physically wrested from the defendant at the location where Mrs. Farber's body was found."

Turning his attention back to the witness, Jaffe continued, "Now, Mr. Kornblau, you have testified that the intruder remained mute while in your presence on May 24, 1977. Is that correct?"

"Yes, sir," Harvey clearly responded, "he did not speak."

"For clarification, sir how did he communicate with you and Roger Farber?"

"He gestured with his hands and the rifle."

"Did you say anything to your assailant – the intruder?"

"I don't believe so. I'm pretty sure I didn't say anything."

"Did Mr. Farber say anything? Did he try to reason with or communicate with the intruder?"

Harvey unconsciously tugged at his chin for a moment, then answered, "To the best of my memory, Roger asked him what he wanted. I believe he asked 'him' not to hurt us. I specifically remember Roger saying, 'My wife comes home at five-thirty.'"

"Now there came a time when Mrs. Farber arrived. Is that correct?"

"Yes."

"What was her reaction upon entering her house? What did she do or say?"

"I heard her come in and she called out that she was home. I heard her cry out when she saw (looking and nodding toward the defendant) him, and us."

"You said heard. What did you see if anything?"

"After tying me up (nodding again toward Ron) 'he' had me lying face down on the floor so, I wasn't able to see much of what happened."

"What then, did you hear?"

"'He' (looking and nodding again toward the defense table) whispered something to Mrs. Farber. I heard 'him' whisper but couldn't make out what he told her. Whatever he told her made her start crying and she pleaded with 'him' not to hurt her. I found out what 'he' whispered though, because I heard Trudy tell Roger, 'He says to call my father before you call the police.'"

"What happened then? Do you recall whether the intruder did anything else – anything that might be considered bizarre – while he was holding you in the kitchen of the Farber home?"

"Yes. I couldn't see what he did but I knew by the sound that he was throwing something at the cupboards and it made Trudy hysterical. She got really upset, was sobbing and pleading with him to please stop. Roger told her to try and stay calm and she wouldn't be hurt."

"What happened next?"

"I heard 'him' (nodding again toward the defendant) and Mrs. Farber leave."

"Please continue, sir. What happened next?"

"Roger got possession of a knife and cut himself free. Then he freed me. While he was cutting my bonds he told me that he had looked out the kitchen window and saw Trudy being pulled through the woods. He told me that 'he' (again looking and nodding at Krom) must have a car parked nearby. Roger told me to go down to the end of the driveway and write down the license number and description of any vehicles that I saw."

"And did you?"

"Yes, I ran down the driveway and looked around but there were no cars."

"What did you do then?"

"I returned to the house. Roger was on the phone when I went in."

"Do you know who he was talking to?"

"Yes, it was the police. I think it was the F.B.I."

"Mr. Kornblau, please describe the Farber driveway. How long is it?"

"Quite long. The house is some distance off the road. Trees and bushes line the drive."

"Did you see Mrs. Farber, her abductor, or anyone else when you went down the driveway?"

"No, sir."

"About what time was it when you returned to the Farber house?"

Harvey tugged at his chin while pondering this question, eventually responding, "I believe it was around five-thirty or five-forty-five."

"What did you do after returning to the house?"

"Well, while Roger was still on the phone, I told him that I hadn't seen anything. The police - I think first a sheriff's deputy and then a trooper – arrived at about the same time I entered the house. I was instructed to go over to the State Police barracks so a detective could question me, and I did."

"While still at the Farber residence, did you and Roger discuss with the police, or with each other, the possibility that Mrs. Farber's abductor could be Ronald Krom?"

"Actually, I mentioned that to Roger while he was cutting me loose and he said that he agreed with me, but he thought it would be in his wife's best interest if we didn't immediately tell the police of our suspicions. He said that if the police went looking for Ron right away, that because Ron was crazy, he might hurt or kill her. He also said that although we both thought 'it' was Ron, there was the possibility 'it' was someone other than Ron."

"Now, sir, there came a time on May 24, 1977, when you left the Farber home and went to the State Police barracks in Ferndale. Is that correct?"

"Yes, sir."

"Who spoke with you there?"

"A BCI Investigator. I don't recall his name."

"Did you provide a signed deposition – statement – to the Investigator?"

"Yes, I did."

"Did the statement that you gave detail the events that occurred on May 24, 1977, as you have testified in this court?"

"Yes, sir, I believe we covered everything."

"Did you indicate or let on to the BCI investigator your suspicion that the disguised intruder, abductor of Mrs. Farber, was Ronald Krom?"

Shaking his head in the negative and displaying a regretful look, Kornblau responded, "No, sir, not at that time."

"When did you inform the police of your suspicion?"

"The next day - in the morning – I called the State Police and told them I thought it could be Ron Krom."

"Mr. Kornblau, several times while seated in the witness chair, you have looked in the direction of defense counsel's table. Who were you looking at?"

Again glancing toward the defense table, Harvey replied, "Ron Krom."

Turning away from the witness and looking at Silverstein, Jaffe stated, "Your witness, Mr. Silverstein."

Silverstein stood and strode quickly to the witness stand. A brief smile quickly changed into steely accusatory stare as he asked, "Mr. Kornblau, you testified that you did not and do not know the defendant Ronald Krom very well. Isn't it a fact, sir, that you came to know him very well, and, in fact, were giving serious consideration about going into business with him?"

Before responding Harvey glanced quickly at Ron and noted that he was no longer focused on the law book. Ron stared back at him. "I, a, well, I got to know Ron fairly well, but I made his acquaintance through Roger and Roger knew him a lot better than me. We discussed going into business, but knowing that he was unstable, convinced me not to get involved with him."

Holding the witness in a steely stare, Silverstein voiced his next question in a tone of voice that suggested disbelief in the witness's previous answer. "Are you suggesting, sir, that you did not lead Mr. Krom to believe that you were interested in partnering with him in ownership of a tavern in New Paltz?"

Harvey met his questioner's gaze with a steely look of his own and answered, "Ron was after both Roger and me to go into business with him. If for some reason he was, or is, under the impression that I was going to partner with him, he was, and is, sadly mistaken."

Silverstein decided to take another tack. Sounding less accusatory, he asked, "You had personally met with and conversed with my client on several occasions prior to May 24, 1977. Is that a correct assumption sir?"

Wondering where his questioner was headed, Harvey responded with trepidation, "'Personally met with' seems to infer that I was looking forward to meeting with Ron and initiating the contact. That, sir, is not correct. The only occasions that I met with him were when he appeared, always unannounced and by surprise, at our Monticello store. I never initiated contact with Ron. It would be correct to say that we conversed on several occasions. Having been made aware of his mental instability, I treated him politely while doing my best to ignore him."

"And, sir, is it your testimony that you did not lead my client to believe that you were interested in joining him in a business venture?"

"I had no interest in entering into business with Ron and when he asked me for a loan so that he could start his own business, I politely turned him down."

Silverstein decided to head down a new path. "Now, sir, you are young and appear to be in fairly good physical condition. Is that a safe assumption on my part?"

This question brought Jaffe to his feet and he called out, "Objection, Your Honor! What has the age and physical condition of this witness got to do with the crimes under consideration?"

Judge Scheinman did not immediately rule. Displaying an inquisitive look he directed that both prosecution and counsel approach the bench. When both arrived, he whispered, "Mr. Silverstein, where are you headed with this?"

Giving His Honor a serious look, Carl whispered in reply, "As you are aware, sir, my client maintains that Roger Farber hatched the plot to abduct his wife and used my client to carry out her abduction. I intend to show that my client is soft-spoken, mild-mannered, has no history of assaulting anyone, and is opposed to violence of any nature. The fact is that two reasonably fit young men - Roger being one of them - failed to take any action to prevent Mrs. Farber's being taken. Especially at a moment when her abductor was not armed, there is strong inference that one or both men were aiding and abetting her abduction."

Jaffe started to respond; however, Scheinman put up his hand, indicating that he did not want to hear argument, and whispered, "I will allow it Carl, but be careful not to stray into the area of making accusatory statements toward unnamed defendants."

Jaffe returned to his seat at the prosecution table.

Turning away from the bench and facing the witness, Silverstein quietly said, "Please answer the question, Sir."

Giving his questioner a curious look, Harvey answered, "I guess you could say that I am fairly young and healthy."

Smiling at the witness, Silverstein asked, "Mr. Kornblau, during the time that you knew Ronald Krom, did he ever give the appearance of being aggressive?"

"No, sir."

"And did Ron Krom display a tough demeanor and speak in a rough, tough tone of voice?"

"No, sir, as a matter of fact he has – had – a very distinctive soft, almost feminine sounding voice, easily recognizable. I am convinced that is why he didn't speak to Roger and me that day."

Continuing to smile and speaking in a polite tone, Silverstein asked, "To bear out what you have just stated as true, sir you are aware that Roger – Roger Farber – in fact recognized Ron's voice over the telephone at the Resnick home. Is that correct?"

"Yes, sir, I am aware that happened."

"Now, sir," Silverstein continued, focusing on the witness with a quizzical look, "you testified under direct, that you – as a matter of fact, both you and Roger – suspected at the moment that Mrs. Farber was being taken from her home, that her abductor was Ronald Krom. You have just testified that you knew Ronald Krom to be non-physical, non-aggressive and soft-spoken. Now, sir, would you please explain to this court, this jury (glancing toward the jury panel), why two young men in good health and physical condition, under the impression that they were being confronted by a man they knew to be non-aggressive and non-violent, did nothing to try and thwart his crime?"

Kornblau did not immediately answer instead casting a brief look of contempt toward the defendant who he now wished he had beaten to a pulp on that fateful day, more than two years ago. He returned his gaze toward his questioner, gave him a frustrated look and with obvious irritation, answered, "Although I now regret not resisting, and God knows I have lived those moments over and over in my mind, the fact is – as I previously stated – I was confused and frightened. If Roger had taken the initiative – after all, as I have said, it was his home – I believe I would have joined him. He did not; consequently, I did not and what happened, happened."

Upon hearing this answer, Silverstein shook his head in the negative, gave the witness an accusatory look and asked, "Sir, could the truth as to why you did not act be that you knew that Mrs. Farber was going to be abducted and that you would not be harmed?"

"Objection!" Jaffe shouted as he leapt to his feet. "Your Honor, Counsel is attempting to influence the jury by inferring that this witness who was a victim of his client's, crimes, is somehow involved in the plot to kidnap Mrs. Farber. I would point out that the police investigation revealed no suspicion, and more importantly, no evidence that Mr. Kornblau had anything to do with the crimes that Ronald Krom is charged with and is on trial for in this court. Counsel's conduct is egregious and he is totally out of line."

"I agree, Mr. Jaffe," Scheinman replied. Giving counsel a stern look, he asked, "Mr. Silverstein, were you, or were you not, cautioned by me not to make accusatory statements toward unnamed defendants?"

Silverstein had fully expected a dress down when he posed the accusatory question of the witness; however, he felt that scoring with the jury was worth the gamble. Giving the Judge an apologetic look he answered, "Yes, you did, Your Honor. I apologize and withdraw my question." (In his mind) He told himself, mission accomplished.

Refocusing on the witness, Silverstein asked, "Mr. Kornblau, you testified that after Mrs. Farber was taken from her home, and while being untied, you and Roger discussed the possibility that the abductor was Ronald Krom. You testified that Roger suggested that you withhold your suspicions from the police; is that correct?"

"Well, not quite correct," Roger responded displaying a troubled, curious look. "As I recall, Roger suggested that revealing our belief that 'he' was Ron too quickly – because of Ron's unstable mental condition – could result in Trudy being hurt or killed. Roger did not suggest that we withhold our suspicion indefinitely and, as a matter of fact, I called the state police the following morning and told them."

"Now consider your next answer very carefully, sir," Silverstein admonished, words emphasized by a serious look. "When Roger agreed with you - immediately after Mrs. Farber was taken – that your assailant, her abductor, was thought to be Ronald Krom and it was suggested that you not immediately report your suspicion as to her abductor's identity to the police, did you doubt the veracity of Roger's reasons for not immediately informing the police?"

Displaying a confused look, Harvey responded, "Well, Roger's reasons did make sense, but I also had mixed emotion as to whether it was the right thing to do. That's why I called the state police the next morning and told them I thought it was Ron."

Turning away from the witness, Silverstein studied the jury's faces for a moment then refocused on the witness. He started to form another question but did not believe it best to leave the jury wondering why Roger and Harvey did not jump the slender, meek-looking defendant, docilely sitting a few feet from them, and why one or both men did not immediately inform the police as to the abductor's suspected identity.

Jaffe gave brief consideration to reexamining the witness but decided against it.

Harvey was visibly relieved when Judge Scheinman said, "Witness excused."

During a recess, members of the media jostled for front row seats as the next anticipated witness would insure that their reports would be front-page fodder.

After calling the court to order, Judge Scheinman asked District Attorney Jaffe if he were ready to proceed.

Flashing a toothy smile at His Honor, Jaffe replied, "Yes, Your Honor. The People call Harry Resnick."

A bailiff exited the courtroom momentarily and returned escorting a man recognized by most of the people filling the chamber. Although impeccably dressed, Harry Resnick, on this day, and at this time, appeared more like the farmer of his roots, than a member of the wealthiest family in Ellenville - perhaps wealthiest in all of the Catskill region.

After the witness was sworn and seated, District Attorney Jaffe left his seat at the prosecution table, and making sure to display a look of sincerity toward the witness who had the power to make or break a career with a telephone call, stated, "Mr. Resnick, I extend heartfelt condolences to you and the Resnick family concerning the tragic and untimely death of your daughter. I regret having to call upon you to testify in this matter; however, I am sure that you understand sir, your being here is absolutely necessary."

Displaying a look of understanding, Harry responded, "Mr. Jaffe, I understand that in the name of justice, although justice can only come from God, my presence here is required. Ask your questions."

Maintaining a considerable distance from the witness, Jaffe asked, "Sir, for the record, would it be correct to say that you are the President of Channel Master Corporation, headquartered in Ellenville, New York?"

Displaying the hint of a smile, Harry answered, "I became President of Channel Master in 1950, and remained in that office until we sold the business to Avnet, Inc. in 1967. I remain on the Board of Directors of that company."

Jaffe smiled in response and said, "Thank you for that clarification, sir." Changing to a serious look, he continued, "Now permit me to take you to the reason we are here today, which is the abduction and tragic death of your daughter Gertrude in May of 1977. I realize that reflection on that horrible time in your life will be difficult and painful for you. We will proceed slowly, and if at any time you wish to take a break, please feel free to say so."

Whatever negative emotions Harry was experiencing were unreadable in the steady gaze he gave Jaffe, and he answered, "Ask your questions, Mr. Jaffe. I have grieved and continue to grieve for my Trudy, but what must be done, must be done in the name of justice, which will never be served for my wife or me."

"Mr. Resnick, for the record, Gertrude, affectionately referred to as 'Trudy,' was your only daughter. Is that correct sir?"

"Yes," Harry quietly answered, adding, "Our Trudy was precious and dear to us."

Jaffe continued, "Now sir, on May 24, 1977, your daughter Trudy was married and living with her husband, Roger Farber, in Sackett Lake. Is that correct?"

"Yes, Mr. Jaffe. They enjoyed their modest home, which was close to Monticello and near Trudy's place of employment."

Displaying a very serious look, Jaffe continued, "Forgive me for asking sir, but to your knowledge was your daughter happy in her marriage?"

Giving his questioner a deadpan look, Harry responded, "Mr. Jaffe, Trudy and Roger in 1977 were practically newlyweds and to my knowledge Trudy was happy in her marriage. My Trudy was not only happy in her marriage, she enjoyed her work and was looking forward to presenting Marcia and me with our first grandchild. Happy, you ask? I believe she was very happy and you can rest assured that if she had not been, I would have known."

"Thank you, sir," Jaffe responded. He then asked, "Now, sir, did there come a time on May 24 1977, when you received a disturbing telephone call from your son-in-law, Roger?"

Reflection on that horrible moment in his life, evoked a look of sadness, but Harry calmly related, "Yes, Mr. Jaffe, Roger called me and I immediately knew something was wrong because he sounded upset and spoke in very fast words."

"Please relate the details of that call sir."

Pain was etched in Harry's face as he slowly related, "He, Roger, told me that my – our – Trudy had been abducted. He told me that an armed intruder had forcibly taken Trudy. He said the intruder was already in the house when he – Roger – and Harvey, his business partner, arrived at the house before Trudy. He told me this intruder threatened to shoot both him and Harvey if they resisted and that he tied them up. He told me that this evil man did not speak and remained silent. He told me that this evil person communicated by showing him notes. One of the notes asked what time Trudy arrived home from work. Another note instructed Roger to call me and not call the police. Marcia overheard my conversation with Roger, recognized that our Trudy had been taken, and she – my poor wife – became hysterical. What Roger was telling made me feel as if lightning had struck me. I tried to convince myself that what Roger was telling me was a cruel joke, but I knew intuitively that my Trudy had been taken."

"Mr. Resnick," Jaffe asked in a quiet voice, "do you recall how you responded to Roger's account of your daughter's abduction?"

Without hesitation Harry answered, "Yes, even while fighting against personal panic, I recognized that the person or persons who had taken Trudy would be making a ransom demand. I instructed Roger to call the F.B.I., tell them what happened, and then come to my home in Ellenville. Then I did my best to calm and reassure my wife that Trudy was all right and would be returned. Then I called the state police. A very polite, professional young trooper came to our home and remained with us that evening. I believe his name was Schetzel, John Schetzel, and he listened on an extension when I received the call from Trudy's abductor. The man said"-

Jaffe interrupted, stating, "Thank you, Mr. Resnick, I will ask you about the ransom call in a minute. First sir, about what time of day was it when Roger Farber called to inform you of your daughter's abduction?"

"I believe it was around six that evening, Mr. Jaffe."

"And, sir, did you say that you contacted the state police immediately after concluding your conversation with Roger?"

Nodding his head in the negative, Harry responded, "Well, Mr. Jaffe, I would not say my call was immediate. I first had to calm my wife, then I called the state police."

"Sir, do you recall when – the approximate time – that Trooper Schetzel arrived at your home?"

"Well, as you can well imagine, it seemed an eternity, but I believe Trooper Schetzel arrived about twenty minutes after my call to his headquarters."

"Now, sir," Jaffe continued, "to the best of memory, what time was it on May 24 1977, when you received first contact from your daughter's abductor?"

"That call, Mr. Jaffe, came at six-forty-five. I remember that Trooper Schetzel wrote down the time."

"Now, sir, do you recall what the caller said and what he instructed you to do?"

"Mr. Jaffe," Harry responded, continuing to speak in a calm voice, "I will recall those horrible words for the rest of my life. The man spoke in a quiet voice, which belied the sort of monster that he was. First he said, 'We have your daughter, Trudy.' I told him that I did not believe him and that he was kidding. He responded by telling me, 'Get into your Rolls Royce and go over to her house and untie her husband and another subject.' I again told him, I don't believe it and asked to whom I was speaking. He then said, 'Our group is well organized and you better transfer some finances into cash.' I told him I could immediately give him two thousand dollars. He responded by telling me, 'we want one million dollars in fifties and one hundreds, if you wish to see her again. We have hired a private courier to pick up the money.' I told him that I did not have access to that sum of money on such short notice. He then told me that I could contact my two brothers for assistance. I explained to him that I had only one brother, as my other brother had passed away some time ago. His response was, 'We want the million dollars and understand it will take some time for you to put that amount together.' He told me not to call the police or FBI - which I had already done - into the case saying, 'If the police got involved, I would never see Trudy again.'"

Harry paused, removed a handkerchief from the pocket of his jacket, used it to dry his eyes and blow his nose. Continuing to hold the handkerchief in one hand, he went on, as he stared at the defendant in a pained look, "He, this evil doer who had taken my Trudy, told me that he had people watching my home and they would know if the police had tapped into my telephone. To emphasize this threat, he described the exact location of my home. Then, he just hung up without explaining how the money was to be delivered in exchange for Trudy. No mention of a date, time or place for exchange. He just like that, was talking one moment and gone the next. As I said, Trooper Schetzel listened on an extension and when the call ended, he told us – Marcia and me – that all we could do from that moment on was let the police conduct their investigation, follow instructions from investigators and hope and pray for Trudy's safe return."

It was noticed that while Harry provided details of the telephone call he received requesting ransom, the defendant momentarily abandoned the open law book in which he seemed to be engrossed and studied the witness with a blank, emotionless stare. When Harry looked at him, he immediately refocused on the open law book.

"Now, sir," Jaffe continued, "did their come a time when you received a second call at your home from your daughter's kidnapper?"

"Yes, Mr. Jaffe. However, I did not personally take the call. Roger was there and he answered our telephone."

"When was this call received, sir?"

"At the time, several members of the FBI and state police were at my home. They had some sort of recording and tracing equipment attached to my telephones. The evildoer called at around 11:30 the following night. Roger answered this call."

"Sir, can you tell the court what transpired, what was said between the caller and Roger?"

"Yes, Mr. Jaffe, as I said, their conversation was recorded and I listened to the recording. The evildoer asked if he was speaking to me. Roger told him, 'No, this is Roger Farber - hold on.' There was no more talk between them because the evildoer hung up."

"Sir, please relate what Roger said after the call ended so abruptly?"

"Roger said that he recognized the voice of the caller. He told the police he believed it was -'him,' (looking and nodding at the defendant)."

"Sir, you just identified the caller as 'him' while nodding in the direction of the defendant. For clarification, did Roger state the name of the suspected caller?"

Continuing to gaze at the defendant, Harry answered, "Yes, Mr. Jaffe, Roger told us – the police and me – that this person was Ron Krom, who lived in the Village of Grahamsville."

"Did you receive any more telephone calls from your daughter's abductor?"

"No, Mr. Jaffe, that was the last call."

"Now, sir, while waiting and hoping to hear from your daughter's abductor again, what did the police instruct you to do?"

"Well, Mr. Jaffe, mostly I just waited for a call or message that would inform me how I could make payment to have my Trudy released. I had called my attorney shortly after learning that Trudy had been taken, and he worked with the police – I believe the FBI – in putting together the ransom money demanded by the evildoer. As time passed and no instructions were received, I began to fear the worst."

"Sir, when Roger said that he believed he had spoken to Ron – Ronald Krom on the telephone, did you know who he was referring to?"

"No, Mr. Jaffe, I did not know this Ronald Krom."

"Now sir, did there come a time when the police introduced you to Ronald Krom?"

"Yes, Mr. Jaffe, I was called by a state policeman, who told me that Ronald Krom was at the Ferndale barracks. I was told that this Krom had agreed to take them to Trudy after being allowed to speak with me. I agreed to go over there and speak to him. When"-

Jaffe interrupted the witness, asking, "And sir, did you go to the Ferndale State Police barracks."

Giving his questioner a frustrated look because he was about to provide the same answer before being interrupted, Harry responded, "Yes, Mr. Jaffe, I was about to tell you that before you interrupted."

"I apologize, sir. When was it that you went to the State Police barracks?"

"It was in the evening of May 26. Two days Trudy had not been heard from."

"Thank you, sir. Now please provide the details of your conversation with Ronald Krom after being introduced to him by the State Police?"

"Please understand Mr. Jaffe that at that time I was willing to do anything for the safe return of my daughter. I would have made a pact with the devil to accomplish that." Staring at the defendant without display of emotion, Harry continued, "I was somewhat surprised that this Ronald Krom I was introduced to did not have the look of evil. It seemed grotesquely ironic that such a harmless - appearing young man could do such a horrible thing by taking my Trudy. I informed him that I was willing to render my assistance to secure the release of my daughter. The first thing this Krom confronted me with was the question as to whether I was aware that my son-in-law, Roger, was involved in Trudy's abduction? I was not surprised by this attempt to shock or upset me because the detectives that I spoke with prior to meeting this Krom, had told me that I should be prepared to hear Krom say incredible, bizarre things. I don't know what sort of reaction Krom was expecting from me when he told me this. I told him that if what he said was indeed true, I would offer the same assistance to Roger as I would to him, in order to secure the safe return of my Trudy. This Krom told me that he knew where Trudy was being held and that he wanted me to pay $400,000 to him and another $100,000 to Roger for him to reveal her location. When this Krom asked for this money, the police told him that his asking me for money was not part of the agreement they had made with him when he told them he would reveal Trudy's location after speaking with me. I informed the detectives that this was not an important issue to me. I then told Krom that my sole interest was the safe return of my daughter and that I was willing to pay the money he requested if such payment would return Trudy without interfering with the official investigation." Hesitating, Harry once again reached for his handkerchief, blew his nose, and continuing in an emotion filled voice, said, "I agreed to pay this money for the location of my Trudy, whether she was found dead or alive. This Krom did not respond directly to me. He just suddenly jumped from his chair and told the detectives, 'Let's go, I will take you to her.' I then spoke with a BCI detective and agreed to wait in the State Police office while they went to find Trudy. That was the last contact and conversation that I had with this Krom."

"Sir, when was it that you learned that Ronald Krom had taken the BCI to the location where he was holding your daughter and learned of her demise?"

"While I waited at the offices of the state police. Later that same evening."

"Mr. Resnick, did you subsequently pay any of the requested ransom to Ronald Krom or any other person?"

"No, Mr. Jaffe, I did not."

Portraying a sympathetic smile, Jaffe intoned, "Thank you, sir. Your witness, Carl."

Silverstein stood and following Jaffe's example did not approach the witness, too closely so as not to give the appearance of intimidation. "Mr. Resnick," he opened, "I also extend my condolences to you on the tragic loss of your daughter. Sir, I only have a couple of questions for clarification. Sir, are you certain that you had not met, and did not know my client prior to May 26, 1977?"

Giving his questioner a sober look, Harry responded, "Mr. Silverstein, it is possible that I met this Krom on a previous occasion; however, if I did it was not memorable to me. I meet many people who remain strangers to me."

Giving the witness a probing, serious look Silverstein asked, "Sir, subsequent to your conversation with Ron Krom on May 26, 1977, have you given any thought, or conducted any investigation to prove the veracity of Mr. Krom's allegation that your son-in-law was involved in the plot to kidnap your daughter?"

Jaffe rose to object but sat down without doing so in response to Judge Scheinman's hand motion indicating that he was to sit down.

Displaying a pensive look, Harry responded, "Mr. Silverstein how does the father of a kidnapped and murdered child ever stop pondering as to why this terrible thing happened? Yes, as incredulous as they seemed, I weighed this Krom's words carefully and arrived at the conclusion that they were mere words without substance. My son-in-law gave me no reason and since that horrible time has given me no reason to suspect or believe that he was involved in these horrible crimes. I was also informed by the State Police that this Krom was a certified schizophrenic, capable of creating fantasies that he could very well believe were true."

Realizing that continued questioning of the witness could adversely affect the jury, Carl flashed a smile at Harry and stated, "Thank you, Mr. Resnick." He then sat down.

After excusing the witness, Judge Scheinman announced that court would recess until the next day.

Reporters scurried from the court building to ensure that their reports on the trial of national interest made the publishing deadline.

Members of the legal community hurried to their offices to read telephone messages and return calls to important clients.

The few spectators who comprised the rest of the audience made their way slowly out of the courtroom discussing with each other personal perceptions of the day's witnesses and testimony.

Harrison and Dorothy Krom, accompanied by son Wayne, would occupy a front row seat throughout the trial. Each one displayed intermittent looks of sadness and dismay as they watched deputies place handcuffs on Ron and then escort him away. As they watched, Ron looked in their direction for a brief moment and the look he gave them was unreadable. They slowly made their way out of the courtroom in silence, minds occupied with trepidation in knowing that the following day's proceedings would only produce more sadness.

The Sullivan County courtroom again filled to capacity the following morning. Opening formalities concluded, Judge Scheinman bade District Attorney Jaffe to call his next witness.

"The People call Investigator Wilfried Holik to the stand," Jaffe announced while looking toward the rear courtroom doors.

A bailiff standing by the entrance to the courtroom opened a door and motioned to a tall male, impeccably dressed in a dark pinstripe suit. The man smiled, entered the courtroom and, displaying confidence, strode quickly to the witness stand. By physical appearance alone, the handsome, square jawed policeman with neatly trimmed salt and pepper hair epitomized the image of a television detective. However, upon hearing him speak in clearly enunciated words, enriched by a recognizable German accent, one might envision that the detective was a doctor or scientist as well. As supervisor of a New York State Police Forensics Investigation Unit, German born Wilfried Holik was all of these, minus the sheepskins that are not awarded for graduation from the school of hard knocks. Holik – or Willy, or Will, as he was affectionately called by friends and co-workers – immigrated to the United States from Germany via enlistment in the United States Navy, which put him on the fast track to citizenship. Upon achieving citizenship and receiving an honorable discharge from the Navy, he became a proud member of a brotherhood that went by the formal name New York State Police. Intelligent and ambitious, Trooper Holik quickly earned promotion into the Bureau of Criminal Investigation (BCI) and soon learned that the manner in which a crime scene was processed played a huge role in solving the case. He also learned that the manner by which evidence was gathered and processed would play heavily on that evidence being admissible at trial and weigh heavily on an outcome of guilty or acquittal.

Knowledgeable and meticulous, Holik soon became recognized as a forensics expert, was promoted to Senior Investigator and placed in charge of the Troop F identification bureau. Holik handled himself well on the witness stand and his noticeable German accent came across as evidence of his knowledge and expertise. Prosecution and defense attorneys throughout southern New York State had been heard to proclaim – in numerous instances - that Holik's testimony had heavily influenced the jury.

Though young, both District Attorney Joseph Jaffe and Defense Counsel Carl Silverstein were aware of Holik's reputation.

After the witness was sworn, Jaffe approached Holik, flashed him a smile and asked, "Sir, please state your name, title and occupation, for the record."

Giving his questioner a smile in return, Holik then looked toward the jury and responded, "Wilfried Holik. The correct pronunciation is Willfreed Hoo-lick. I readily respond to Willy, Will, and Ooh-lick as well. I am a Senior Investigator in the New York State Police. I presently supervise the Troop F Identification Bureau headquartered in Middletown."

It would be reported that a magical connection was immediately established between this witness and nearly everyone present in the courtroom. Some would report that Holik appeared warm, genuine and comfortable on the witness stand. Others would relate that this attractive man with twinkling eyes seemed sincere and seemed to be speaking directly to them when he spoke. Somehow, this experienced police officer who spoke in a quaint accent and was dressed in a wrinkled suit that had possibly not seen the inside of a dry cleaning establishment in months, established a positive connection with the jury and this fact was recognized by prosecutor, defense attorney and judge.

A member of the jury would tell this author, "The witness spoke directly to us when answering, and his eyes twinkled with sincerity lending credibility to his answers."

Jaffe continued, "Investigator, how many years have you been a member of the New York State Police?"

Again facing the jury, Holik answered, "Approximately sixteen years."

"Sir," Jaffe continued, now displaying a serious look, "what are your duties as a Senior Investigator?"

Having already settled in and appearing calm and relaxed, Holik faced the jury and answered, "I supervise the Troop F Identification Bureau, which gathers and processes evidence, processes fingerprints, and we maintain criminal record files on all subjects arrested for crimes within our troop area."

"Investigator, would it be accurate to say that one of your primary duties as supervisor of F Troop's Identification Bureau, is the process of major crime scenes?"

Flashing a twinkle in the eye smile at his questioner, Holik answered, "As professionals, sir, we prefer to be referred to as Troop F so as not to have anyone associate us with a certain television comedy serial."

Willy's answer elicited laughter from just about everyone in the courtroom familiar with the fumbling, bumbling antics of the popular television series – at that time – "F Troop."

As the laughter subsided, Holik explained, "Yes, Mr. Jaffe, one of my most important duties is processing crime scenes for evidence. We are trained in photography, securing latent fingerprints for identification, drawing crime scene diagrams and gathering evidence believed applicable to identifying a motive for the crime. That will also aid in identifying the person or persons responsible."

Jaffe smiled at Holik and responded, "Thank you for that clarification Investigator. I am certainly glad that you are a member of Troop F, rather than F Troop." After waiting for the laughter to again subside, he continued, "Now on a serious note Investigator, did you respond to a Sackett Lake home on May 24, 1977, concerning a reported abduction?"

Remembering to look at the jury before answering, Holik flashed them a serious look. He then faced Jaffe and answered, "Yes, sir."

Jaffe continued, "What time – the approximate time, sir – did you arrive at the Farber home in Sackett Lake?"

"I arrived there at precisely seven thirty-five in the evening."

"Was there anyone at the Farber home when you arrived?"

"Yes, sir, a trooper and a sheriff's deputy, both in uniform."

"Investigator, what did you do after arriving at the Farber home?"

"Well, I had been called by Senior Investigator Don Scherpf, supervisor of the Ferndale BCI unit and asked to respond to the Farber home. Scherpf filled me in on what had transpired at the Farber home. When I arrived there, I slowly walked about the premises to obtain a visual perspective of the areas pertaining to the crimes. I saw that a screen had been cut on an open window in the master bedroom. I saw that the bed in the master bedroom was in disarray and one sheet had been torn or cut. Closer examination indicated that it was cut and most probably with a hunting knife that was lying on top of a nightstand in the same room. I saw that the kitchen was in disarray. A kitchen chair was lying on its back, several pieces of string and strips of sheet were scattered about the floor, a steak knife was embedded in a kitchen cabinet and other steak knives were scattered about the countertop and floor. I took several photographs, then I drew diagrams of the bedroom and kitchen, took measurements and indicated the location of each of the items of evidence that I would subsequently gather."

"Investigator, did you note or find anything of evidentiary value in any other areas of the premises?"

"Yes, sir, I also observed a footprint in soft dirt at the rear of the house, on the edge of a wooded area; following in the assumed direction the perpetrator had taken with the victim, I came out on Sunset Drive Extension. This was the approximate location where – as I was told – a neighboring resident had observed a car parked. I found a tire imprint on the shoulder of the road. I photographed the footprint and tire imprint and used plaster-of-Paris to obtain casts of both impressions."

"Investigator Holik, what evidence did you secure from the residence, and where was each item located?"

Holik smiled at Jaffe as he asked, "Would it be permissible to look at my notes, sir?"

Jaffe responded, "Certainly, Investigator. If need be, please consult your notes."

Reaching into a breast pocket of his suit coat, Willy produced a small notebook of the sort carried by most police detectives. Turning to the appropriate page, he read: "I secured from the bed in the master bedroom one sheet which had two pieces cut out of it; a hunting knife that was lying on top of a nightstand in the master bedroom; a three foot long piece of nylon string that was found lying on the floor just inside the front door of the residence; a two and one-half foot long piece of nylon string found in the upstairs hallway; a three foot two-inch long piece of nylon string found on top of the kitchen counter; a two foot five-inch long piece of nylon string found draped over an open, (under the sink) cabinet door; two pieces of dark fabric, both two feet in length, found on the kitchen floor; two pieces of bed sheet, one measuring two feet ten-inches in length and the other two feet five-inches in length, also found on the kitchen floor; a one-foot, one-inch long piece of cotton string found lying on a kitchen chair; a Middletown Times-Herald Record newspaper, found on top of the kitchen table; six matching steak knives, one removed from an upper kitchen cabinet door, four found in various places on top of the kitchen counter and one found on the kitchen floor; the victim's passport, found lying on top of a bedroom dresser and one plaster of Paris cast of a footprint believed left by a male and one plaster of Paris cast of a tire tread, believed to be from a tire on a car used by the perpetrator." Looking up from his notes, Willy added, "The newspaper was missing a piece of its cover page. I duly noted on my diagrams the location where each of the items was found."

Turning away from the witness, Jaffe looked at Judge Scheinman and asked, "Please give me a moment Your Honor."

Scheinman nodded his head in the affirmative, but did not verbally respond.

Jaffe walked to the prosecution table, picked up a large envelope, opened it and sorted out a quantity of 8 x 10 black and white photographs. He carried the photos to the witness stand, handed them to Holik and questioned, "Investigator, I show you People's 1A thru 1S, and ask if you recognize these photos?"

Willy quickly examined the reverse side of each photo and after seeing the notations he had placed on each photo answered, "Yes, sir, they are photographs that I took at the Farber residence on May 24, 1977."

Jaffe retrieved the photos from the witness and flashed him a smile as he did so. He then approached the jury, handed the photographs to the foreman and stated, "Ladies and gentlemen, please examine these photographs which are in evidence, and which depict the Farber residence on the day Mrs. Farber was abducted. Please note the condition of the premises and each item of physical evidence that the witness has described."

The courtroom was abuzz with whispered conversation while the jury examined the photographs; however, by the time the foreman handed the photographs back to the District Attorney, the chamber was silent.

After placing the photos on his worktable, Jaffe approached the witness and asked, "Investigator, did you subsequently make a comparison of the footprint cast and tire cast to any person and vehicle?"

Smiling, Willy answered, 'No, sir, it was determined that the casts were of insufficient quality to make a positive identification."

Momentarily turning away from the witness, Jaffe walked to the prosecution table, examined his legal pad and then refocused his attention on Senior Investigator Holik. He asked, "Now Investigator, did there come a time when you were notified that Mrs. Farber had been located and that she was deceased?"

"Yes, sir," Holik answered displaying a somber look.

"Investigator, were you directed to proceed to the location where Mrs. Farber's body had been found to take photographs and search for evidence?"

"Yes, Mr. Jaffe. Senior Investigator Scherpf called me and gave me directions to the location where Mrs. Farber's body had been found. I went immediately and had no difficulty finding the location because a trooper had been posted on Route 55, at the turnoff into the woods."

"When was this that you went there, Investigator?"

"I arrived at the location at precisely 10:25 p.m., May 26, 1977."

"Please describe to the best of memory the exact location where Mrs. Farber was found."

Looking directly at the jury, Holik answered, "The crime scene was located in woods on the south side of Route fifty-five, in the Town of Wawarsing, Ulster County, approximately five-hundred yards from the Sullivan County line. The precise location was on a small level area about one-third of the way up the side of a mountain. I surmise that in a direct line it was six hundred thirty yards from the south shoulder of Route 55. The Rondout Reservoir is located on the north – opposite - side of Route 55. The scene was accessed via a dirt trail, which may have served as a logging trail running diagonally up the hillside, then upon reaching the end, by an uphill walk of approximately two hundred yards, reaching the level area in the woods."

"Was it a dark night, sir?"

"Yes, sir, it was a very dark night; however, lighting powered by generators had been set in place prior to my arrival and I was able to see quite well."

"And what did you see, Investigator?"

Providing his answer directly to the jury, Holik slowly answered, "I observed the body of a white female - who had already been pronounced deceased by the Ulster County Coroner, who preceded me to that location - and told me that the woman had already been identified as Trudy Farber. She was crammed into a hole in the ground and lying on her back in a curled up position. Her arms were frozen in a raised position slightly above her body. Her hands – very obviously damaged – were in a clenched position. There were bruises on her face and nose. The victim's eyes and mouth were open and her face appeared frozen in a look of terror. The plywood cover, which had covered the pit and entombed Mrs. Farber, had been opened and removed before my arrival. I would later ascertain that Mrs. Farber's hands were bruised and bloodied from trying to claw her way out of the pit. The ends of her fingers were torn, bloody and one side of the plywood cover was found to have scratch marks."

Giving the witness a grim look, Jaffe asked, "Investigator, when you saw this gruesome scene, what was your impression – your reaction?"

"Objection!" Silverstein called out from his seat. "Your Honor, the witness is a trained professional, who has undoubtedly observed many victims of various causes of death. One would believe that as a professional, he would be focused on his work without show of emotion."

"Your Honor," Jaffe argued in response, "I thank counsel for recognizing this witness as a professional; however, he is still a human being subject to occasional displays of emotion. I believe the jury would be interested in whatever emotions Mr. Holik felt upon viewing Mrs. Farber's body."

"I will allow it," Sheinman responded without clarification.

Returning his attention to the witness, Jaffe asked, "Investigator, approximately how many death scenes have you examined over the course of your career?"

After a few moments of reflection, Holik answered, "Perhaps a hundred. I do not maintain a tally sheet on the number of death cases I have investigated."

"Now, sir, would it be reasonable to conclude that forming an impression of how the victim died is part of the evidence gathering process?"

"Yes, sir, that would be a reasonable statement."

"Now I ask, Investigator, what was your initial impression – reaction – upon observing Mrs. Farber's condition in that pit?"

"Well, sir," Holik responded and then faced the jury as he finished answering, "although I have observed many faces of death, none was as shocking as this one. It was immediately obvious that Mrs. Farber was in absolute terror and suffered greatly."

"Thank you, Investigator," Jaffe quietly responded. Then raising his voice he asked, "After observing Mrs. Farber's body in the pit, what did you do?"

"I took photographs of the victim, then her body was lifted from the hole. We – the Coroner and I - conducted a cursory examination of the body, noting several contusions and abrasions, which seemed consistent with attempts by Mrs. Farber to escape her confinement. Then she was placed in a body bag and taken up to the Kingston morgue by Coroner Corcoran. Then, with the assistance of other officers at the scene, I drew a diagram, took photographs, measurements and searched the immediate area for any evidence."

"And did you find and take into custody any evidence?"

Several jurors faces revealed amazement, as Will answered, "Yes, Mr. Jaffe, I was at the location until five the next afternoon, leaving solely for the purpose of attending the post mortem examination on Mrs. Farber, which took place at nine in the morning. At the conclusion of the autopsy, I returned to the hillside, finished processing the scene and left at five that afternoon. In the vicinity of the pit, next to a log, partially buried in the ground and covered with leaves – the exact location noted on my diagram – we found a metal box. The box contained 500 rounds of twenty-two caliber long rifle ammunition, a knife, a pair of sunglasses, two ski masks, a jumpsuit, a pair of men's sneakers, a peanut butter sandwich and an apple."

Momentarily turning away from the witness, Jaffe walked to his worktable, removed more 8 x 10 black and white photographs from an envelope; then, he returned to the witness. Handing the photos to Holik, he asked, "Investigator, I show you People's 2A thru N and ask if you recognize these photos?"

Once again, Holik immediately examined the rear of each photo and observing his initials, date and time on each, answered, "Yes, sir, these are the photographs I took at the location where Mrs. Farber was found."

Taking the photos from the witness, Jaffe began handing them one at a time to Holik asking that he describe what each photo depicted.

Studying each, Will answered, "This photo depicts the overall general appearance of the area. This photo depicts Mrs. Farber's body as found in the pit. This photo depicts the pit or hole, after Mrs. Farber was removed. This photo depicts the lock that secured the cover to a hasp connected to an iron bar. This photo depicts the plywood cover that covered the pit. This photo depicts a close up of the five bullet holds in the plywood cover. This photo depicts the aluminum box found by the log. The remaining photographs depict the items found in the aluminum box."

Turning from the witness, Jaffe walked to a slide projector that had been set up prior to calling Holik as a witness. The projector was pointed at a portable screen strategically placed to permit viewing of slides by all participants in the trial process. While turning the slide projector on and letting it warm up, he asked, "Investigator, at my request did you have the photos you have just described developed into slides?"

"Yes, sir." Holik answered, "As you requested, I developed the photos, made 16x20 prints and set of viewable slides."

"Now, Investigator, I am going to present the slides that you turned over to my office for viewing by the jury." Directing his attention to jury, he added, "Ladies and gentlemen, I must advise that the photographs you are about to see are quite graphic and horrific. If"-

Interrupting, Silverstein called out, "Your Honor, defense will stipulate that the photos taken by this witness are a true and accurate representation of the scene where Mrs. Farber was found. Therefore, there is no need for the jury to see them."

"Your concern is duly noted," Judge Scheinman replied. "However, I will permit the jury to see them. Mr. Jaffe, you may proceed."

Jaffe triggered the device that he was holding in his hand and as the first slide depicting the area where Trudy's body was found, he asked, "Investigator, as I scroll through this presentation, please describe what is portrayed in each slide."

As the first image filled the screen, Holik stated, "This is the area where Mrs. Farber was found. I refer to it as 'the crime scene'."

Jaffe scrolled slowly through the slide presentation, holding each image on the screen long enough for the witness to describe what was depicted. He had placed the horrific photo of Trudy's body in the hole as the last slide, intending to ignite emotion, have it mount and finish in a crescendo of horrified awe. When that moment came, almost every juror shuddered and a collective gasp rippled through the previously silent courtroom. Trudy's wide-open blue eyes portrayed unimaginable horror and suffering. Raised, bloody, clenched hands, even in death, seemed to fight for escape from the makeshift coffin lid that denied her freedom and life. Jaffe intentionally left the death mask slide on the screen as he continued questioning the witness. "Investigator, did you take measurements of the hole, pit, or better said, tomb where Mrs. Farber's body was found?"

"Yes sir," Holik replied. While focusing on the jury, he stated, "the pit appeared to have been dug with hand tools and as you can see, it was quite small. It measured three feet seven inches in depth, two feet six inches in width and it was five feet two inches long."

"And Investigator, did you learn or personally measure the height of Mrs. Farber?"

"Yes, sir, Mrs. Farber was five feet five inches tall."

"Please describe Mrs. Farber's size. What was her build?"

"Mr. Jaffe, I would describe Mrs. Farber as being of medium build for her height. At autopsy, she weighed 135 pounds."

"Now, sir, as you have described Mrs. Farber, would it have been possible for her to stretch or move about in the hole, or pit where she was imprisoned?"

Shaking his head in the negative, Holik answered, "No, sir, as depicted in the photo, she was forced to remain in a curled position, especially after the cover was closed. She would have been very cramped and very uncomfortable. She had virtually no mobility."

"Now, sir, did you examine and measure the plywood cover that sealed Mrs. Farber in the hole?"

"Yes, sir, the piece of plywood was five feet six inches by three feet one inch and it was seven eights inch thick, which would be referred to as one inch when sold."

"Now, you testified that this plywood cover had five bullet holes in it, apparently fired through the plywood for the purpose of admitting oxygen. Would you describe these bullet holes as round, clean holes that you could readily see through?"

No, sir, the bullets that made the holes were small caliber bullets and the composition of plywood, which in essence consists of multiple thin sheets of wood glued and pressed together to form a specific thickness or ply, resulted in the bullets ripping their way through rather than cleanly puncturing. After the bullets passed through the slivers of wood forced open by the bullets, they re-closed leaving only a miniscule opening."

"Investigator, did you make any determination as to the caliber of the gun that made the holes in the plywood and did you in fact identify the specific gun that was used?"

"Well, sir, as I said, it was obvious the holes were made by a small caliber weapon and, as the suspect told the arresting officers, he used a twenty-two rifle to make the holes; a twenty-two rifle was taken from him at the time of his arrest and finding twenty-two caliber ammunition in the box found at the same location, made it apparent the holes were made by a twenty-two rifle."

"Mr. Holik, did you determine if the bullet holes in the cover would allow sufficient air into the hole so Mrs. Farber could breathe?"

"Well, sir, as I said, they were not large enough to see light through and therefore it was reasonable to believe very little air was admitted into the hole."

"Did you subsequently perform tests to determine the caliber of the gun that made the holes and the amount of oxygen or air that could come through them?"

"We did, sir. We – myself, with assistance by members of my unit, fired several twenty two-caliber bullets into and through plywood of the same size and thickness as the cover on the pit. We found that – using the same type solid jacketed .22 long rifle ammo – in order for the bullets to pass completely through the sheet of wood, we had to hold the muzzle of the rifle no farther than one foot from the surface of the board. We found that – as I testified – although the bullets passed completely through the sheet when fired from that distance, they did not leave a clean round hole. The combination of multiple thin wood strips pressed together with glue, resulted in the bullets tearing their way through rather than cleanly puncturing. The splinters of wood torn and pushed aside at the time of the bullets passage closed back in, permitting very little air. As to whether there was sufficient oxygen being admitted to sustain life, the Medical Examiner concluded that Mrs. Farber died as the result of asphyxiation."

Though Holik had attended the post mortem examination of Trudy Farber, Jaffe decided not to ask him questions that might produce answers, which could conflict with the pathologist who would later testify. He did ask, "Investigator, when you attended the autopsy of Mrs. Farber, did you secure any items in evidence?"

"Yes, sir," Holik answered, then he asked, "may I, refer to my notes?"

"Please do," Jaffe responded.

After producing the notebook from an inside breast pocket of his jacket, Holik leafed through it and finding what he was looking for, faced the jury and read, "One pair of lady's combination gold and silver earrings, one lady's white gold ring with an orange stone, one lady's Seiko silver wristwatch, and assorted personal papers."

"Investigator, Jaffe continued, "were any of these items pertinent to the crimes under investigation?"

"No, sir," Will responded, "these items were released to a Mr. Jeffrey Farber, on June 1, 1977."

"Investigator Holik, did you participate in any other phase of the investigation concerning the abduction and subsequent death of Mrs. Farber?"

First smiling at Jaffe, then facing the jury, Holik answered, "Yes, sir. I processed a red/orange Chevrolet Corvette, that belonged to the defendant, and, I processed a red/orange Pontiac Firebird belonging to a Mr. John Rogers."

"What - if any – evidence did you find when you processed the defendant's Corvette?"

"Nothing of consequence, sir."

"What – if any – evidence did you find when you processed Mr. Rogers' Pontiac?"

Looking directly at the jury, Willy answered, "I found Mrs. Farber's palm and fingerprints on the inside of the trunk cover."

"Investigator, how did you determine that the palm and fingerprints had been left in the trunk of the Pontiac by Trudy Farber?"

"I obtained Mrs. Farber's palm and fingerprints during her autopsy. I subsequently compared the latent prints found in the trunk of the Pontiac against Mrs. Farber's."

"A positive comparison, Investigator?"

"Yes, sir, an absolutely positive comparison. Mrs. Farber had at some point been inside the trunk of Mr. Rogers' Pontiac."

Jaffe flashed Holik a warm smile as he said, "Thank you, Investigator. Your witness, Carl."

Silverstein arose from his chair but remained at the defense table as he asked, "Investigator, on May 24th, when you arrived at the Farber residence and, as you have testified, examined the premises, how many windows did you find open?"

"Just one, sir," Holik responded.

"And was that window in the master bedroom and the same window having the screen cut?"

"Yes, sir."

"Investigator, did you find any evidence that the window had been jimmied or forced open?"

"No, sir."

"Now Investigator, in your analysis of the Farber residence, where two young, healthy men were allegedly restricted and tied up by a lone male, subsequently identified as the defendant, did you find any evidence to indicate a struggle, fight or some sort of resistance had taken place?"

"No, sir, my observations and the evidence I found were consistent with what I was told as to how Mrs. Farber's abduction occurred."

"Thank you, Investigator," Silverstein responded while retaking his seat.

The prosecutor's first four witnesses had provided several hours of testimony establishing the defendant's guilt of the crimes he was charged with; however, many more witnesses were waiting in the wings.

Susan Katz would follow Holik to the stand. After being sworn and answering questions establishing that she was a neighbor of the Farbers, Jaffe asked, "Mrs. Katz, on the afternoon of May 24, 1977, did you observe a vehicle parked alongside Sunset Drive Extension, in an area near your home?"

Appearing nervous, but composed, the young housewife and mother answered, "Yes, I did."

Jaffe gave the witness an encouraging smile as he asked, "Please relate the circumstances of that sighting, as you best recall."

"I recall the car very well," Susan answered, "because it was a sporty looking car and I had not seen it in that area before. You see, Sunset Drive Extension is sort of remote and used only by residents. Therefore, the car seemed out of place. I was returning home when I saw the car, and my two children were with me. I was concerned that as the car was unoccupied and no one was around it, that it could belong to someone breaking into a house or, that it was stolen and had been abandoned there. When I arrived home, I wrote down everything that I remembered about the car and called the Sheriff's department. By the time a deputy arrived, the car was gone."

Jaffe encouraged, "Please describe the car that you observed parked alongside Sunset Drive Extension that day."

Without hesitation Susan testified, "It was a Pontiac Firebird, red-orange in color and the license plate contained a combination of four letters and numbers. I did not write down the plate number; however, I specifically remember that there were only four characters on the plate. The car was parked on the north side of Sunset Drive Extension – facing west."

"Do you recall the approximate time that you observed this vehicle you have described?"

"It was about quarter to five that afternoon. I had picked up my kids from their school in Monticello and was returning home."

Continuing to give the witness a friendly look of encouragement, Jaffe continued, "Mrs. Katz, you testified that the red-orange Firebird was unoccupied. Did you at any time observe anyone on foot any where in the vicinity of this vehicle?"

"No, sir, I did not."

"Madam, did you know, or were you acquainted with Roger and Trudy Farber?"

"I did not really know them, but I knew where they lived, recognized them as neighbors and we waved to each other in passing."

"Mrs. Katz, this Firebird that you saw parked - how far was it from the Farber residence?"

After pondering her answer for a moment, Susan responded, "It was some distance, certainly not within sight of their place. I would say the shortest distance to their home from where the car was, was several hundred yards through a patch of woods."

"Mrs. Katz, subsequent to your sighting of the Firebird, did you learn of Mrs. Farber's abduction and provide a statement to the state police concerning your observation?"

"Yes, sir, I did. A BCI man accompanied by a Sheriff's Deputy came to my residence and I signed a statement for the BCI guy. They told me what had happened at the Farber's and I was hopeful that my seeing that car might help them find her."

Turning from the witness, Jaffe stated, "Your witness."

Silverstein remained seated as he responded, "I have no questions of this witness."

After briefly consulting a legal pad lying on his worktable, Jaffe called out, "The People call Helen Redmond to the stand."

A moderately attractive, middle-aged, blonde woman, dressed in a dark pants suit, entered the courtroom and proceeded to the witness stand. While being sworn in, her face and slight shake of her raised right hand displayed a hint of nervousness; however, her voice was resolute and firm while responding to the oath administered by a court attendant.

Jaffe approached the witness stand but (to lessen her tension) stopped short, leaving a zone of comfort between himself and the witness. Displaying a smile, he directed, "Please state your full name and occupation for the record."

The witness's attractive blue eyes alternately darted from prosecutor to defendant and eventually focused on Jaffe, as she answered, "Helen Irene Redmond. I am a real estate agent employed by John Rogers Realty Agency located in West Hurley, New York."

Jaffe would continue to focus on this witness with an encouraging smile throughout his questioning of her. He asked, "Were you so employed on May 24, 1977?"

Helen found that focusing on the handsome and pleasant appearing young prosecutor put her at ease, so that is what she did as she responded, "Yes, sir, I was."

"Mrs. Redmond, were you acquainted with the defendant Ronald Krom, prior to May 24, 1977?"

The question caused Helen to glance at the defendant, and their eyes briefly met as he looked up from the book in which he seemed to be engrossed. She felt a shiver of coldness, because although looking directly at her, Ron's eyes and face did not reveal a trace of emotion. Returning focus on the pleasant face of her questioner, she answered, "Yes, I knew Ron Krom prior to May 24th 1977."

"Mrs. Redmond, please tell the court how you came to know the defendant and describe your relationship with him."

"I first met Ron, I think in 1975, when he appeared at our office and introduced himself as a realtor from Grahamsville, and that he was interested in maintaining a business relationship."

"What was your impression of Ron Krom?"

"He seemed like a nice young man. He was always polite in my presence. The only thing that troubled me about him is that he seemed to have a need to make himself out as bigger and more successful than he was."

"Did you see Ron Krom on May 24, 1977?"

"Yes, Ron unexpectedly appeared at our office in West Hurley at about eleven that morning. Ron told me that he had a big deal in the works; a deal that involved the sale of a large portion of Sullivan County. He said that he was picking up clients at an airport and his Corvette wasn't suitable for passengers. He asked if he could borrow my car for the day, which was a 1974 Cadillac El Dorado. I told him that my car was in the garage for repairs – which it was and suggested he rent a car. He told me that he only needed a larger car for a few hours and didn't want to pay out the money for a full day's rental. John – John Rogers – was in his office, had heard my conversation with Ron, and he came out to join our conversation. John asked Ron about his potential big sale – what he was selling. Ron said that he wasn't at liberty to discuss the sale because his clients wanted it kept hush-hush. He did tell us that it would be his biggest deal ever and he would make a lot of money. Ron then asked John if he could borrow his Cadillac for the rest of the day. John told him that his wife had the Cadillac and was already on the road with it. I heard him say that if he, (Ron), was interested he would let him use his Firebird, which, although sporty, would accommodate passengers. He would make the swap if Ron left his Corvette for John to use. It now seems strange, but not at that time, John's Firebird and Ron's Corvette were the same color. They agreed to exchange cars and laughingly agreed that the gas tanks on both vehicles should be full when Ron returned the Firebird. Ron left at about 11:45 that morning driving the Firebird. After Ron left, John told me that he was going down to Saratoga for the rest of the day with Ron's Corvette. That was the last time I saw Ron Krom until today."

Flashing a smile, Jaffe stated, "Thank you, Mrs. Redmond. I have no more questions – no wait, when did you learn of Mrs. Farber's abduction?"

"When I read about it in the Kingston paper. I believe it was two days after Ron came to borrow the car."

"Did you know Gertrude Farber?"

"No, sir. Of course I knew of the Resnick family, but had no personal association or relationship with them."

"Did you know the Farber family?"

"No, sir."

"When did you learn that Ron Krom had been arrested for the abduction and murder of Mrs. Farber?"

"The same way I learned about her abduction – it may have been in the same article. I read in the Kingston paper that Ron had been arrested."

"What was your reaction?"

"I was surprised and shocked. Although I perceived Ron as an odd ball and a braggart, I would never have imagined he was capable of such a horrible thing."

"Thank you," Jaffe concluded, as he returned to the prosecution table and sat down.

Looking toward defense counsel, Judge Scheinman asked, "Mr. Silverstein, do you wish to cross?"

Carl remained seated as he responded, "No, Your Honor, I have no questions of this witness."

"Then we will take a ten minute recess," Scheinman stated

When court had been called back into session, Jaffe stated, "The People call John Rogers to the stand."

The gallery studied the middle aged, pleasant looking, slightly overweight man dressed in a blue blazer, tan slacks and loafers, as he made his way slowly to the stand. Those present who did not know the successful realtor, possessing a gregarious personality, might mistakenly believe him to be a used car salesman. As John Rogers had a strong affection for automobiles – especially of the sporty variety – their assessment was not far off the mark. After John settled into the witness chair he appeared relaxed and confident.

Again leaving a comfortable space between himself and his witness, Jaffe asked, "For the record, sir, please state your full name and occupation."

Seeming to focus entirely on his questioner, the witness answered, "John Francis Rogers. I am a realtor and own Rogers Realty in West Hurley."

"Mr. Rogers," Jaffe continued, "how long have you known the defendant, Ronald Krom?"

Rogers glanced over at the defense table; then, returning focus on his questioner, he responded, "Ron appeared unannounced in my office in the early spring of 1977, or perhaps winter of 1976. He introduced himself as a realtor operating from his family's agency in Grahamsville. He claimed that he wished to establish a relationship with Roger's Realty because he frequently had clients interested in purchasing property in the Woodstock area and would refer them to our agency for a finder's fee, if a sale occurred. As I recall we received no referrals from him."

"Did you see Ronald Krom on May 24, 1977?"

"I did. That day, I was in my office and my office door was open. I heard someone come in the outer office and when this person spoke with my associate Helen Redmond, I recognized that it was Ron. I listened as they conversed and heard Ron ask Helen if he could borrow her Cadillac because he had a big deal going and would be picking up clients at the airport. He"-

"Excuse me sir," Jaffe interrupted, "what time was it when Ron Krom appeared in your office that day?"

"I would say it was around ten thirty or eleven that morning."

"Thank you, sir, please continue. What happened next?"

"Ron wanted to borrow a larger car for the day because he drove a Corvette, which doesn't accommodate more than one passenger. I heard Helen tell him that her car was in the garage for repairs. Upon hearing this, I went out and greeted Ron. I was interested in the big sale he had cooking and asked him about it. He told me that it was very substantial and the commission would make him a wealthy man. Said he couldn't tell me the tract he was selling because the purchasers wanted it kept quiet until the deal was closed. Ron then asked if he could borrow my Cadillac for the day. I told him my wife was using the Cadillac – which she was – and then he asked to borrow my Firebird. I told him my Firebird was too small to accommodate a lot of passengers. He told me that the customers were all men and they would be comfortable enough in it. I agreed to let him use my Firebird in exchange for my using his Corvette. We agreed but with the proviso that both cars would be returned with full gas tanks. We exchanged car keys and Ron left, driving my Firebird. I then took a spin down to Saratoga in the Corvette. I arrived home from Saratoga at about two the next morning and my Firebird was in my driveway. Ron was asleep behind the wheel. I woke him up and asked, Ron, what the hell he was doing there that late.' He told me that he was in the area and figured he would wait rather than come back in the morning. We exchanged cars and that was the last time I saw him until seeing him in court."

"Mr. Rogers, what is or was, the license plate number on your Firebird on May 24, 1977?"

"It was my initials JFR with the number 2."

"A total of four digits?"

"Yes, sir, JFR2."

"What was Ron's physical appearance when you found him sleeping in your car early in the morning of May 25th?"

"Well, it was pretty dark, but I recall that his hair was quite rumpled and unruly; I had never seen him like that before."

"Did you carry on a conversation with him as to where he had been or how his sale had gone?"

"As a matter of fact, I did. He told me that his clients were pleased and had agreed to the purchase price. He said that because of this sale and other deals he had in the works, he would soon be a wealthy man."

"Do you recall what Ron was wearing when you came upon him in your driveway that night?"

"As I said, it was dark and I didn't pay much attention to what he had on. I seem to remember that he was wearing a light weight, waist length sports jacket."

"Did you loan your Firebird, or any other vehicles to Ron Krom before May 24, 1977?"

"No, sir."

"Throughout the period of time that you were acquainted with Ronald Krom, what was your impression of him?"

Rogers unconsciously rubbed his chin while thinking about his answer, eventually responding, "He presented himself well. He seemed intelligent. He was soft-spoken and always had a neat appearance, which was a plus in my book. On the negative side, he had grandiose ideas, made himself out to be more successful than he actually was and therefore, I was leery about making any investments with him."

"Mr. Rogers, when did you learn of Mrs. Farber's abduction?"

"I was listening to the radio and heard it as a news broadcast."

Turning away from the witness, Jaffe stated, "Thank you, sir." He then took his seat at the prosecution table.

Silverstein did not move from his chair as he asked, "Mr. Rogers, during all the time that you knew Ronald Krom, did he give you any reason to believe he was capable of committing the crimes he is presently charged with?"

Taking a moment to study the scholarly, bespectacled, meek-looking defendant before he answered, Rogers shook his head in the negative and responded, "No, sir."

Giving the witness a smile, Silverstein stated, "Thank you, sir. No further questions."

Almost immediately, Jaffe stood and called out, "The People call Marilyn Horn." This announcement triggered a whispered buzz throughout the courtroom, because no members of the media or audience in general knew or recognized this name. A moderately attractive, middle-aged blond - medium height and build, dressed in a dark skirt topped by a white blouse - entered the courtroom and made her way to the witness stand. The courtroom quieted as this surprise witness was sworn.

Again opting to leave a zone of comfort between himself and the witness, Jaffe remained in front of his worktable as he opened questioning. His handsome face displaying a smile, he asked, "Please state your full name and occupation for the record."

The witness flashed a nervous smile at Jaffe, quickly replaced by a serious look as she answered, "Marilyn Marie Horn. I am a supervisor in the Sullivan county Mental Health Clinic, located in Ferndale."

"Ms. Horn," Jaffe asked in a quiet, pleasant tone of voice, "as a supervisor in the Sullivan County Mental Health Unit, were you acquainted with Gertrude Farber?"

"Yes," the witness responded, explaining, "Trudy was a psychiatric therapist working in our unit. I was her supervisor; however, I would classify our relationship as co-workers and friends. Trudy enjoyed her work and was very conscientious."

"Did you know Mrs. Farber prior to her employment at the Mental Health Clinic?"

"No, but she had a wonderful personality and we quickly became friends."

"As your friend, did she share personal or confidential information with you?"

"Our relationship was such that we trusted each other and yes, frequently shared private matters and concerns and looked to each other for advice."

"How well did you know her husband, Roger Farber?"

"I knew Roger; however, my relationship was with Trudy."

"Ms. Horn, Trudy had been married – what, about two years – when she started employment at the clinic. Is that correct?"

"Yes, I believe so."

"Did she ever confide in you any problems in her marriage?"

"No, I believe she was reasonably happy in her marriage. She also seemed upbeat and happy at work, which to someone specializing in the recognition and treatment of human behavior was indicative that she was not undergoing stress or strain of an unhappy marriage."

Upon hearing this answer Jaffe smiled and then asked, "Are you acquainted, or were you acquainted, with the defendant Ronald Krom?"

Staring directly at the defendant, Marilyn answered, "I never personally knew him; however, I knew of him because of a conversation I had with Trudy."

"Please continue. What did Trudy tell you about Mr. Krom?"

"It was six or seven months before she was abducted. She seemed very upset one day and when I asked what was troubling her, she told me that the prior afternoon she had received a telephone call from Ronald Krom. She described Mr. Krom as a person who lived in Grahamsville and who had been after her husband to either loan him money or join with him in some sort of business enterprise. She told me that this Ronald Krom wanted her to persuade Roger to invest with him. She said that when she explained to Mr. Krom that she did not involve herself in her husband's business affairs, he became angry and his anger was so pronounced that he began calling her names, making threats and eventually became incoherent. She told me that this Ron Krom concerned and frightened her because his threats sounded real and she knew that at one time he had been under psychiatric care. I advised her to call her attorney to have Krom's behavior and threats put on record. I don't know if she did that, but she did tell me sometime later that Roger was taking, or had taken, care of the problem."

"Thank you, Ms. Horn," Jaffe said, while displaying a smile of appreciation. He then turned toward Silverstein and stated, "Your witness."

Following Jaffe's example, Silverstein also remained standing in front of the defense table as he asked, "Ms. Horn, subsequent to hearing of Mrs. Farber's abduction, you spoke with the state police. Is that correct?"

Staring stonily at her questioner, Marilyn answered, "Yes, two members of the BCI came to the clinic and spoke with me."

"And did you provide those officers a list of the clinic's patients?"

If this question was intended to rattle the witness, there was no visible sign that it did as Marilyn continued to give her questioner an emotionless stare as she answered, "Yes, I did."

"Ms. Horn, isn't that some sort of violation of ethics? Aren't you prevented by law from releasing the names of patients under treatment for some sort of mental disorder to the authorities?"

In an icy tone of voice, the witness responded, "It is not unlawful or unethical to provide patients names to the police. It would, however, be unethical and unlawful to release information concerning their diagnosis and course of treatment without a court order."

Silverstein pointed at his client and asked, "Was Mr. Krom a patient at your clinic?"

"No, sir."

"So you can offer no professional opinion, or information, concerning Mr. Krom's mental condition. Is that correct?"

Continuing to respond firmly and coldly Marilyn responded, "I do not know Mr. Krom and cannot attest as to his mental condition."

Silverstein re-took his seat at counsel's table without verbal response, tacitly dismissing the witness.

Jaffe's next witness would be a young, sandy-haired, tall, slender male, a young officer dressed in the uniform of the Woodstock Town Constabulary. Jaffe flashed the handsome young officer his patented smile and asked, "Please state your name, title and occupation for the record."

Sitting tall in the witness chair, looking very military and answering like a member of the military, Constable Hicks answered, "Gerald Richard Hicks, sir. I am a member of the Woodstock Town Constabulary."

"Constable Hicks, were you on duty in the Town of Woodstock on the night of May 24, 1977?"

"Yes, sir! That night I worked the six to two in the morning shift with Constable Henry Williams."

"In the course of your patrol that night, did you happen to meet the defendant Ronald Krom?"

"Yes, sir! We were patrolling Route 212 and near the Hamlet of Bearsville, we observed an orange car parked on the westerly side of the highway. The car was facing in the direction of Phoenicia. We stopped to check this vehicle and examined the interior of the car with the aid of flashlights. There was a man lying in the back seat who, sat up immediately when our lights illuminated him. After sitting up he put glasses on. I asked what he was doing parked there and he responded that he was sleeping in the car because he was on his way to visit an elderly person, did not want to wake him up and so was sleeping in the car until morning. I advised him that there was an ordinance against sleeping in a car while it was parked on the highway. He told me that he had been unaware of that and would leave. We then drove away and when we returned about twenty minutes later, the car was gone.

"Constable, what time of night was it when you checked this orange car?"

"It was between eleven and midnight sir."

"Did you ask the man in the car for identification?"

"No, sir, I did not."

"Did you write down or record any information concerning the car or its occupant?"

"No, sir, the man did not appear intoxicated or under the influence of any drugs and he was very cooperative, so, we didn't make any written notes."

"Did you make a strong enough observation of this individual in the orange car to remember what he looked like?"

"Yes, sir." Looking at and pointing at the defendant, Hicks stated, "The man in the car is presently seated right over there."

"You are pointing to the defendant, Constable?"

"Yes, sir."

"Did you see the orange car again during the remainder of your shift that night?"

"No, sir."

"Thank you, Constable," Jaffe concluded. He then re-took his seat at the prosecution table.

Silverstein stood, took a couple of steps toward the witness, then stopped, smiled and asked, "Constable Hicks, you testified that you made no notes and filed no reports concerning your encounter with the man sleeping in the orange car. Is that correct?"

Constable Hicks remained erect in the witness chair as he responded, "Yes, sir."

"Do you recall the make or model of the orange car?"

"No, sir. I can say that it was sporty looking."

"Did you memorize the license plate number on the sporty-looking orange car?"

"No, sir."

"Did you issue a citation to the individual in the orange car for – what is the violation – sleeping in a parked car?"

"No, sir. The violation observed was actually parking on the pavement, not sleeping in a car, and, as the car was parked on the shoulder of the highway and just slightly on the pavement, we decided against issuing a citation."

"Now Officer – I mean Constable – let me get this straight; you made no notes, wrote no citations, cannot recall the make or model of the car or its license plate number and yet you are certain, more than two years after that night, that the man you saw and spoke briefly with that night is the defendant?"

Constable Hicks recognized that his honesty and integrity were being questioned, but he remained military in appearance and unfazed because he was certain that Ron Krom was the individual in the car and he had no motive or reason to make a false identification. He firmly responded, "Yes, sir!"

Recognizing that browbeating this witness would gain him no points, Silverstein turned and sat once more at the defense table.

Jaffe immediately got up, calling out as he stood, "The People call Investigator James Chandler."

A tall, ruggedly handsome man, with short sandy-brown hair entered the courtroom. His muscular physique was hidden under a white dress shirt, striped necktie, blue blazer and black dress slacks; these items of clothing were brought out of the closet for special occasions and when providing testimony in a superior court. His normal workday garb was a faded, well-worn brown sport coat over some sort of open neck sport shirt. The young-appearing police detective walked confidently toward the witness stand and once there automatically raised his right hand. After being administered the oath, he took his seat in the witness chair.

Jaffe was confident that the testimony from this man, whom he knew to be a consummate professional, would heavily influence the jury. Flashing his introductory trademark smile, Jaffe opened his questioning of this witness from a position in front of his worktable; he would subtly position himself in different areas as he continued (for maximum effect on the jury). He opened with the standard "Please state your name, title and occupation for the record."

As a 'squad detective' or 'street cop', Chandler took great pleasure in solving crime and locking up 'scumbags,' a common police term for felons having committed particularly despicable crimes. However, like most excellent detectives, he disliked being wrung through the wringer by defense attorneys who – from his biased perspective - easily bent, twisted and warped the truth to achieve victory for their client. Of course he knew that when the 'scumbag' didn't cop a plea, it would be necessary to prove guilt in a court of law. As the prosecution was required to focus on known facts, testimony and admissible evidence, the issues that the prosecutor would cover with each of his witness's were carefully reviewed prior to trial. Therefore, to most experienced police officers, providing testimony under direct examination was not overly stressful. Giving the appearance of being calm, cool and collected, he answered, "James Chandler. I am an Investigator in the New York State Police working out of the Ferndale Bureau of Criminal Investigation Unit."

"Investigator, how long have you been a member of the New York State Police?"

"Approximately fifteen years."

"Did there come a time in May 1977 when you were involved in an investigation to find a kidnap victim by the name of Gertrude Farber?"

"Yes, sir."

"And during your investigation, did you meet with a person by the name of Wayne Krom, the brother of the defendant Ronald Krom?"

Making sure to look toward the jury while answering, Chandler, in a firm voice, answered, "Yes, sir."

"Investigator, describe the circumstances of your meeting with Wayne Krom."

"On the morning of May 26, 1977, two days after Mrs. Farber's abduction, Investigator Ralph Fuente and I were assigned by our supervisor to locate and interview Ronald Krom, who was suspected of being involved in the kidnapping. We proceeded to the Green Hills Realty office in Grahamsville, where the suspect was employed, arriving there at about nine that morning, and there we met Wayne Krom. We told Wayne that we were interested in speaking with his brother and asked where we could find him. Wayne told us that Ron lived with his parents and he believed him to be home. We asked Wayne to describe Ron's car. He told us Ron drove a leased orange Chevrolet Corvette and the car had a New Jersey license plate. We asked if Ron owned any firearms and he told us that he owned several rifles. Wayne also told us that Ron worked as a salesman in the family-owned realty firm, but usually only made a morning appearance in the office, then disappeared the remainder of the day. We asked Wayne to call Ron to ascertain when he was coming in to the office. Wayne called and asked that question; however, Ron was evasive as to a time and told Wayne that he might not come in at all. We then asked Wayne if he would take us to his parent's home and he agreed to do so. When we arrived there, we immediately observed an orange 1976 Chevrolet Corvette, bearing New Jersey registration 978-FPR, parked in an open garage. We waited outside while Wayne went into the house to tell Ron there was someone outside waiting to speak with him. Wayne was in the house about five minutes and re-appeared accompanied by Ron. Wayne remained while we questioned his brother, but that was basically the end of our involvement with him."

"Did Wayne Krom ever surface as a suspect in your investigation?"

"No, sir."

"Investigator Chandler, now please relate the circumstances of your first meeting with Ron Krom."

"We identified ourselves to Ron and informed him that we were investigating the kidnapping of Gertrude Farber, and his name had come up as possibly being involved. As he was a suspect, Investigator Fuente proceeded to advise him of his Constitutional Rights pursuant to the Miranda Decision. Ronald interrupted Fuente and told us, 'I know my rights. I could have been a lawyer.' We ignored his statement and Ralph provided him the entire Miranda Warning. We then asked Ron if he would like to speak with 'his' lawyer and he responded, 'I don't need a lawyer.' We then informed him that we really needed to locate Mrs. Farber, and asked him where she was. Ron responded that he might be able to locate her. Having said this, he turned his attention on his brother Wayne and chewed Wayne out for bringing us to the Krom home. Then he – Ron – suddenly took off running toward the house and entered it through a sliding glass door, which entered directly into his bedroom. Ralph – Investigator Fuente – and I were right behind him and we were concerned because we did not know what he intended to do when he ran into the house. Upon entering his bedroom, Ron opened a closet and came out with a small toy safe. He opened it and produced a piece of paper. He then placed the paper back in the safe and stated"-

"Excuse me, Investigator," Jaffe interrupted, "after providing Ron Krom his Miranda Rights, he ran from you, entered his residence and into a bedroom. Did you place him under arrest at that time?"

"No, sir, at that time he was still only a suspect and we were trying to get him to reveal Mrs. Farber's location."

"Weren't you concerned that he was running into his bedroom to arm himself?"

"Yes, sir, and that is why both Ralph and I drew our weapons when we entered the room behind him. When we saw that he was only after the piece of paper, we breathed a sigh of relief and holstered our weapons."

"What happened after Krom returned the paper to the safe?"

"He – Ron – started cursing and told us that he worked for the CIA. He said, 'if you don't believe me, contact Donovan in Washington, D.C. at CIA headquarters.' As soon as he said this, he ran back outside, through the same sliding glass door and ran into the garage. He got into the Corvette, started it up and started to back it out of the garage. Investigator Fuente and I blocked his exit by standing in back of the car. He started screaming that he would run over us if we didn't get out of his way. Ralph remained standing behind the car, while I went up beside it, reached in, turned the ignition off and removed the car keys. Ron jumped out of the car and started to walk away. Investigator Fuente said something to him, which made him stop and return to us. We informed him that we really needed to find Mrs. Farber, and it would be in his best interest to help us. Ron then told us that he could 'help' find Mrs. Farber, but for his assistance, he wanted $300,000 for himself and $100,000 for Roger Farber. He said that Harry Resnick was certainly able to pay that amount of money. We asked Ron to accompany us to our office in Ferndale, so we could contact Mr. Resnick and work out the arrangements for Mrs. Farber's return. He agreed and we went to the Ferndale state police station. We"-

"Excuse me, Investigator," Jaffe again interrupted, "about what time did you arrive at your office with Ronald Krom?"

"It was approximately eleven that morning."

"Okay, now, it is approximately eleven on the morning of May 26, 1977, and you have Ron Krom at the state police barracks. What did you do then?"

"We – Investigator Fuente – and I, escorted Ron to a room specifically designated for interviewing witnesses and suspects. We offered him a seat and"-

"Was Krom restrained in any fashion at this time?"

"No, sir, at that particular time he was not restrained in any fashion."

"Pardon my interruption," Jaffe stated displaying a smile. "Please continue."

"We started to discuss with Ron what he could do to aid us in finding Trudy Farber. He repeated his demand for $300,000 for himself and $100,000 for Roger Farber, and said that once he received the money, he would divulge Mrs. Farber's location. He – Ron – then told us that he wanted to talk personally with Harry Resnick. We told him that we would call Mr. Resnick, but he needed to give us something that would convince Mr. Resnick of his involvement. Ron told us to tell Resnick that the person who called in the original ransom demand asked for $1,000,000 cash, in fifty and one-hundred dollar bills. We could also tell Resnick that the caller had advised him to contact his brothers and liquidate some assets if he could not raise the money. We informed him that we would have Mr. Resnick called, and that did occur. While waiting for a response from Harry Resnick, we – Investigator Fuente – and myself continued questioning Ron Krom. Ron assured us that Mrs. Farber was in good health and alive. He also told us that he had called the Resnick residence sometime between eleven and midnight on May 25 and asked for Mr. Resnick. When Roger Farber identified himself, he immediately terminated the call. We spent considerable time trying to get Ron to reveal Mrs. Farber's location, to which he responded that we should ask Roger Farber. He also told us that Mrs. Farber might be in an air-conditioned room eating chicken. He then started talking negatively about Mr. Resnick. He said that Harry Resnick was the man responsible for unemployment in Ellenville and that Resnick was responsible for his uncle losing his job. He claimed that Harry Resnick had made him suffer for five years, as he – Ron – had not been invited to Trudy and Roger's wedding and as a result he lost a girlfriend whom he loved very much. He claimed that he and Roger Farber had planned Trudy's kidnapping about three years before, saying that they started planning it even before Roger and Trudy married. He also told us that after Trudy was found, he would not tell her that her husband was involved and that the police would never be able to prove that Roger was involved. He also told us that he gained entry to the Farber residence by cutting a screen in a window, which Roger had opened and this was part of the pre-arranged plan. During this time, he told us many times that Trudy Farber was alive and well and that he knew her location. About two that afternoon, Ron told us that he was going to leave. At this time Ralph – Investigator Fuente – informed him that he could not leave because he was now under arrest. Ron responded by saying he wanted to contact a lawyer. We provided him access to a telephone and he called Barry Martin, a Monticello attorney. We stopped questioning Ron when he asked to speak with his attorney."

"Did Mr. Martin come to the Ferndale barracks?"

"Yes, sir, he conferred privately with Krom and then informed us that as Ron was not able to provide him a retainer, he was not going to represent him."

"What happened then? Did you continue questioning Mr. Krom?"

"When Mr. Martin informed us that he was not going to represent Ron, we – Ralph and I – returned to the interview room and asked Ron if he wanted to call another attorney. At this time, he told us that he did not want any other lawyer and would represent himself because he did not want to be represented by a legal aid attorney. We again commenced discussing the importance of locating Mrs. Farber, and Ron told us that he would write out a contract for presentation to the District Attorney. He said that if the D.A. agreed to the terms specified in the contract, he would take us to Mrs. Farber."

"And did this occur?"

"Yes, District Attorney Emmanuel Gellman was already in the Ferndale station, having responded there after being advised that a suspect had been brought in. Mr. Gellman was introduced to Krom. Before conversing with Ron, Mr. Gellman – again – informed him of his rights and asked Ron if he wished to consult an attorney. Ron told him that he did not need a lawyer and was representing himself. He"-

Jaffe interrupted, "Were you in the room when this conversation between Gellman and the defendant occurred?"

"Yes, sir. Both Inv. Fuente and I were present and listened to their conversation."

"What was the conversation between Gellman and Krom?"

Chandler stared at the defendant while answering, "Ron told Mr. Gellman that he would reveal Mrs. Farber's location in exchange for a signed agreement that no criminal charges would be filed against him. Mr. Gellman refused and informed Ron that if he cooperated in recovering Mrs. Farber, the District Attorney would inform the court of his cooperation, which would weight heavily on any sentence. Krom refused to reveal Mrs. Farber's location."

"What happened next?"

"Mr. Gellman asked to speak with me privately. When we were outside the room, he told me to go ahead and let Krom write out a contract, specifying any terms he wanted, if it would aid in recovering Mrs. Farber. He said that any such contract wouldn't be worth the paper it was written on because it was being forced by duress."

"And did Mr. Krom write out a contract?"

"He did, and it was presented to Mr. Gellman, who took it with him."

"Do you recall the terms specified by Krom in the contract?"

"To the best of memory, it stated that for the payment of $300,000 to Ron Krom, $100,000 to Roger Farber, and a favorable sentence, Mr. Krom would divulge the location of Gertrude Farber."

"Did Ron Krom reveal Mrs. Farber's location after completion of this contract?"

"No, sir, he insisted upon receiving the money prior to divulging this information."

"Please continue; it is now afternoon on May 26 and Ron Krom is at the Ferndale barracks. What happened next?"

"Well, we provided Ron food and drink purchased at McDonald's. We continued asking him to reveal Mrs. Farber's whereabouts and explained how it was in his best interest to do so. At around six that evening, we introduced FBI Agent Leo McGillicuddy to Ron. From that point on, Agent McGillicuddy remained with Ralph and me throughout the remainder of our involvement with Ron Krom. Agent McGillcuddy again advised Ron of his Constitutional Rights. Ron maintained that Mrs. Farber was alive and well and he would take us to her when the terms of his contract were met. He also reiterated that Roger Farber was involved in the conspiracy to kidnap his own wife. In continued discussion, he told us that if he received guaranteed bail, legal expenses, a cash payment of $10,000 and was allowed to confront Harry Resnick, he would reveal Mrs. Farber's location."

"Now Investigator, did Ron Krom confront Mr. Resnick?"

"Yes, sir, Mr. Resnick came to the Ferndale station and spoke with Ron in my presence."

"About what time did this occur?"

"It was around eight that evening."

"Please relate the details of that meeting."

"After being introduced, Mr. Resnick related that his purpose in meeting with Krom was to accomplish the safe return of his daughter. He told Ron that he would offer any assistance to accomplish this goal. Ron asked Mr. Resnick if he were aware that his son-in-law was involved in his own wife's abduction. Mr. Resnick responded that he had been advised of this allegation and, if in fact this was true, he would offer the same assistance to Roger that he was offering Krom. Krom told Mr. Resnick that he wanted $400,000 for himself and $100,000 for Roger Farber, and then he would reveal Mrs. Farber's location. Mr. Resnick responded that his sole interest was the safe return of his daughter and that he would comply with Krom's demand, to the degree that he could comply, without interfering with the official investigation. He added that he would make this agreement for the recovery of his daughter, whether she were dead or alive."

"Investigator, what happened when Mr. Resnick agreed to pay Krom for his daughter's return?"

Chandler again eyed the defendant, who did not return his gaze, as he answered, "Krom just suddenly stood up and said to us, 'let's go, I'll take you to her'."

"About what time did this occur?"

"It was about eight forty-five that evening."

"Please continue, Investigator. What happened next?"

"We – Investigator Fuente, Agent McGillicuddy and myself - left the Ferndale station accompanied by Mr. Krom. Ron told us to drive to Grahamsville, proceed on Route fifty-five toward Ulster County and when we were on fifty-five"-

"Excuse me, Investigator, Jaffe interrupted, "Was the defendant shackled or restrained in any manner when you left your office?"

"No, sir."

"And what were your positions in the car?"

"We took my assigned car. I drove, Agent McGillicuddy sat in the front and Investigator Fuente sat beside Ron in the back seat."

"Okay, you reach Route 55 outside Grahamsville. What happened next?"

"Shortly after entering Ulster County, Ron directed me to turn right onto a dirt road. This road led up the mountainside and it was in terrible condition. This dirt road – better described as a logging trail – ended a short distance up the mountain. I stopped the car and Ron immediately got out and hurried – sort of running – up a footpath. We had flashlights in our possession, and we followed him up the path, which ended at a level area in the woods. Ron ran across this area, then stopped and pointed to the ground. He said, 'here. She's here.' He then bent down, and using his hands, brushed branches and leaves aside revealing a sheet of plywood, which was secured and held in place by a steel bar, secured to the plywood by a padlock. He asked for a flashlight, which he used to illuminate a rock near the plywood. He removed a key from beneath this rock and used it to unlock the padlock. He then lifted the plywood, which covered a hole in the ground. Mrs. Farber was in the hole and she was obviously dead." Reflection on that horrific moment caused the hardened police detective to pause and take a deep breath.

Displaying an empathetic look, Jaffe quietly encouraged, "Please continue. What happened next?"

Chandler's face revealed sadness as he looked toward the jury and responded, "It was readily apparent that Mrs. Farber had suffered a horrible death. Krom seemed startled and he started gagging. I thought he was going to throw up. For a moment, we – Ralph, Agent McGillicuddy and myself -

were in shock. We had hoped to find Mrs. Farber alive and when we saw her condition, it knocked the wind out of us."

"What happened next?" Jaffe quietly encouraged.

Before answering, Chandler glared at the defendant who stared back at him without any recognizable display of emotion. Then Chandler turned his attention to the jurors who were completely focused on him. Returning his attention to his questioner, Chandler answered, "Ron took off running and I ran after him. He didn't go far and stopped at a log, just a short distance from the hole. He reached down behind the log and came up holding the rifle that was stashed there. I tackled him and wrenched the rifle out of his hands. Krom was then handcuffed and restrained so as to avoid resistance or escape."

Jaffe had approached his worktable while the witness answered the question, picked up a rifle lying on the table and returned to the witness. Handing the rifle to the witness he asked, "Investigator, do you recognize this weapon?"

After searching for and finding his initials that he had etched on the gun at the time of its seizure, Chandler answered, "Yes, sir, this is the twenty-two caliber rifle that I took from Mr. Krom, immediately after the discovery of Mrs. Farber's body."

"And Investigator, was this rifle loaded with ammunition and in firing condition when you wrested it from Mr. Krom?"

"Yes, sir," Chandler responded, glaring at the defendant as he did so. He added, "It is a semi-automatic. There was a round of solid point twenty-two long rifle ammunition in the chamber and ten rounds in the magazine tube. The gun's safety was in the 'off' position and pulling the trigger would have fired a bullet. Fortunately, Mr. Krom did not get to press the trigger."

"Investigator, please describe Mrs. Farber's condition when you saw her in the hole."

Silverstein had remained silent for a long time; however, having viewed photographs and slides depicting Trudy's open eyes and frozen look of horror, he knew every detailed description of her condition had a profound effect on the jury. Therefore, he left his seat and called out, "Objection!" He then argued, "Your Honor, this witness is not a medical professional and therefore should not be required to provide testimony as to the medical state or appearance of Mrs. Farber's death. Such testimony is better left to the medical examiner or coroner, whom I presume will be testifying in this matter."

Jaffe, standing beside the slide projector, which he intended to turn on, alternately looked at Judge and Counsel, but did not respond.

Judge Scheinman gave Silverstein a sober stare as he responded, "On the contrary, Mr. Silverstein. The witness is certainly qualified to relate his personal observations. Please answer the question, Investigator."

The condition of Trudy Farber's body in that small, makeshift grave was forever etched in Chandler's mind and many a night he was jarred from sleep by the subconscious vision of her reaching out to him for the rescue that never came. Focusing on the jury, he slowly related, "Mrs. Farber was lying on her back in a curled up position, facing upward. Her eyes were fully dilated, her mouth was open – apparently forming a scream - and her face was frozen in a look of horror. Her arms were bent, forearms raised giving the appearance that even in death, she continued pushing against the wood that sealed her in the hole. Her hands were clenched and bloody, fingernails torn away from clawing at the plywood. During the course of my career, I have viewed many faces of death, but none was as horrific as what I confronted that night."

Jaffe switched on the slide projector as the witness described the death scene and Trudy's frightened image filled the screen.

The courtroom was silent and remained so for several seconds after Chandler had stopped talking, and many observers, including several members of the jury, used a handkerchief or tissue to wipe away tears.

It would be reasonable to believe that as Defense Counsel Silverstein listened to the witness's description of the victim, which adequately described the image portrayed on the screen, he silently wished he had pursued a different law specialty, or had not accepted the post of Legal Aid Attorney.

Breaking the silence, Jaffe quietly asked, "Is the image displayed on the screen an accurate depiction of Mrs. Farber's condition when you found her?"

Nodding in the affirmative, Chandler answered, "Yes, sir, that is how Mrs. Farber looked when we found her."

"After locating Mrs. Farber and subduing the defendant, what did you do?"

"We called in on the car radio and reported our situation. I requested that the Coroner and troop identification unit respond to the scene. We set flares at the turn off from the main highway and remained at the scene until other police personnel arrived. Then we returned to the Ferndale station with the defendant."

"Did you engage the defendant in conversation subsequent to the discovery of Mrs. Farber's body?"

"Yes, sir. Actually, Krom became very verbose, almost to the point of what could be described as babbling. We didn't have to ask him questions. He just started talking and continued talking. He reiterated that he and Roger Farber had planned Mrs. Farber's abduction for some five years, even before the Farber's married. He told us that he had personally dug the hole and made the cover for it. He claimed to have spent one night sleeping in the hole. He told us that he cut the window screen and entered the Farber home at around 2:30 in the afternoon of May 24th. That he wore a"-

Jaffe interrupted, "Excuse me, Investigator. Who are the 'us' – the people listening to the defendant when you returned to Ferndale?"

Flashing a brief smile at his questioner, Chandler answered, "Investigator Fuente, Agent McGillicuddy and myself. We had returned to the interview room in the Ferndale station."

"Thank you, Investigator. Please continue. I believe you were about to relate what the defendant told you about the clothing he was wearing."

Nodding his head in the affirmative, Chandler responded, "Yes, sir, Ron – the defendant – told us that while he was in the Farber home, he was wearing a dark color ski mask. He also told us that the rifle taken from him where Mrs. Farber was found was the rifle he had while in the Farber house and that he had purchased it about two weeks before at the Woolworth store in Middletown. He told us the jacket he was presently wearing – which was a lightweight waist length, zip up – was the jacket he wore during the kidnapping. He told us that he had placed the remainder of the clothing he wore during the kidnapping in the metal milk box that he had hidden under a tree near the hole where we found Mrs. Farber's body. He told us that he had purchased handcuffs and other items of clothing originally intended to be used, but after burying these items in the woods, he forgot their location and couldn't find them. He told us that he purposely did not use his Corvette during the abduction and had planned to borrow John Rogers's Cadillac, but used Rogers's Firebird because the Cadillac was not available. He told us that after taking Trudy – Mrs. Farber – from her home, he placed her in the trunk of the Firebird and drove directly to the site where she was imprisoned. He told us that he had used a typewriter in the Green Hills Realty office to type the note asking Roger what time Trudy arrived home from work. He told us that after showing Roger the note, he pocketed it and later threw it away, but could not remember where. He told us that he shot five holes through the plywood cover in Mrs. Farber's presence – to convince her that she would have to get into the hole or be shot and that the bullet holes would permit her to breathe for the anticipated short duration of her entrapment. He told us that after securing Mrs. Farber in the hole, he drove directly to Woodstock to return Rogers's Firebird, and called Harry Resnick from a pay phone along the way."

Satisfied he had gleaned every essential detail from the witness, Jaffe gave Chandler an appreciative smile, then turned toward the defense table and stated, "Your witness, counsel."

Silverstein stood and approached the witness. He decided not to appear accusatory or go on the attack, believing to do so would adversely affect the jury. He would remain smiling, polite and cordial throughout his cross and opened by asking, "Investigator, were any of your conversations with Mr. Krom electronically recorded?"

Chandler studied his questioner with a sober look, as he would continue to do so throughout the questioning session. He firmly answered, "No, sir."

"Did you or any other officer obtain any signed statements from Mr. Krom?"

"No, sir," came the answer.

"Investigator, did you believe everything Mr. Krom told you throughout the hours you were speaking with him?"

This question puzzled the veteran detective and his face revealed that puzzlement. He did not immediately answer and thought carefully before answering. "Much of what Mr. Krom told us was incredible and bizarre. I felt the need to pay close attention to what he said and weed fiction from fact."

"Did my client sound credible when he persisted in telling you that he did not conceive the kidnap plot on his own and that Roger Farber was his accomplice in the abduction?"

After pondering this question for a moment, Chandler answered, "I did not know what to make of this claim. I did report Krom's allegation to my supervisor, and I am aware that other Investigators spoke with Mr. Farber and investigated that possibility. The focus of my assignment was Ronald Krom, and I had no involvement with Mr. Farber."

"Investigator, were you aware that Ronald Krom was under psychiatric treatment?"

The witness immediately answered, "I was not told that Mr. Krom was under psychiatric care. I was informed that he had previously spent time in Middletown State Hospital and had been diagnosed as schizophrenic."

"Investigator, are you familiar with the characteristics and behavior of persons suffering from schizophrenia?"

Jaffe briefly considered objecting to this question and started to rise from his seat but changed his mind because the witness appeared composed and able to handle the question.

Chandler met his questioner's bland look with a steely gaze as he responded, "Sir, I am a policeman, not a psychologist or psychiatrist; however, I have had experience in dealing with delusional people and am aware that schizophrenics are often delusional."

"Investigator, would it be fair to say that during all the hours you were with Mr. Krom, you believed he was telling the truth when he told you he knew Mrs. Farber's location and could take you to her?"

"Yes, sir, that is a fair statement."

"Then sir, wouldn't it also be fair to say that Mr. Krom was also telling the truth about Mr. Farber's involvement in his wife's abduction?"

Silverstein was gambling that the question would pose a small dilemma for the witness and if the witness hesitated or appeared confused, the seed already planted in the minds of the jurors – that the defendant did not act alone - would begin to sprout. However, the witness continued to hold his questioner in a steely gaze and showed no sign of confusion as he answered, "Sir, as I previously stated, I made no assumptions and formed no opinion as to Mr. Krom's allegations about Mr. Farber. My task, as also previously stated, was to locate Mrs. Farber, and that is what I was focused on."

Silverstein displayed a forced smile and concluded, "Thank you, Investigator, I have no more questions."

Investigator Chandler's testimony had consumed several hours and, believing it a good time to call a recess, Judge Scheinman announced that court was adjourned and would resume promptly at nine the next morning.

The day had gone well for the prosecution and being fully prepared for the 'morrow, District Attorney Jaffe would get a good night's sleep.

Having already concluded that his client would be convicted, Defense Counsel Silverstein was reasonably satisfied that he had most members on the jury wondering if Ron had been aided and abetted in his crimes. This would be a formidable task, because – as he related to the author many years later – he never believed that Roger Farber was involved in having his own wife kidnapped. He would, however, focus on nurturing those seeds and introduce the supposition that because his client was a schizophrenic, an intelligent person with a diabolic mind could easily manipulate him. He just might be able to convince the jury that his client was under the control of a demon by the name of schizophrenia, acted under extreme emotional disturbance and therefore was not competent to understand the gravity of his actions. However, Carl knew this was a long shot and hoped that at least he could convince the jury that his client never intended that Trudy Farber die and, in his delusional mind frame, truly believed that Roger Farber acted with him in committing his crimes. This could result in his client either receiving a less than life sentence or incarceration in a mental hospital rather than a maximum-security prison. It is likely that as Carl pondered these prospects, he was not sleeping as well as the District Attorney.

Court was called to order at precisely nine the following morning, and as it would continue throughout the trial, every seat in the courtroom was occupied.

Appearing fresh and immaculately dressed in a dark power suit, District Attorney Jaffe called for State Police Investigator Ralph Fuente to take the stand. A ruggedly handsome, tall, broad-shouldered male; dressed in a dark, pinstripe suit reserved for weddings, funerals and superior court testimony - entered the courtroom and strode confidently to the witness stand. Like the preceding witness, Ralph Fuente was a veteran member of a brotherhood known as the New York State Police. Some onlookers were heard to remark that it seemed every member of the State Police testifying at this trial was tall and appeared to be in excellent physical condition. Those familiar with the State Police organization would respond that these men epitomized all members of the (prior to 1970) all male force. All applicants for the position of trooper – in addition to passing a difficult entrance exam – were required to meet a minimum height and maximum weight requirement, pass a rigorous physical exam, psychological exam, oral interview by veteran officers, a comprehensive background investigation and graduate from a rigorous training program before being permitted to don the gray uniform denoting membership in the New York State Police brotherhood. By demonstrating skill at solving crime, Trooper Fuente had earned early promotion to the esteemed Bureau of Criminal Investigation and was recognized by his supervisors and peers for quick wit, street savvy and conversational skill.

Jaffe flashed Fuente his patented introductory smile and after establishing the witness's credentials, proceeded to cover the same ground covered by Investigator Chandler the previous day. As expected there were no inconsistencies or surprises and, as a plus, Fuente testified well and appeared to make a good impression on the jury.

During cross, Silverstein posed basically the same questions he had asked Chandler, and Fuente – although in different words – provided basically the same answers.

The prosecution parade of witnesses continued and FBI Special Agent Leo McGillicuddy was called to follow Fuente. The big, round-faced Irishman, a veteran federal agent with a pronounced Irish brogue, corroborated the testimony of the two State Police investigators who had preceded him to the stand. During cross examination Silverstein asked, "Agent McGillicuddy, were any federal charges placed against Ronald Krom?"

"No, sir," McGillicuddy responded, explaining, "as Mrs. Farber was abducted from her 'ome in the state of New Yark, was found in the state of New Yark and the defendant was apprehended in the state of New Yark, it was decided that state charges were applicable."

"Agent McGillicuddy, did you participate in any part of the investigation that you have not testified about?"

"No, sir, I was assigned to work with the State Police fellas to locate Mrs. Farber and to ascertain, what if any, federal laws had been broken."

"In your tenure as a Federal Agent have you spoken with any suspects who had been diagnosed as schizophrenic?"

"Tis safe to say that I have, sir, but I do nah recall the last."

"Agent, did you believe Ronald Krom when he told you that he knew Mrs. Farber's location?"

"Well, sir, as he did in fact take us to the hole that contained the poor woman, I would have to say that he was certainly tellin' us the truth."

The agent's answer evoked a smile on many faces in the court, including Silverstein's, who continued, "Agent McGillicuddy, did you believe Ronald Krom when he told you that Roger Farber – the victim's husband – was involved in having his own wife abducted for ransom?"

McGillicuddy answered in a straight face, "my assignment was dealin' with Mr. Krom and tryin' to convince him to reveal where he was hidin' Mrs. Farber, which he obviously knew. Other agents and State Police fellas were dealin' with Roger Farber and whether he was, or was not involved. It was not my concern."

Returning to the defense table, Silverstein stated, "Thank you, Agent."

Jaffe immediately got up and called out, "The People call Susan Horton."

A short, dark-haired, reasonably attractive woman with only a hint of makeup, appearing to be in her mid to late twenties, dressed in a white blouse atop a dark skirt, entered the courtroom. A court attendant directed her to the witness stand. As she took the required oath the noticeable tremble of her raised right hand indicated nervousness. However, she would respond to the oath and following questions in a clear, crisp voice.

Once more leaving a comfort zone between himself and the witness, Jaffe displayed a warm smile as he directed, "Please state your full name and occupation for the record."

"Susan Ann Horton. I am a sales clerk at the F.W. Woolworth store in Middletown, New York."

Recognizing the witness's nervousness, Jaffe continued display of a warm smile as he stated, "Ms. Horton, you are here today to provide testimony concerning the sale of a twenty-two caliber semi-automatic rifle which occurred on May 13, 1977." He then handed the witness the two pieces of paper he was holding in one hand and asked, "I show you People's Exhibit 11 and ask if you recognize this record of sale?"

Susan scanned the document, then, answered, "Yes, this is the record of sale that I filled out when I sold a rifle to a customer."

"Ms. Horton, would you please read aloud the information on this record of sale?"

As previously instructed, Susan slowly read and stated, "The number on this sales invoice is three-dash-zero-three-six-dash-six-one-seven. It is dated

May 13, 1977, and represents the sale of a twenty-two rifle; bearing serial number, two-one-zero-six-one-two, to Ronald H. Krom, date of birth July 9, 1951, address, Moore Hill Road, Grahamsville, New York. The customer provided New York driver's license number K-one-eight-five-six-eight-six-three-nine-seven-zero-four-nine-four-five-nine-one-dash-five-one, as proof of identity. The other record of sale indicates Mr. Krom also purchased a block of five hundred twenty-two, caliber long rifle bullets."

Jaffe momentarily returned to his work table, picked up the rifle lying there and presented it to the witness, while asking, "Ms. Horton, I show you People's Exhibit – and ask if this is the rifle you sold to Ronald H. Krom?"

Susan examined the gun and after comparing the serial number listed on the record of sale answered, "Yes, this is the rifle purchased by Mr. Krom."

Jaffe retrieved the rifle, returned it to his worktable, then turned to face the witness and asked, "Ms. Horton, do you recognize the Mr. Krom to whom you sold this rifle as present in this courtroom?"

A negative head movement as she was asked this question, emphasized her answer, "I know that Mr. Krom is the defendant, but in all honesty, I do not recall his purchasing the rifle. When the police detectives came to the store, they showed me a picture of Mr. Krom, and even back then, I could not remember him."

"Thank you, Ms. Horton," Jaffe concluded. Then he glanced in the direction of the defense table and said, "Your witness counsel."

Aware that it would not be possible to disconnect his client from purchase and possession of the rifle, Carl asked just one question of the witness. "Ms. Horton, are you certain that the information that you recorded concerning the sale of the rifle is correct?"

Susan gave her questioner a look that translated to 'that's a dumb question.' Then she answered, "Yes, the buyer showed me his driver's license and I wrote the information it contained onto the record of sale. If the purchaser were not Ronald Krom, how did he end up with the rifle?"

Silverstein had not anticipated this witness would come back at him with a question that made his question of her sound foolish. Regretting having asked the question, he returned to his seat at the defense table without response.

Jaffe's next witness was Dr. Roberto Benitez. The doctor was a well-known highly respected pathologist in Ulster County, but at the time – virtually unknown in Sullivan County. Tall, with thinning dark hair and physically resembling one's perception of a college professor, Dr. Benitez frequently displayed a warm smile on his handsome face and enjoyed hearing a good joke. However, he was not known to be a prankster and attended to the morbid profession he had chosen with sincerity and dedication.

The author attended numerous autopsies during his 17 years in Ulster County, many of which were conducted by Dr. Benitez, and learned a great deal about death. Doctor Benitez was a man of few words, but when he spoke his words were full of meaning and substance.

Some spectators in the courtroom that day would later remark that the dark haired doctor, dressed in a gray two-piece suit and wearing dark rim glasses made them think of Clark Kent, Superman's alter ego. Like Clark Kent, the good doctor was mild-mannered, smiling easily and often. No stranger to the witness stand, Dr. Benitez stood tall as the oath was administered and answered in a clear, pleasant voice.

Jaffe stood in front of the jury panel as he opened questioning of the doctor, and, of course, exhibited a warm smile. "Doctor, for the record, please provide your name, title and occupation."

The witness's warm, sincere smile and pleasant tone of voice appeared to establish immediate rapport with all members of the jury, as he answered, "Roberto Benitez, I am a medical doctor, specializing in pathology and at present, I am Chief of Pathology at Kingston City Hospital."

"Thank you, Doctor," Jaffe responded. Then he asked, "Were you so employed on May 26, 1977?"

"Yes, sir."

"Now, Doctor, on May 26 1977, did Coroner Corcoran ask you to examine the body of a woman identified as Gertrude Farber?"

"Actually, sir, Mrs. Farber's body was brought into the Kingston City Hospital on May 26, 1977. I first examined her on the morning of May 27, 1977, after Ulster County Coroner Stephen Corcoran contacted me and reported that Mrs. Farber had been kidnapped from her home in Sullivan County, had become the victim of homicide and her body was found in Ulster County. I was asked to conduct a postmortem examination to ascertain the cause of her demise."

"And did you conduct this examination sir?"

"Yes, commencing at approximately nine on the morning of May 27, the victim, identified to me as Gertrude Farber, was autopsied by me in the morgue at Kingston City Hospital."

"And were other persons present during this autopsy?"

"Yes, sir: Ulster County Coroner Stephen Corcoran, Sullivan County Medical Examiner Doctor Sydney Schiff, and State Police Investigator Will Holik."

"Doctor, what did this examination of Mrs. Farber reveal?"

The witness gave Jaffe a pleading look and responded, "May I consult my written report?"

Flashing a smile in return, Jaffe answered, "By all means, Doctor, feel free to do so."

The witness removed a one page typewritten report from an inside pocket of his suit jacket, unfolded it and read: "The body is that of a well developed, well nourished adult white female of approximately the given age of 30 years. Her height is approximately 65 inches, weight approximately 150 pounds; She had blue eyes, light brown to blonde hair. The corners of both eyes are remarkably clear. Over the right sclera in the conjunctional sac, there is a fragment of loose dirt. The victim has several abrasions on her forehead and lacerations beneath her upper lip; facial livid with pinkish blotches more pronounced on left side than the right. Superficial lacerations noted on both hands, on both feet. There is a superficial linear laceration on her left foot that suggests the victim was dragged. The most striking aspect of external examination is the skin color and its lividity. It is estimated that death occurred within 12-24 hours after burial in the pit."

"And, Doctor, what did you conclude as having caused Mrs. Farber's death?"

"After consulting with Doctor Schiff, who had examined the pit and taken temperatures therein, combined with the retention of oxygenated blood in the victims peripheral tissues and the blood stream, Doctor Schiff and I concurred that death was the result of entombment asphyxia. Entombment asphyxia occurs when a person trapped in a small space experiences fear and stress, which increases his rate of oxygen consumption. Not enough oxygen was admitted to the pit and Mrs. Farber died as a result."

District Attorney Jaffe recognized that most medical terminology would sound like a foreign language to the jurors and the term entombment asphyxia might be especially confusing, so he asked, "Doctor, asphyxia is readily understandable to the layman, but would you please explain – so the jury has a better understanding of – what made you determine and conclude that Mrs. Farber's death was the result of 'entombment asphyxia'?"

Nodding in the affirmative, Benitez replied, "Gloister's Book on Forensic Pathology describes, "that bodies which have been kept in a cold chamber most frequently show reddish patchy coloration on the body surface, and sometimes in the organs. The blood is of a brighter reddish color and surface injuries, such as bruises and abrasions, have an intensified appearance. Blood has a bright red color due to the lack of dissociation of oxygen from hemoglobin. There is a similarity of the colored markings on the skin as to carbon monoxide poisoning. Lividity is reddish in death from freezing because oxygen and hemoglobin binding become greater as the temperature decreases."

The blank, puzzled looks on the jurors faces were indicative that after hearing the witness's explanation as to the cause of entombment asphyxia and the clues it left in death, they still did not have a clue what entombment asphyxia was. However, there was no doubt in their minds that the victim had been buried alive and lack of oxygen had caused her death.

"Doctor, in layman's terms, would it be correct to say Mrs. Farber died from asphyxiation due to the lack of oxygen?"

"Yes, however, I would clarify this by stating that a very small amount of oxygen was admitted through the small splintered holes in the plywood cover. The amount admitted was not sufficient to sustain Mrs. Farber's life due to her state of stress. Also, the low temperature in the confined pit increased the rate of oxygen consumption as well. Therefore - although seeming a matter of semantics - it would be medically correct to say that death was due to a lack of 'enough' oxygen."

"Doctor, you testified that a laceration on Mrs. Farber's left foot resulted from being dragged. Did her injuries suggest that she was unconscious prior to, or while being placed in the pit?"

"We found no blunt force trauma indicating forced unconsciousness; however, psychologically induced stress could have produced unconsciousness."

Displaying a smile of thanks, Jaffe stated, "Thank you, Doctor." Then he returned to his seat at the prosecution table.

Silverstein would open his cross by asking, "Doctor, I heard in your testimony, that whoever fired the bullets through the plywood did so to provide an oxygen supply. Is that a correct assumption on my part?"

Benitez held his questioner in a sober look as he answered, "Sir, my expertise in this matter was solely to examine the deceased and determine what caused her death. I had nothing to do with determining why the bullets were fired through the plywood. I do know that whatever oxygen was emitted into the pit was insufficient to sustain the life of the person confined therein."

Not receiving the answer hoped for, Silverstein next asked, "Doctor, did you render a legal verdict concerning Mrs. Farber's death?"

"No, sir. I believe such finding was rendered by either Doctor Schiff or Coroner Corcoran."

Having no more questions for the witness that might aid the defense, Silverstein returned to his seat without comment.

Jaffe next called Doctor Sydney Schiff to the stand. After administration of the required oath, he requested, "Please state your full name, title and occupation for the record."

'Doc' Schiff – as he was fondly referred to by police detectives, friends, relatives and many patients – was a popular general practitioner in Sullivan County and saw patients at his office located within his Liberty residence. Of Jewish heritage, the gnomish-appearing, bespectacled 'Doc' was blessed with a quick wit, wonderful sense of humor, a mischievous smile and could have played the role of 'Happy' in "Snow White and the Seven Dwarfs." A rapid-fire orator and master of one-liners, 'Doc' could have just as easily performed as a one-man standup comedian in any of the many Catskill Mountain resort hotels. Instead, he treated patients with doses of rapid-fire humor and this prescription often worked wonders toward curing their illness. Over the years 'Doc' had also endeared himself to the many members of the New York State Police who passed through the Ferndale barracks. He treated them with respect, humor and – during the era when troopers made poverty wages – provided 'his' boys in gray, and their families, free medical service. Many of Doc's boys in gray earned promotion during their careers, some attaining high rank in the esteemed police agency; they found a way to honor and reward the good 'Doc' from Sullivan County, who while treating sickness and injury, had boosted their spirits as well. At the time of Trudy Farber's horrible and untimely demise, 'Doc Schiff' was one of a handful of physician's throughout the state duly designated as a New York State Police Physician. This elite cadre of trusted doctors on retainer with the New York State Police were called upon to treat the many injuries and illnesses - such as gunshot wounds, knife wounds, exposure to infectious diseases, etc. - resulting from the performance of members' duties. Although never one of Doc's patients, the author personally witnessed a patient visit to the good Doctor. It was a memorable experience and when reflected upon, evokes a smile. This is that story in a nutshell. Frankie P., one of my brothers in gray had been working in an undercover capacity, impersonating a New York City Organized Crime figure to purchase illegal firearms from a known suspect. During the investigation, the suspect was hospitalized with an unknown illness and died. It was subsequently learned that death was the result of a severe case of infectious hepatitis that had overwhelmed his immune system. We were unable to learn how the individual contracted the contagious disease. As Frankie had had numerous personal contacts with the suspect, including one just before he died in the hospital, it was decided that Frankie needed to be immunized. An appointment was made with Doc Schiff and I accompanied Frankie to the Doc's office in Liberty. On arrival, Doc greeted us cordially and inquired about the health and status of numerous members of the State Police while ushering us into his inner-sanctum, a room which more resembled the chamber of a practitioner of witchcraft than a medical doctor. Doc proceeded to put my worried companion Frankie at ease by informing him how horrible infectious hepatitis was and how fortunate he was to be able to receive the magic serum that would "hopefully" prevent him from dying a horrible death. After providing us stools to sit on, Doc momentarily left our company, informing Frankie that he had to go prepare the syringe needed to administer the shot. While waiting, Frankie was sweating bullets and relating to me his concern that he might somehow pass the illness to his wife and family. I did my best to calm his nerves and assured him that it was reasonably certain that getting inoculated would prevent that from happening. About five minutes later, Doc re-appeared and when Frankie saw the syringe Doc held in his hand, he turned pale, his eyes opened wide and his face displayed a look of panic. Doc was holding the largest syringe I had ever seen. It looked to be at least six inches long, its tube an inch thick and the needle looked more like a hollow ice pick than a needle. This syringe was filled with a putrid looking yellow liquid. While instructing Frankie to roll up his sleeve and close his eyes, Doc pushed the plunger on the syringe slightly, squirting some of the horrible looking liquid into a plastic drinking cup. Frankie did not make a move to roll up the sleeve of his shirt and instead, sat frozen in confusion and terror. As Doc studied his panic-stricken patient, his face broke into a broad smile, his eyes sparkled like those of a mischievous leprechaun and he began to laugh. While laughing, he placed the monstrous syringe on his desk, opened a desk drawer and took out a sealed package containing a small syringe, which he subsequently used to administer the shot.

Realizing that he had been had, Frankie began to laugh and informed Doc, "Good thing you put that torture stabber down when you did Doc because I was about to jump up and run for the door."

Having previously observed someone being inoculated for hepatitis, I had correctly guessed that Doc was playing a joke on Frankie and I played along with the scam, trying to look concerned, while masking a smile. Many years have passed but I will never forget the look of terror on Frankie's face when Doc Schiff produced that monstrous syringe.

After the three of us had wiped away tears of laughter, Doc apologized, saying, "Sorry, Frankie, I couldn't help myself, and the look on your face was priceless."

Such was the humorous side of Doc Schiff; however, on this day in the Sullivan County courtroom, attired in a hounds tooth sport jacket, dark slacks, white dress shirt and rust colored bow tie, Doc was all business and demonstrated pure professionalism. He responded, "Sydney P. Schiff. I am a general practitioner with office in Liberty. I am also Medical Examiner for Sullivan County."

"Doctor, in the course of your duties as Medical Examiner, did you participate in the post mortem examination of Gertrude Farber at Kingston City Hospital, on May 27 1977?"

"Yes, Mr. Jaffe, I did."

"Who else attended this autopsy?"

"Doctor Roberto Benitez, Chief Pathologist for Ulster County, and Investigator Holik of the New York State Police."

"Doctor, during your tenure as Medical Examiner, have you presided over or attended many such post mortem examinations?"

"Yes, Mr. Jaffe, sad to say, too many."

"Doctor, prior to attending the autopsy on Mrs. Farber, what had you been told concerning her demise?"

"I learned of Mrs. Farber's abduction from the Middletown Times-Herald Record newspaper. Then, a couple of days later I was notified by the State Police that Mrs. Farber's body had been found in a pit in Ulster County. I went to the location and met with Ulster County Coroner Steve Corcoran, who had already pronounced Mrs. Farber deceased. I offered my assistance and attended the autopsy performed by Doctor Benitez. As it turned out, it was decided that prosecution of her killer would occur in Sullivan County."

"Doctor Schiff, Doctor Benitez earlier testified that Mrs. Farber's death resulted from entombment asphyxia. Do you concur with that finding?"

"Yes, Mr. Jaffe, I personally researched the causes and symptoms of entombment asphyxia and concurred with Doctor Benitez that was what caused Mrs. Farber's death."

"Doctor, what did your research reveal regarding entombment asphyxia?"

"Mrs. Farber's skin color and lividity were suggestive of entombment asphyxia. I examined the pit where she was found, took temperature readings in the pit and contacted the local weather service to ascertain the approximate outside temperatures in the vicinity of the pit May 24 through May 26. I determined that the temperature within the pit, during Mrs. Farber's period of confinement, ranged from 38 to 40 degrees, which is similar to the temperature in the holding room of the morgue. A person confined to these temperatures and wearing light clothing, combined with being in severe stress from fear and shock, requires more oxygen than normal. Although oxygen may have been admitted to the pit, through the small bullet holes in the plywood cover, it was not sufficient to sustain Mrs. Farber's life. She was entombed and asphyxiated, hence the term entombment asphyxia."

"Doctor, to what did you attribute the injuries you found on Mrs. Farber's body?"

"Mr. Jaffe, the contusions and abrasions on Mrs. Farber's face and forehead indicated she had been forcibly placed in the hole - head down – and with considerable effort, she managed to turn so that she was lying on her back."

"Doctor Benitez previously testified as to a laceration on Mrs. Farber's left foot, which appeared to have resulted from Mrs. Farber being dragged. Do you concur with that finding?"

"Yes, Mr. Jaffe, I do."

"Doctor, you stated that Mrs. Farber was forcibly placed in the pit – I believe you said hole. Was it possible she was unconscious when that occurred?"

"It is quite possible because the hole was very small and if she physically resisted being confined therein, it would have been very difficult for a man acting alone to have placed the cover in the position required to apply the padlock to the hasp."

"Doctor, did you issue a legal ruling concerning Mrs. Farber's death?"

"Yes, Mr. Jaffe, I issued the ruling – agreed upon by Ulster County Coroner Corcoran – that Mrs. Farber's death was a homicide."

"Doctor, did you have any other involvement in the investigation concerning Mrs. Farber's abduction and subsequent homicide?"

"Yes, I examined the hole, took temperature readings inside it and directed the State Police to conduct tests on a comparison sheet of plywood by firing twenty-two caliber bullets through it. During this test, a total of 126 bullets were fired through the plywood and, accumulatively, they allowed only a trickle of air to pass through the wood. Also my examination of the injuries on Mrs. Farber's hands and claw marks on the inside cover of the plywood indicated that Mrs. Farber vainly fought to escape from the hole."

Giving the witness a smile of appreciation, Jaffe concluded, "Thank you, Doctor. Your witness, Counsel."

Silverstein arose from his seat, displayed a sober look, approached the witness, and asked, "As a doctor and medical examiner, how many cases have you seen of entombment asphyxia?"

Giving his questioner a look of aplomb, the witness responded, "Mrs. Farber was the first," immediately adding, "needless to say, not many people are buried alive in Sullivan County."

Detecting a note of hostility in the answer, Silverstein continued to hold the witness in a critical stare and probed, "You testified as to finding contusions and abrasions on Mrs. Farber. Did you determine that these injuries resulted from any sort of physical assault?"

"Most of these injuries appeared associated with Mrs. Farber's struggle to free herself from her tomb. As previously stated, a laceration on her left foot was consistent with having been dragged."

"There has been considerable testimony provided that some bullets were fired through the plywood cover to permit oxygen into the space where Mrs. Farber was confined. You have testified that these holes provided an insufficient supply of oxygen to sustain life. Would it be accurate to assume that the person shooting the holes through the plywood intended that Mrs.

Farber would survive but, lacking expertise in the technology of airflow was unaware of the amount of oxygen required for her survival?"

"It would be more accurate to say," Doc snapped in reply, "that anyone who would even consider burying another person alive is a sadistic animal having forfeited his right to be classified as a human being!"

Silverstein glared at the witness and responded, "I did not ask you to express your personal feelings! You are on this witness stand as Medical Examiner of Sullivan County, a medical doctor and supposed expert on causes of death. I am asking your expert, professional opinion as to whether the person responsible for Mrs. Farber's demise intended that she live or die when he placed her in that space below ground?"

Doc glared at the defendant as he answered, "What 'he' intended is of no consequence! The fact is Mrs. Farber was forcibly placed in that cramped hole, then sealed in by a cover secured with a padlock and she subsequently died as the result of 'his' action. Any reasonable thinking human being would have to believe that burying another person alive could likely result in that person's death!"

Clearly frustrated, Carl responded, "As you insist on expressing opinion rather than answer the question concerning whether Mrs. Farber's death was intentional or unintentional, what is your professional opinion as to why the bullets were fired through the plywood cover?"

Continuing to focus sternly on the defendant, the witness answered, "His intent may have been to create openings for air, or to frighten his victim. Whatever the intent was, the fact is, the victim – Mrs. Farber – was forcibly placed in that hole and subsequently died from a lack of oxygen!"

Jaffe slowly came from his seat and interjected, "Your Honor, it seems Counsel is berating the witness over an issue that has no bearing on this, as the law is perfectly clear that when death occurs during the commission of a felony, in this case the felony of kidnapping, the person or persons responsible are guilty of Murder. It has been well established by evidence and testimony that the defendant forced Mrs. Farber into a hole to secrete her while waiting to collect ransom for her release and that while confined in that hole, she died."

Silverstein rebutted, "I am fully cognizant of the circumstances that constitute crimes within the Penal Law; however, the prosecution by its grotesque slide presentation is intent on inflaming the jury. My intent is to point out that there was no intent that Mrs. Farber die; in fact, as testimony has shown, Mr. Krom was shocked, very upset and became sick when she was found deceased. I believe that his lack of intent in this regard, diminishes culpability."

"I believe Counselor," Judge Scheinman responded, "you just succinctly made this clear. Please address a different issue or sit down."

Re-focusing sternly on the witness, Silverstein asked, "You and Doctor Benitez testified that you concurred that Mrs. Farber died as the result of entombment asphyxia. Doctor Benitez related that he arrived at this conclusion after consulting some medical publication known as Gloister's Book on Forensic Pathology. Are you familiar with this publication?"

"I am." Schiff tersely responded, then added, "and after our examination of Mrs. Farber, I suggested that Gloister's addressed the issue of reddish splotches of coloration and bright red blood. What we saw closely resembled the appearance of victims I had examined who died of carbon monoxide poisoning and I recalled that Gloister's addressed that issue. We consulted Gloister's, conducted temperature tests and concluded that Mrs. Farber's death was the result of entombment asphyxia as described and defined in Gloister's."

Carl studied the witness and continued, "Sir, you have established your credentials with this court as a medical general practitioner and hold the office of Sullivan County Medical Examiner. Would you consider yourself an expert concerning the cause of death?"

Wondering why he had been asked this question, Doc displayed a look of curiosity as he replied, "I have been called upon to provide expert medical testimony in many court cases."

"As a medical expert doctor, I presume you can tell this court how many bones there are in the human body?"

"Of course," the witness smugly replied, "there are 202 bones in the human body."

Silverstein smiled, stated, "Thank you for this expert reply Doctor; however, for your information, there are 206 bones in the human body."

Jaffe immediately called out, "Objection! The number of bones in the human body has absolutely nothing to do with the matter under consideration!"

Continuing to smile, Carl immediately responded, "Your witness, I have concluded with this witness."

Realizing there was no need to rule on the objection, Judge Scheinman displayed the hint of a smile as he waited for Jaffe's response.

"I have just one question, Doctor," Jaffe asked from his chair, "is there anything equivocal concerning the cause of Mrs. Farber's death?"

Appearing un-rattled by the defense's attempt to embarrass him, Doctor Schiff responded in a firm voice, "No, Mr. Jaffe. Mrs. Farber died as the result of forced entombment which caused her to asphyxiate."

"Thank you, Doctor," Jaffe concluded.

"The witness is excused," Judge Scheinman said.

Jaffe immediately started to call his next witness but was interrupted by Judge Scheinman who announced that court would recess and reconvene the next morning.

Jaffe returned to his office, where he met briefly with his staff, to obtain their opinion as to the progress of the trial. There was unanimous agreement that 'the boss' was doing a magnificent job, no surprises had come forth and, without some sort of defense surprise, conviction was sure.

Defense Counsel Silverstein returned to his office, read his telephone messages, and returned the ones he considered important. He then placed calls to his intended defense witnesses to put them on notice that it appeared the prosecution was about to run out of witnesses and it would be his turn in the batter's box. He felt a small sense of victory at having shown the jury that the smug Medical Examiner was not the expert that he portrayed himself to be.

The matter of the 'People of the State of New York against Ronald Harrison Krom', resumed at precisely nine the following morning. Well rested, looking particularly handsome in a double breasted blue blazer and displaying a welcoming smile to Judge and jury, Jaffe called Marilyn Jennings as his first witness of the day.

The courtroom was again abuzz as media and spectators in whispered voices asked who this woman was and wondered what she would bring to the case. A short, slender blond woman, appearing to be in her mid to late thirties, entered the courtroom and was directed to the witness stand. The woman's garb of a print blouse, atop tight fitting denim slacks seemed a poor selection of clothing for a court appearance and made her appear even thinner than she was. However, the witness responded to the oath in a clear, pleasant voice.

Jaffe would leave a comfort zone of approximately eight feet between himself and this witness. "Ms. Jennings," he opened with a smile, "please state your full name, employment and community of residence for the record."

The witness returned a forced smile as she answered, "Marilyn Jean Jennings, I am a waitress at Ed's Snack Shack and live in Grahamsville, New York."

"Ms. Jennings, do you know and are you acquainted with the defendant, Ronald Krom?"

Marilyn glanced nervously at the defendant – who met her gaze with a blank look – then returned focus to her questioner and answered, "Yes, I know Ron and his brother, Wayne. I have known them for a number of years."

Continuing to smile, Jaffe continued, "Ms. Jennings, I will get right to the point of your being here today. Would you please relate a conversation that you had with Ron Krom in May of 1976?"

The witness spoke directly to Jaffe as she answered, and frequently paused to look over at the defendant to see his reaction. She seemed surprised that Ron seemed unaffected by her testimony. "During May 1976, I moved into a trailer that I rented through Krom Realty. Mr. Ron Thomas, a salesman with the Krom agency, arranged the lease for me. Mr. Thomas and Ronnie Krom helped me move my furniture into the trailer. My younger sister Susan was also helping. While we were taking a break, Ronnie asked if my parents had any money. I told him that if they did I would be moving into a chalet and not living in a trailer. Then I asked him – Ronnie – why he asked the question. Ronnie told me that if my parents had money, he would kidnap my cute sister, hold her for ransom, and we could all split the money. We all laughed because we thought Ronnie was joking."

"And were either you or your sister subsequently harmed or threatened in any way by Ronald Krom?"

"No, sir."

"What caused you to contact the state police and report the comment made by Ronald?"

"When I learned that he – Ronnie – had been arrested for the kidnap and murder of Mrs. Farber, it sent chills up my spine because if my family had money, he probably would have done the same thing to my sister."

"Ms. Jennings, you also told the State Police about another troubling conversation that you had with Wayne Krom, the defendant's brother, subsequent to the statement Ron Krom made in 1976 about kidnapping your sister. What was that conversation?"

"It took place sometime around the ninth or tenth of May 1977. Just a short time before I learned of Ronnie's arrest. I stopped in Marty's tavern in Neversink to have a drink and Wayne Krom was in the place. He was there with a couple of his friends that I did not know. At the time Wayne and I were not getting along at all because he had threatened to sue me for not paying a bill that I had already paid. Wayne offered to buy me a drink and I refused to accept it. He bought the drink anyway. When the bartender put it in front of me, I took it, and poured it into the garbage can located in a corner of the room. Wayne walked over to me and said that he did not want to press the issue of the lawsuit because he had a million dollar real estate deal working at the present time and would soon be able to buy and sell all the little people in Sullivan County. I told him to get lost and he left Marty's accompanied by his two friends."

Jaffe moved closer to the witness and displayed a questioning look as he asked, "It was Wayne Krom who told you this, not Ronnie?"

"Yes, sir, at the time, I thought he was just shooting off his mouth and trying to impress me, but then, I learned that Ronnie had been arrested and had asked Mr. Resnick for a million dollars ransom. I recalled Wayne's conversation telling me that he had a million dollar deal working, (just a couple of weeks before), which made me think he and Ronnie might have been involved together."

"Did you have any more conversations or dealings with either Ron or Wayne Krom subsequent to the conversation in Marty's Bar?"

"No, sir."

Jaffe returned to the prosecution table, stating as he did so, "Thank you, Ms. Jennings. Your witness, Carl."

Silverstein gave serious consideration to a rigorous cross examination of this witness, eventually deciding not to because he knew the prosecution had a supporting deposition from Ron Thomas, who would not be called upon to testify unless his testimony were required to corroborate Jennings' account. He would subsequently count on defense witness Wayne Krom (Wayne would not testify) to refute Jennings' testimony about their meeting in Marty's Bar. Therefore, he responded, "I have no questions of this witness."

Jaffe's next witness was Giuseppe Giordano, a suave appearing middle-aged male, having a thick mane of dark, wavy hair. Giordano, dressed in a camel tan leisure suit, strode confidently to the witness stand. A gold Italian horn good-luck pendant was prominently displayed amidst a patch of dark chest hair visible in the open V-neck of a white, wide-collar dress shirt. It was noted that Mr. Giordano answered the required oath in a pleasant-sounding, deep base voice.

Jaffe stood in front of the prosecution table, displaying his smile of greeting as he asked his first question of the witness. "Sir, please state your full name, occupation and community of residence for the record."

The witness gave his questioner a wary, penetrating look in return as he answered, "Giuseppe Alphonse Giordano. I am the owner of G.G.'s bar in New Paltz, New York, and I live in that community."

Continuing to smile, Jaffe asked, "Mr. Giordano, are you acquainted with the defendant Ronald Krom?"

Maintaining a sober look of wariness, the witness answered, "Yes, I have known Mr. Krom for perhaps four to six years. He is a regular, or should I say, was a regular customer at my business establishment."

"Mr. Giordano, did you have a conversation with Ronald Krom concerning selling your business?"

"Yes, Ronald was continually asking me if I wanted to sell and told me that if I was, he was interested in buying. I remember telling him that I had already turned down an offer for fifty grand. I told him that if he made an offer it would have to be a much higher amount. I did not think that Ron was serious and we never discussed an actual price that would entice me to sell. I remember asking Ron where he would get the money if he did buy my place and he told me that he had a source."

"When did this conversation concerning his wanting to buy and having a source of money take place?"

"Well, he mentioned that he was interested in buying my place several times and the last time we spoke about it was sometime in the fall of 1976."

"Would that conversation have taken place about six months prior to his arrest for kidnapping and murder?"

"Yes, that is about the time he told me he wanted to buy."

"Did Krom identify the individual that was his supposed source of money?"

"No, he did not."

"Was anyone else present when Ronald Krom spoke to you about purchasing your business?"

"No, sir."

"When was the last time you spoke with Ronald Krom?"

"He was at the bar about two months before I learned of his arrest. We briefly spoke then, but he made no mention about wanting to purchase my place."

"Thank you, Mr. Giordano." Jaffe concluded. Then he glanced at the defense table and stated, "Your witness."

Silverstein's only question of this witness was, "Mr. Giordano, did you have an outside relationship with my client?"

Giordano stared blankly at Silverstein as he responded, "He was a customer. Outside my place we had no contact."

Jaffe immediately called Robert Carsoni of New Paltz to the stand. The male entering the courtroom closely resembled the preceding witness in physical appearance, except he had a heavier build. He was of medium height, had thick, dark hair and like Giordano, was wearing an open neck leisure suit, popular in that era. However, his leisure suit was dark brown, the open neck shirt was mauve and no neck jewelry was visible. Although loose fitting, the leisure suit did not conceal Carsoni's girth and combined with a round face, he appeared older than his thirty-six years.

As a matter of standard routine, Jaffe greeted the witness with a smile as he asked the ritual opening question, "Please state your full name, occupation and community of residence for the record."

This witness would display the smile and charisma of a car salesman – which was precisely what he was. "Robert Carlson Carsoni," he answered, "I am a car salesman employed by Johnny B's Cadillac in Kingston, New York, and I reside in New Paltz."

"Mr. Carsoni, are you acquainted with the defendant Ronald Harrison Krom?"

Carsoni glanced briefly at the defense table, then, refocused on his questioner as he answered, "I have known Ronald, and I guess all of the Krom family, since 1963 or 1964. I met them at Albee's Auto Sales in Accord, New York, where I worked at the time. Since that time, I have sold cars to Ronald, his brother and their dad, Harrison. I also saw Ron and his brother Wayne a lot at G&G's bar in New Paltz."

"When was the last time you spoke with Ronald Krom?"

"I believe it was about six or seven months before he was arrested."

"Where did that conversation take place?"

"At that time I was working as a bartender at Donny's Tavern in West Park. Ron came in to the bar, had a few drinks and we chatted. He told me that his purpose in driving all the way to West Park to see me was to ask me if I would like to partner with him in purchasing G&G's Bar over in New Paltz. Ron told me that he had discussed purchase with Mr. Giordano and if he could come up with the money, Giordano would sell. Ron told me he needed $50,000 and that he had 'somebody' – he didn't give me a name – who would loan him the money. I presumed he was referring to his father. I knew that Ron often had big ideas and plans, but none of them ever seemed to take off. I was interested though in the G&G deal because I knew the place was a real popular hangout for the New Paltz college crowd. So I called Ron's mother and asked if she or her husband were loaning Ron money to buy a bar. She told me that they had no intentions of loaning or giving any money to Ron. After speaking with Mrs. Krom, I lost interest in going into any business deal with Ron."

"Did you speak with Ron subsequent to your conversation at Donny's?"

"No, I didn't. As I said, Ron was arrested about six months later and we haven't spoken."

"Thank you, Mr. Carsini," Jaffe concluded, displaying a smile. "Your witness, Counselor."

Not bothering to stand, Silverstein responded, "I have no questions of this witness."

"The People call Michael Thompson" Jaffe immediately responded. A young man of medium height and build, having long dark hair and dressed in a gray cable knit sweater, over a light blue sport shirt and dark slacks, entered the courtroom and was directed to the witness stand. While the required oath was administered Thompson's face revealed discomfort; however, his voice was firm and clear.

Displaying his trademark introductory smile Jaffe asked, from a standing position in front of the prosecution table, "Please state your full name, occupation and community of residence for the record."

The witness took a deep breath, exhaled slowly, forced the hint of a smile and replied, "Michael James Thompson. I am a collection clerk for RJ Collections and I live in New Paltz, New York."

Sobering slightly, Jaffe continued, "Mr. Thompson, are you acquainted with the defendant Ronald Krom?"

"Yes, sir, I am."

"How did you come to know Mr. Krom, sir?"

"I met Ron about six years ago. We were in the same class at New Paltz University. We struck up a conversation and became friends."

"How often did you see Ronald Krom prior to his arrest in 1977?"

The witness cast frequent glances at the defendant while testifying and it was noted that Ron smiled back at the witness while they exchanged looks. This was the first witness that the defendant had revealed any visible emotional connection with. Thompson answered, "We went to class together once or twice a week and sometimes we went to G&G's for a beer afterwards."

"Mr. Thompson, do you recall the last time you saw Ron Krom prior to his arrest?"

"I was asked this same question by the State Police two years ago, and they took a statement from me. So I know it was on May 20 1977, at about two in the afternoon. I was about to leave New Paltz that day to go to Long Island, when my landlady told me that Ron had stopped by and left the message that he was waiting to see me by the lake on campus. I found Ron there and he told me that he was studying for his insurance broker exam. We spoke for about five minutes, then I told him I had to get going because I was leaving for Long Island."

"When did you learn about Ron's arrest?"

"It was on May 28 1977. I was still in Long Island and read in the New York Post about the kidnapping, that the girl taken had died and Ron had been arrested for it."

"What did you do after reading this?"

"I called Ron's house and spoke with his brother Randy. Randy told me the State Police had come to the house a couple of days previously and arrested Ron. I asked Randy where Ron was being held and if he knew what the visiting hours at the jail were. Randy told me Ron was in the Sullivan County jail in Monticello. After speaking with Randy, I immediately left Long Island, drove to Monticello and tried to get in to see Ron. They wouldn't let me in, as I was not a relative. While returning to my car in the parking lot, I met Randy who was able to get me into the jail and we visited with Ron for about thirty minutes."

"What did you converse about during that thirty minutes?"

Before answering Michael looked at Ron, apparently intending to see how he was reacting to his testimony. Noting that Ron seemed unaffected and was still smiling at him, he returned focus on his questioner and responded, "I asked Ron if it were true that he had kidnapped the woman. He told me that he did. I asked him why he did it and he said he did it for the money. He told me that the woman's husband was involved with him and that they had planned the kidnapping for two years. He also told me that he had been digging the hole he hid her in for a couple of years. He told me that he borrowed a Firebird to transport the woman from her home to the pit where he hid her. He told me that he believed the ransom would be quickly paid and he did not intend for her to die. He told me that he had placed a peanut butter sandwich and drink in a box he left near the pit for the woman to eat." Before continuing, Michael glanced apprehensively at Ron, who winked and smiled at him in return.

Jaffe regained the witness's attention by asking, "What was your reaction when Ron told you all of this?"

"I was stunned! It was incredible and as Ron seemed cool and collected while telling us this bizarre tale, plus what else he said, convinced me that he had flipped and was out of his mind."

"What else did he say?"

"He was so cool, so unaffected, by what he had done and by the woman's death. After telling us about taking the woman from her home and burying her alive, he just rambled on about how he would soon be released on bail, would have $10,000 to boot and couldn't wait to drive his Corvette with the sun roof open and Cynthia – his girl friend by his side. He was unconcerned about the death of the woman, or the seriousness of the charges he was facing. He told us that when he got out he was going to marry Cynthia. I assured Ron that I would do whatever I could to help him and then Randy and I left the jail. That was the last time I spoke to him."

"Mr. Thompson, did you have prior knowledge that Ron Krom was planning to abduct Mrs. Farber, or for that matter, any other person?"

"No, sir."

"What did you do – if anything – to aid the defendant?"

"Randy invited me to stay at his parents home that night and I did. The following day, we – Randy and I – went out to South Hill Road, by the Rondout Reservoir, to examine the hole where Ron hid the woman. When we arrived we found Grahamsville Attorney Joseph Brunson there. Randy introduced me to Brunson, who said that he was giving consideration to representing Ron. The three of us looked at the hole and Mr. Brunson told Randy and me not to touch anything. We were at the hole for about an hour and then Mr. Brunson invited us to his office in Grahamsville. Randy and I went there, told Mr. Brunson about what Ron told us when we saw him in the jail, and then, we left Brunson's office. After that I remained in contact with Randy, but came to the realization that I really couldn't do anything to help Ron."

Having concluded with the witness, Jaffe stated, "Thank you Mr. Thompson." He then retook his seat at the prosecution table.

Silverstein had listened carefully to the witness's testimony under direct examination and believed that he could possibly score points with the jury if the witness responded in cross-examination the way he hoped he would. Displaying a warm smile, he slowly began, "Sir, throughout your relationship with Ron, did he ever give you cause or reason to believe he was untruthful?"

Anticipating that Ron's attorney would go on the attack, Michael gave his questioner a curious, inquisitive look, as he answered, "No, sir."

"Sir, did you believe Ron when he told you that he was involved in the kidnapping of Mrs. Farber, for the money?"

"Yes, I had no reason to not believe him."

"Did you believe Ron when he told you that the victim's husband Roger Farber was involved in the plot to have his wife taken for ransom?"

Michael thought about his answer for a moment and finally responded, "As bizarre as it seemed, I had no reason to disbelieve him."

Giving the witness an appreciative smile, Silverstein stated, "Thank you sir. I have no further questions."

Jaffe next called a witness whom he felt sure would seal a conviction with the jury. This witness could prove to be the diva whose aria would make the prosecution's case, a stellar performance. He stood confidently at the prosecution table and called out in a dramatic flair, "The People call Cynthia Black"

Very few spectators in the courtroom knew Cynthia Black, and as her name had not appeared in any news account concerning the kidnapping and murder, a murmur rippled through the room as reporters and spectators asked the person beside them if they knew this mystery witness and what was she going to bring to the case.

A reasonably attractive young brunette, short and having a petite figure, appearing to be of oriental extraction, dressed in a navy blue pants suit entered the courtroom and was directed to the witness stand. The noticeable tremble of her right hand and arm and tense look on her face were indicative of the fact that this woman was nervous and either regretted or resented having been called as a witness.

Jaffe would leave a large zone of comfort between this witness and himself for most of his questioning of her. He naturally opened by giving the witness a warm smile as he asked, "Please state your full name, occupation and community of residence for the record."

The witness's face revealed discomfort and wariness as she answered, "Cynthia Marie Black, I am a hairstylist employed at Village Salon in Monticello and I reside in Swan Lake."

Jaffe would continue to smile as he asked in a pleasant tone of voice, "Ms. Black, are you acquainted with the defendant Ronald Krom?"

"Yes," she answered in a quiet voice.

"Please describe your relationship with Ron Krom?"

"We were dating."

"How did you happen to meet Ron?"

"He came in to the salon to get his haircut. We talked and he seemed friendly. After his third visit, he asked me to go out with him and I did."

"During what period of time did you know and date Ron Krom?"

"He started coming in to the salon in April of 1977, and our first date was on April 20, 1977. I – we – continued to see each other until he was arrested."

"Ms. Black, you were interviewed by the state police on May 26, 1977, and you provided a deposition to them concerning your relationship with Ron and in that statement you describe a conversation that occurred between you and Ron on May 22, 1977. Please relate the substance of that conversation. You may refresh your memory by looking at your deposition if necessary."

"I do not need to look at the deposition. That night – May 22 1977 – I was at Ron's parents home and we were watching television. Ron told me that he was going to pick up a girl and drive her somewhere. I thought that was a strange thing to tell me and I asked him why he was picking up this girl. He – Ron – told me that someone was going to pay a lot of money for her. He didn't say anymore at that time about picking up this girl and I assumed he meant that he was going to pick up a girl and drive her somewhere for money."

What time did this conversation take place on May 22, 1977?"

"It was around eight or nine in the evening."

"On the evening that Ron told you he was going to pick up a girl, what time was it when you left the Krom residence?"

"We left at about two-thirty in the morning and Ron drove me home."

"What was Ron's car? Did he drive you home in his car?"

"Yes, he drove me home in his Chevrolet Corvette."

"Can you describe Ron's car more specifically?"

"It was an orange, nice looking Corvette and it had New Jersey license plates on it."

"Are you sure about the New Jersey license plates?"

"Yes. I know, because I asked Ron why he was driving a car with New Jersey plates and he told me that he had had a lot of accidents and it was cheaper insurance to drive on Jersey plates."

"While Ron was driving you home on the night of May 22, 1977, I presume you conversed?"

"Yes."

"What did you talk about during that ride?"

"Our relationship was starting to become serious and we discussed a lot of personal things."

"Do you recall telling the police about something Ron told you during the drive that night, that didn't mean much at the time but bothered you after learning of his arrest?"

"Well, Ron said that perhaps we shouldn't see each other for a few days so we could think things over."

"Now, after the ride home on the night of May 22, 1977, when did you next see Ron Krom?"

"Ron came to get me on May 25, 1977, at around eight-thirty in the evening. We drove around for a while and he took me home at around eleven-thirty. He promised to give me a call the next day."

"When you saw Ron on May 25 1977, did he appear nervous, upset or act different than normal?"

"Not that I noticed. He was his usual self."

"How was he dressed - what was he wearing - when you saw him on May 25, 1977."

"Like I told the police, I am not sure. I think he was dressed casual, maybe a light colored shirt and dark pants."

"When Ron picked you up on May 25, 1977, what car was he driving?"

"His orange Corvette."

"Did Ron call you on May 26, 1977?"

"I got a call at about nine-thirty that morning and I was pretty sure it was from Ron, but I never heard him say anything. I just heard another person in the background and I'm pretty sure they were talking to Ron. This person was saying, 'you can trust us. Why can't you trust us? You don't have to keep anything from us.' Then I thought I heard Ron say, 'I will call you back,' and that was the end of the call."

"When did you learn that Ron had been arrested?"

"When the State Police and an FBI agent came to the salon on May 26."

"Did you see or speak to Ron after learning of his arrest on May 26, 1977?"

For the first time, Cynthia turned her head to look directly at the defendant who winked and smiled at her. She quickly returned her attention to the prosecutor and whispered, "No, what he supposedly did to that lady shocked, horrified and frightened me. I didn't want anything more to do with him."

"Has the defendant, Ron Krom, tried to communicate with you during the past two years?"

"Yes, Ron wrote letters – continues to send me letters."

"Did you, or have you responded to his letters?"

"I did at first. I told him we were through and asked him to stop writing to me, but he didn't. His letters no longer make any sense."

For the first time during questioning of this witness Jaffe displayed a serious look as he asked, "Ms. Black, did you participate in or have any knowledge of the planned abduction of Mrs. Farber?"

Face now ashen and voice trembling, the witness responded in a strained whisper, "No sir, I did not."

"Thank you, Ms. Black," Jaffe concluded. He then retook his seat at the prosecution table.

Silverstein approached the witness, leaving a smaller comfort zone than that provided by the prosecution and positioned himself so that the defendant would be in the witness's line of vision while looking at him. Displaying a look of compassion he opened, "Ms. Black, throughout your relationship with Ron, did he ever give you any reason to believe he was capable of committing the crimes he is charged with?"

Cynthia did her best to avoid looking at Ron as she answered and found she could do so by focusing on the jury. Her face remained ashen, as she tersely answered, "No."

"You testified that your relationship with Ron was getting serious. Did you love him?"

Cynthia shot a glance at Ron, noted he was studying her, then turned quickly away, looked down at her hands and in a strained whisper replied, "At the time I thought I did."

"Would it be accurate to say that Ron treated you very well?"

"Yes," came the whispered answer.

Displaying a smile, Silverstein concluded, "Thank you. I have no more questions."

Jaffe moved from his seat, faced the bench and asked, "Your Honor, the People will rest their case with the stipulation that if the defense introduces expert testimony concerning the defendant's mental state, that we be permitted a rebuttal witness."

Jaffe's request to the bench brought Silverstein to his feet and he responded, "Your Honor, Mr. Jaffe knows full well that I intend to introduce expert psychiatric testimony. The defendant has been examined by both prosecution and defense psychiatric specialists and it would better serve the flow of these proceedings if the prosecution experts testified prior to my presentation."

Judge Scheinman responded, "Gentlemen, approach the bench." When both District Attorney and Defense Counsel were leaning over the rail, Judge Scheinman leaned forward in his seat and whispered, "To my calculations, during the past two years nine specialists in psychiatry have examined the defendant. I do not want to turn this trial into a forum on psychiatry. How many specialists do you intend to call Carl?"

"Just two," Silverstein whispered in response.

Jaffe immediately responded, "I believe it appropriate that I be provided the opportunity to respond with my own psychiatric specialist, Your Honor."

"That witness should testify first, Your Honor," Silverstein argued.

Jaffe retorted, "Your Honor, the prosecution has focused entirely on proving the crimes the defendant has been indicted for. There is no need for me to confuse the jury with psychiatric testimony until such time defense makes it an issue. Therefore I request"-

Raising one hand in a silencing gesture, Judge Scheinman interrupted and stated, "Enough, gentlemen. I will allow the prosecution a rebuttal witness to the defense experts. Please take your seats so that we can proceed."

As Jaffe and Silverstein returned to their respective work tables, Judge Scheinman faced the jury and apologized for the brief delay. Then turning his attention to the District Attorney, he asked, "Mr. Jaffe, do you wish to call another witness?"

Jaffe stood and responded, "Not at this time, Your Honor. The People rest with the stipulation that rebuttal witness's may be called."

"Then we will recess," Scheinman responded. Then focusing his attention on Defense Counsel he stated, "Mr. Silverstein, court will reconvene at 2:00 p.m., at which time you will be asked to call your first witness."

"Yes, sir." Silverstein responded, "The defense is ready."

Silverstein knew that the prosecution had presented a very strong case for conviction of his client; however, 'in proving the crimes the defendant had been indicted for' the District Attorney had left the door slightly open for the defense to persuade the jury that Ron Krom had committed those crimes because of a diminished capacity caused by a debilitating mental disorder known as schizophrenia. This is a mind fracturing disorder that caused its victim to suffer delusions, hallucinate and motivated unpredictable and, sometimes, criminal behavior. Carl had mentally juggled whether to have Ron testify and attempt to elicit a personal display of schizophrenia for the jury, but after evaluating Ron's performance on the witness stand during the Huntley Hearing, he decided against having his client testify in front of the jury. Performing before a larger audience might result in Ron going all out to prove to everyone that he was in control, knew precisely what he was doing and absent any display of emotion, his testimony would have a negative impact on the jury. Silverstein decided that the best route to take toward establishing his client's lack of responsibility due to mental illness, was by having Ron's father establish the history and progression of his son's illness, bolstered by testimony from professionals in the field of psychiatry.

Silverstein had skipped lunch, instead using the time during recess to freshen up and prepare his first witness, who physically displayed the angst displayed by a mouse under the shadow of a swooping hawk. He met with the defendant's parents in his office. Both had testified during the Suppression Hearing, so he anticipated no resistance from them over testifying at trial. Harrison and Dorothy Krom were red-eyed from lack of sleep and both appeared on the verge of physical collapse.

Judge Scheinman reconvened the matter of the People of the State of New York against Ronald Harrison Krom, at precisely 2:00 p.m., directed his attention to Defense Counsel and asked, "Is the defense ready to proceed?"

"May I approach the bench, Your Honor," Silverstein asked?

Judge Scheinman responded by motioning with his hand for both Defense Counsel and Prosecutor to come forward.

When gathered, Silverstein whispered, "I apologize to the court, but my witness is not available. I am requesting an adjournment until tomorrow, at which time I will be ready to proceed."

Jaffe studied Judge and Counsel without responding.

As the attorney's returned to their respective tables, Judge Scheinman announced, "We will recess and reconvene at 9:00 a.m. tomorrow."

Carl had acquiesced to Harrison and Dorothy Krom's request not to put them through the devastating trauma of testifying either for or against their son. He would rely solely on the testimony of psychiatrists who could establish what he had initially intended through Harrison. He recognized that no matter the outcome of the trial, Harrison and Dorothy Krom would be serving a life sentence of confusion, loss, rejection, humiliation and depression. He would not add to their woe by making them fodder for the media. He returned to his office, picked up the telephone and called the offices of New York City psychiatrists B. Thomas Houghton and Romero Malcagnon and was assured that both would appear in the Sullivan County Court the following day.

Dr. B. Thomas Houghton arrived at Carl Silverstein's office at 8:00 a.m. the following morning. Dr. Romero Malcaganon would arrive at 11:00 a.m. Both of these gentlemen were well known psychiatrists with offices in New

York City. Both had examined Ron several times since his arrest at request of the defense and both had previously testified at the Suppression Hearing.

When Judge Scheinman called the packed courtroom to order at 9:00 a.m., Defense Counsel was at his worktable and ready to proceed. Krom sat impassively beside him and as he had done throughout most of the trial, gave the appearance of being engrossed in a hardcover book titled, "Criminal Procedure Law of the State of New York."

District Attorney Joseph Jaffe was at his worktable, appeared relaxed and exchanged a smile and nod of greeting with Defense Counsel.

"Mr. Silverstein, is your witness here and are you ready to proceed?" Judge Scheinman inquired.

Silverstein stood and responded, "Yes, Your Honor, the Defense calls Dr. B. Thomas Houghton to the stand."

A tall male of medium build, appearing to be about fifty years old, having dark hair with a receding hairline, impeccably dressed in a dark pinstripe suit, and purple tie, entered the courtroom and strode with a confident air to the witness stand. Gold cufflinks bearing the initials BTH fastened the cuffs of his silk white shirt were readily observable as was the purple handkerchief in the left breast pocket of his suit jacket.

After being sworn and seated, Silverstein – revealing the trace of a smile – greeted, "Good morning, Doctor. For the record, please state your name and expertise."

The witness smiled and nodded in return, then turned serious as he responded, "Dr. B. Thomas Houghton. I am a doctor of psychiatry with office in New York City. I have been in practice for twenty years."

Greetings and introduction aside, Carl held his witness in a serious look and asked, "Doctor, I will get right to the purpose of your being here. Did you have the occasion to examine my client Ronald Krom?"

Houghton glanced briefly at the defendant, turned his attention back to his questioner and replied, "Yes, I have examined Mr. Krom on two occasions during the past two years.

"Would it be accurate to say that those examinations were conducted at my request to determine my client's mental state, whether he understood the seriousness of the crimes he was charged with and was capable of participating in his defense?"

"Yes, that would be correct."

"What did you determine, Doctor?"

"I personally examined the patient, spoke with his parents, and studied his medical and psychiatric history, which revealed Mr. Krom had started demonstrating delusional behavior and acting out violently at a very young age. He was diagnosed as schizophrenic and hospitalized twice while still in high school. My examination revealed that Mr. Krom continues to suffer from schizophrenia."

"And schizophrenia is a severe mental disorder is that correct?"

"Yes, Mr. Silverstein. Schizophrenia is a severe mental disorder and its cause is unknown; however, there is a consensus among many psychiatric practitioners that it is genetically induced. It is also widely held that the disease is influenced by environmental factors and the use of certain drugs. The disease is characterized by disorganized speech and behavior, delusions, and in more advanced stages- paranoia."

"What symptoms led you to conclude that my client is schizophrenic?"

"Mr. Krom experiences delusions and frequently responds inappropriately to stimuli. He has manifestations of grandeur and easily becomes braggadocio."

"Doctor, you testified that the cause of schizophrenia is unknown. Is there a cure for this illness?"

"There is no known cure; however, inducing prescribed anti-psychotic medications has proven effective in reducing the frequency of inappropriate behavior. The normal course of treatment involves hospitalization in a psychiatric treatment facility for a time to observe the patient's behavior accompanied by the administration of medication and, in severe cases, shock therapy. When the patient responds well to treatment and is determined to present no danger to society or his person, he is placed on a prescribed medication and sent home."

"Doctor, would it be accurate to say that a schizophrenic may believe that his hallucinations are real?"

"Quite accurate," Houghton replied, while nodding his head in the affirmative. He added, "In Mr. Krom's case, he deluded about having been an agent in the Central Intelligence Agency, and in his mind, he believed this true."

"Now sir, the law provides that mental incompetence negates criminal intent. I presume that you are aware of that fact?"

"Yes, I am."

"The law also provides that a person acting under extreme emotional disturbance may not be culpably responsible for his actions. Are you aware of that fact sir?"

"I am."

"And the purpose of your examinations of my client were to determine if one or both of those factors existed?"

"Yes, sir."

"And what did you conclude?"

"I determined that Mr. Krom did not fully understand the severity of his actions, was incapable of making a knowledgeable waiver of his Constitutional rights and"-

"Objection, Your Honor," Jaffe called out while rising from his chair, "the matter of the defendant knowing and understanding his Constitutional rights was addressed at a Suppression Hearing in this court. It was decided by this court that the defendant understood and knowingly waived his rights."

"You are quite right," Judge Scheinman answered. "However, I will give the witness some latitude here because it appears this statement is inclusive in his complete analysis of the defendant's mental state." Turning to face the jury he added, "For your information, it was previously decided that the defendant understood and knowingly waived his rights. Please discount that part of the witness's answer which, addresses that issue. You may continue, Counselor."

Silverstein flashed a smile at the witness and stated, "Please relate your conclusions as to my client's mental state."

Having testified in numerous court proceedings, the Doctor appeared calm and unfazed by the interruption. Projecting his best look of expertise toward the jury he responded, "I concluded that Mr. Krom is severely affected by schizophrenia, is very delusional, hallucinates and has infrequent bouts of paranoia. His condition caused him to believe that he was being both seduced and pressured by a second party to carry out the acts he confessed to. Therefore, he was acting under extreme emotional disturbance."

"Thank you, Doctor," Carl responded displaying a smile. "Your witness, Mr. Jaffe."

Jaffe stepped from his place, walked to an area in front of the jury, gave the witness a sober stare and asked, "Doctor, just a few months ago, you testified at a Suppression Hearing in this matter, is that correct?"

"Yes, that is correct," Houghton, responded.

"At that Hearing, you testified that you had not reviewed the defendant's mental history and reached your conclusion that the defendant was not mentally capable of knowing and waiving his rights, based on one four and a half hour consultation with him. Was that your testimony then?"

"That may be true," Houghton responded sounding defensive, "but after my second session with Mr. Krom, I examined his history."

Holding the witness in a cold stare Jaffe responded, "Doctor, I presume you are familiar with the Bible of psychiatric practitioners referred to as DSM (Diagnostic and Statistical Manual of Mental Disorders)?"

"I am," the witness responded - displaying a curious look.

"Then, I would presume that as an expert on schizophrenia, you are aware that the DSM section that addresses schizophrenia provides that there is no test that can definitely identify schizophrenia. The diagnosis depends on excluding causes such as epilepsy and brain tumors as responsible for the patient's behavior, combined with a study of the patient's history of behavior?"

"I am aware of that fact."

"All well, and good, but the truth is Doctor, it does not seem feasible that after spending a mere four and one-half hours with a new patient and not knowing his history, that you could arrive at the conclusion that he – Krom – was not mentally capable of knowing and waiving rights that were carefully provided and reviewed with him several times by several different people. Thank you sir. I have no more questions."

Silverstein started to object but realized that Jaffe had made his point and having dismissed the witness, an objection would serve no purpose. Instead, he asked his witness, one more question, "Doctor, did you conduct an in depth study of my client's mental health history?"

"Yes, I did." Houghton answered.

"And how much time did you spend with my client in the second session?"

Appearing uncomfortable for the first time, the witness answered, "As you can well imagine, I have a very busy practice. Our second session was approximately four hours."

"And since being so rudely treated by the prosecution is there any equivocation regarding your previous answer that the defendant was acting under extreme emotional disturbance?"

"No, sir."

Forcing a smile of thanks, Silverstein responded, "Thank you, Doctor." He then turned his back on the witness and returned to his chair at the defense table.

Doctor Houghton exited the courtroom and seeing colleague Doctor Romero Malcaganon standing in the hallway, flashed him a smile and said, "Your turn in the box, Doctor."

Malcaganon entered the courtroom as Silverstein was calling his name as his next witness. A psychiatrist with impressive credentials, Malcaganon was as well known in the field of psychiatry as the witness who preceded him; however, there was a sharp contrast in physical appearance between the two. As a Filipino-American, Malcaganon was small, slight of build and dark skinned. He was more casually attired in a dark sports jacket, dark brown slacks, highly polished cordovan loafers and mauve turtleneck sweater. Having testified in many court cases – usually for the defense - Dr. Malcaganon appeared calm, cool and collected on the witness stand. After establishing the doctor's credentials and experience, Defense Counsel Silverstein asked him the same questions that he had posed of Dr. Houghton and received basically the same answers, albeit in slightly different words and terms. Dr. Malcaganon concurred with Houghton that it was his professional opinion that the defendant was severely affected by schizophrenia, had frequent bouts of delusion, believed his delusional manifestations as true and was acting under extreme emotional stress when he committed the 'acts' he was on trial for.

In cross, Jaffe elicited testimony that Dr. Malcaganon had testified at an earlier Suppression Hearing at which time he told the court that the defendant understood the seriousness of the crimes he was charged with, understood the rights provided him and had made a knowledgeable determination to waive those rights. He concluded, "Doctor, your analysis of the defendant during the hearing appears to be in direct conflict with the analysis you provided today."

This caused Silverstein to re-direct and he asked, "Doctor, please disregard the prosecutions unwarranted comments. Do you hold to your testimony of today?"

Displaying a serious look, the witness answered, "Yes, Mr. Silverstein, I believe Mr. Krom's illness had progressed to the point that he was behaving irrationally and acted under extreme emotional stress."

When the witness was excused, Jaffe requested a short recess to notify a rebuttal witness that he was required for testimony.

Judge Scheinman announced that court would recess until two that afternoon, "At which time I expect that all parties will be ready to proceed."

Although noted for patience and understanding, Judge Scheinman insisted on punctuality and therefore, when he entered the courtroom at precisely 2:00 p.m., he was pleased to note that defendant, defense counsel, prosecutor, jury and court reporter, as well as a standing-room only audience were in place and ready to proceed.

"If it please the court," Jaffe opened, "the People call Doctor Daniel Schwartz."

To those acquainted with the world of psychiatry, Dr. Daniel W. Schwartz was the modern day image of Dr. Sigmund Freud, although somewhat smaller of stature and build. The doctor sported a Freud-like black and white goatee and a dark mustache sat above his upper lip. Large, horned rim glasses were perched atop his nose and the size of the glasses made his dark, piercing eyes, seem larger than they were. Small of stature, Doctor Schwartz, was attired in a black pinstripe, three- piece suit, large collar, white dress shirt and purple or mauve necktie sprinkled with white dots. Like the preceding witnesses, Doctor Schwartz was a renowned psychiatrist with office located in the Manhattan borough of New York City.

Jaffe began his questioning of this witness, standing in front of the prosecution table, asking several questions that established the witness's identity, education and expertise. He then asked, "Doctor Schwartz, at the request of my predecessor and myself, you examined the defendant to first determine if he was capable of knowingly understanding his constitutional rights. Is that correct?"

It was noted by the jury that the witness focused his attention on his questioner while each question was asked, then faced the jury as he answered and displayed a sober, serious look throughout the exchange. "That is correct, Mr. Jaffe."

"And sir, what conclusion did you draw and testify to at the Suppression Hearing?"

"I concluded that Mr. Krom at the time he gave his statement to police, did not as a result of mental disease or defect, lack substantial capacity to know or appreciate that he was waiving his right to counsel and incriminating himself."

"In more succinct terms, Ronald Krom understood full well what he was doing. Is that correct?"

"Yes, that would be correct."

"Now, sir, during the past two plus years, how many times have you examined the defendant?

"I personally examined Mr. Krom twice, and conducted an in depth study of his psychiatric history."

"Who provided you that history?"

"Mr. Krom's parents, siblings, and examination of records pertaining to his hospitalization at various times in his life."

"What conclusion did you arrive at after being provided the known facts surrounding the crimes for which the defendant is on trial and your investigation as to whether the defendant knowingly committed those acts?"

"I concluded that, although there is no question Mr. Krom suffers from schizophrenia, his actions were not inspired by delusions. The motivations for his actions were jealousy, anger and greed. In my opinion Mr. Krom knew precisely what he was doing and understood the possible consequences of his actions."

"Would it then be accurate to conclude that the defendant is mentally competent, understands the severity of the offenses with which he is charged and is capable of assisting in his defense?"

"Accurate and succinctly stated Mr. Jaffe."

"Thank you, Doctor." Jaffe concluded with a smile, then turned and walked to his seat.

Upon cross- examination, Defense Counsel Silverstein pressed Dr. Schwartz on the possibility Krom could have been behaving under a delusion, were it not for his allegedly placing Mrs. Farber in the pit and locking it.

Dr. Schwartz responded, "Except for the bunker situation, Mr. Silverstein, she's alive. It was the act of placing Mrs. Farber in the bunker that eliminated the theory of delusion."

Out of questions, Silverstein turned away from the witness and returned to his place.

Upon conclusion of Dr. Schwartz's testimony, both prosecution and defense rested their cases. It was agreed that both sides would be ready for summation the following morning.

On December 11, 1979, each attired in their most impressive dark power suit, Defense Counsel and District Attorney, exchanged nods of greeting and each informed Judge Scheinman their summation was ready.

Silverstein was focused on convincing the jury that the defendant acted under extreme emotional disturbance, which diminished culpability and negated guilt. "Ladies and gentlemen of the jury," he began, "I thank you for your attentiveness throughout this arduous trial, a trial during which it has been clearly established that the defendant is a victim of a cruel and horrible mental illness known as schizophrenia. The quiet, young man you have had privilege to observe throughout these proceedings has a demon inside his skull and periodically, this demon forces him to do things that he would not do if freed of the demon's control. The prosecution produced many witnesses, all of whom, provided testimony intended to link Ronald Krom to the crimes he is on trial for. I submit, that several of these witnesses also testified as to the defendant having grandiose ideas, making bizarre statements and exhibiting strange behavior, all of which are symptomatic of schizophrenia. You heard testimony from specialists in psychiatry who unanimously agreed that the defendant suffers from schizophrenia and two of these highly acclaimed experts testified that the defendant was not culpable for his actions because in his delusional mind, he believed that he was acting at the behest of and cooperation of the victim's husband. He maintained this in every conversation with authorities. The prosecution has attempted to overwhelm you with testimony and evidence of the defendant's guilt; however, I beseech you to carefully consider and weigh the irrefutable evidence that Ronald Krom's ability to understand right from wrong was overwhelmed by the demon within his brain and he acted under extreme emotional stress. The only just verdict in this tragedy would be a finding of not guilty by reason of extreme emotional disturbance, and directing that Ronald Krom receive the treatment needed to rid his brain of the demon that controls him." Carl's summation was over in slightly less than ten minutes and intentionally so. He could not refute the prosecution's mountain of testimony and evidence and would not frustrate the jury in trying to do so. He was satisfied that he had taken the right path and only path available to win a satisfactory outcome for his client.

When Carl returned to his chair at the defense table, Ron glared at him and hissed, "You made me out to be some sort of freak! I am not under a demon's control Roger was involved with me, but he can't control me - nobody controls me - and I knew what I was doing. I will beat this rap and after I get out, I will become rich and famous."

Carl studied his client with a look of compassion but did not respond.

Sensing victory and seeming super-charged, District Attorney Jaffe was immediately on his feet and approached the jury box. Standing tall and displaying a smile, he spoke, "Ladies and gentlemen, I also offer you my sincere appreciation and thank you for your dedication and attentiveness. During the past three weeks you have heard testimony from numerous citizens, police officers, medical experts and experts in psychiatry. Many of these witnesses provided testimony linking the defendant to the horrific crimes he is charged with and which revealed that the defendant acted alone. A wealth of evidence was introduced which connected the defendant to those horrific crimes and proved that he acted alone. You heard testimony from several police officers and a former district attorney that the defendant confessed to them his unconscionable crimes and corroborated his admission of guilt by taking the police to the place where he had secured his victim. The defense would have you believe Ronald Krom is himself a victim, alleging he suffers from a mental illness that controls his mind and forced him to commit the unimaginable act of burying a woman alive. Ladies and gentlemen, the truth is, the defendant harbored a longstanding grudge against his victim's family, was jealous of their wealth, angry at the victim's husband and calculatingly plotted – over the course of several years - to get even. The defendant acted alone in stealing Gertrude Farber from her home, burying her alive, and took pleasure in her suffering while waiting for a ransom to be paid. You heard testimony that the defendant confessed to personally digging the hole for the purpose of secreting Gertrude Farber. You heard testimony that the defendant disguised himself and avoided speaking to avoid recognition. You heard testimony that the defendant calculatingly borrowed a car to transport the victim to her burial spot, to thus avoid detection. Such planning and precaution to avoid recognition refutes argument that a delusional influence was directing the defendant's actions. You heard testimony that when questioned by police as to Gertrude Farber's **location**, Ronald Krom readily admitted that he knew her location but **refused to** divulge that information over the course of approximately twelve hours. **He only** divulged her location after being assured of being paid for her **release from** Harry Resnick. A delay, ladies and gentlemen, which very possibly **contributed** to Gertrude Farber's death. The truth is, Ronald Krom is not a victim! He is a cold-hearted, cruel, calculating individual - who motivated by jealousy, anger and greed - stole Gertrude Farber from her home, buried her alive and abandoned her to the fate of a horrible death. Ladies and gentlemen, there are many people afflicted by schizophrenia, but they do not plan, plot and commit the despicable crimes that were committed by Ronald Krom. I submit that the defendant, Ronald Krom, was in total control of his faculties when he envisioned a way to extort one million dollars from Harry Resnick and he was in total control of his faculties when he carried out his plan. Ronald Krom is a heartless punk and must be held accountable for his acts of depravity." Pausing for a brief moment, Jaffe projected a look of seriousness and sincerity, concluding in an appealing tone, he said, "Only a verdict of Guilty as charged on all counts will provide a small measure of justice to all who suffer the loss of Trudy Farber. Thank you."

Jaffe's footsteps could be heard in the silent courtroom as he returned to his seat. Many in the room reached for a handkerchief or tissue during the silence.

Judge Scheinman broke the silence by informing the jury that the decision as to the defendant's guilt or innocence was in their hands. Before excusing them to begin deliberation, he reminded them that a guilty verdict must be unanimous and the burden of proof was on the prosecution. If any questions came up during deliberation, the foreman would have the assigned bailiff present their question or concern to the Judge.

Not surprisingly, it did not take the jury long to agree on a verdict. On December 12, 1979, Judge Scheinman received notice that the jury had reached a verdict. Upon being notified that the verdict 'was in,' prosecution and defense teams began gathering in the courtroom, and, as the Sullivan County jail was located immediately behind the Court House, it did not take long for the Sheriff's Department to produce Ron in court. District Attorney Jaffe, whose office was located in the Court House, learning that the verdict was in, was one of the first to appear in the courtroom and if he felt any nervousness, a confident smile hid it well. Although not confident of winning a 'not guilty' verdict, Defense Counsel Silverstein felt that he had put on a good defense as to his client's mental condition and non-responsibility for knowing criminal conduct. Judge Scheinman had directed that all parties affected by the crimes and impacted by the verdict be notified, and set a reasonable time period for them to gather in the court for reading of the verdict. A gaggle of reporters, members of the legal community, employees from various offices in the building, relatives and friends of the victim and the defendant, and a few curious citizens, who had followed the trial, eventually filled the courtroom to capacity. The venerable courtroom was soon abuzz with whispered conversations inspired by nervous tension, excitement or dread.

When the jury was seated, Judge Scheinman faced them and asked, "Ladies and gentlemen, have you reached a verdict?"

The Foreman stood and responded, "We have, Your Honor."

"How do you find on the first count of Murder in the Second Degree?"

"We find the defendant guilty as charged." A response of guilty would follow to each of the remaining charges.

Judge Scheinman thanked the jury for their service and advised that the verdict would be so noted and filed. They were then excused.

There was minimal reaction from the gallery to the verdict because most present anticipated a finding of guilt. The only flurry came from the reporters who hurried from the court to file their stories. Members of the Resnick family, gathered to exchange hugs and tears. The Kroms sat in stoic silence, their faces revealing sadness and pain.

Ronald Krom who had stood passively beside his attorney through the reading of the verdict, suddenly erupted in fury. He pushed his attorney aside and screamed, "This has all been a farce! I was framed! The CIA screwed me!" Then he rushed toward District Attorney Jaffe, screaming obscenities and sputtering, "You put a fix on the planted agents! This trial was arranged to get even with the man who took down Nixon!"

Sheriff's Deputies and court officers, grabbed Krom before he was able to reach Jaffe and it took four of them to wrestle him to the floor, where he was shackled and then roughly lifted to his feet. He was then forcibly escorted to a cell in the county jail, which was conveniently located adjacent to the court building.

After the brief brouhaha, Joe Jaffe and Carl Silverstein shook hands, gathered up their files, and returned to their respective offices. Judge Scheinman felt a sense of relief, but only small relief, for he still had to sentence the defendant and anticipated future scrutiny by the Court of Appeals.

Epilogue

On December 31, 1979, a shackled Ronald Harrison Krom reappeared in Sullivan County Court for sentencing. Members of the Resnick family and Krom family attended; however, no statements were made either in condemnation or on his behalf. On this cold winter day, Judge Scheinman focused an icy stare on the defendant and pronounced the following sentence: "Mr. Krom, on the first count of Murder in the 2nd degree, I hereby sentence you to serve two indeterminate terms of imprisonment having a minimum of twenty-five years and a maximum of life. On the count of Murder in the 2nd Degree –Depraved Indifference, I hereby sentence you to an indeterminate term of imprisonment having a minimum of twenty-five years and maximum of life. On the count of Burglary in the 2nd Degree, I hereby sentence you to a concurrent term having a minimum of five years and a maximum of fifteen years."

Although also convicted on two counts of Kidnapping in the 1st degree, prior to sentencing, those convictions were set aside as lesser offenses in the crime of Murder.

Ronald Harrison Krom remains in prison at the date of this writing. Since his arrest on May 26, 1977, he has been shuffled numerous times between secure psychiatric facilities and various state prisons. At the time of this writing he is an inmate in Auburn Maximum Correctional Facility. Parole has been denied and numerous appeals in State and Federal Courts have been denied.

Sullivan County District Attorney Stephen Lungen advised that during his 30years of incarceration, Krom has been a prolific letter writer - sending hundreds of letters to his office, members of the legal community, members of the judicial system, members of the media, members of the New York State

Police and Sullivan County Sheriff's Department, political leaders, former friends, relatives, Trudy Farber's parents, and even people he did not know. All of Ronald Krom's letters were bizarre and one manifestation that began appearing in them was particularly troubling. In his initial correspondence, he would close with the words, "Yours truly" or just "Truly, Ron Krom." This closing evolved into, "Trudy," or "Trudy yours, Ron Krom," which, may or may not have been a way to torment or harass the recipient.

The Resnicks were outraged and considered the unsolicited letters from the killer of their daughter a deliberate attempt to harass them. They met with the District Attorney and begged him to do everything within his power to deny their daughter's killer the ability to harass them from his prison cell.

On September 28, 1988, District Attorney Lungen drafted the following letter, which was sent to the Superintendent of Mid-State Correctional Facility, located in Marcy, New York – where Krom was under custody and treatment at the time – with copy also sent to New York State Corrections Commissioner Thomas A. Coughlin and the Resnick's Attorney, Ronald S. Kossar:

OFFICE OF THE DISTRICT ATTORNEY
SULLIVAN COUNTY

County Courthouse
Monticello, NY 12701
914-794-3344

STEPHEN F. LUNGEN
District Attorney

FRANK J. LABUDA
K.C. GARN
BONNIE M. MITZNER
ANTHONY M. GIORDANO
GORDON T. SAKOW
ELISSA YAVNE
Assistants

September 28, 1988

Mid-State Correctional Facility
P.O. Box 216
Marcy, NY 13403-0216

Attention: Garry Stevens, Superintendent

Re: Ronald Krom
    80A-0001

Dear Superintendent Stevens:

The above named individual was convicted in Sullivan County on December 31, 1979, for the kidnapping and murder of a young woman named Trudy Resnick Farber. The crime and the circumstances surrounding the defendant's conduct represented one of the most heinous and notorious crimes that we have had in the county. The defendant has exhausted all of his appellate rights and is confined to the state prison system for at least 25 years to life.

Throughout his period of incarceration, he has been a prolific letter writer. My office, the Sullivan County Legal Aid Society and others have received numerous letters from him on all sorts of bizarre issues. These letters are simply filed without response.

Mr. Krom has again commenced his letter writing. I received a letter dated September 18, 1988, and legal aid received another dated September 22, 1988. Most importantly the mother and father of the female victim also received a letter dated September 22, 1988. I am enclosing a copy of all three of those letters.

page 2 of letter:

```
Superintendent Stevens
September 28, 1988
Page two
```

I have been contacted by a representative of the family to see if there is anything I can do to prevent any further communication by the defendant to the aggrieved family. Letters such as this rekindle the horrible memories and grief that this family has had to endure because of this defendant's egregious conduct. Simply put, something must be done to prevent this from <u>ever</u> happening again.

I know that the state prison system has an ability to review an inmate's postal privileges. I want to be able to assure the Resnick family that they will never hear from Mr. Krom again. I would ask that you look into this matter and request that you advise me of what actions can and will be taken in this regard. I would further hope that the procedures employed will follow Mr. Krom to whatever facility he may go during his period of incarceration. Thank you for your attention to this matter.

Very truly yours,

[signature]

Stephen F. Lungen
District Attorney

```
SFL:db
Encs.
pc   Thomas A. Coughlin III, Commissioner (enc)
     Ronald S. Kossar, Esq. (enc)
```

District Attorney Lungen received the following letter of response, dated October 4, 1988, from Mid-State Correctional Facility Deputy Superintendent of Programs Daniel J. Alexander:

STATE OF NEW YORK
DEPARTMENT OF CORRECTIONAL SERVICE

MID-STATE CORRECTIONAL FACILITY
P.O. BOX 216, RIVER ROAD
MARCY, NEW YORK 13403-0216
315-768-8581

Thomas A. Coughlin III
Commissioner

An Equal Opportunity Employer

John J. Cassidy
Superintendent

October 4, 1988

Mr. Stephen F. Lungen
District Attorney
Sullivan County
County Court House
Monticello, New York 12701

RE: KROM, Ronald
80-A-0001

Dear District Attorney Lungen:

    This is in reply to your September 28, 1988 letter to our former Superintendent, Gary Stevens, in which you complained that the above-named inmate had been improperly corresponding with the family of the person whom he was convicted of kidnapping and murdering in Sullivan County in 1979.

    Please be advised that we do not have this person in our inmate population at Mid-State Correctional Facility. A check of the Department of Correctional Services Records indicates that he is currently confined at our Green Haven Correctional Facility, Stormville, New York and has been in Green Haven's population for several years.

    Regardless, on October 3, 1988, I telephoned Green Haven's Assistant Deputy Superintendent of Programs Paul Kimelman relative to your concerns about this inmate, and made him aware of the inmate's inappropriate correspondence with the victim's family.

    Assistant Deputy Superintendent of Programs Kimelman at that time indicated to me that he would see to it that the inmate is immediately instructed that he is not to correspond with the victim's family, and that disciplinary action would be taken against the inmate in the event that he continued to do so.

    Likewise, Assistant Deputy Superintendent of Programs Kimelman indicated that inmate Krom would be immediately referred for psychological evaluation.

    I have attached your letter regarding this inmate to the carbon copy of this letter which I am forwarding to the Superintendent at Green Haven Correctional Facility.

                                              Sincerely,

                                              Daniel Alexander
                                              Deputy Superintendent Programs

CC: Charles Scully, Superintendent
      Green Haven Correctional Facility

    It became a concern in the minds of a multitude of folks familiar with the Trudy Farber case as to whether corrections personnel or the inmates were in control of the New York State Correctional System, as the flow of unsolicited, unwanted correspondence from inmate Ronald Krom continued unabated. District Attorney Lungen continued to receive complaints from recipients of Krom's confusing, bizarre, schizophrenic inspired letters. An exchange of letters also continued between the District Attorney and various supervisors in the New York State Department of Corrections, who continued to advise the District Attorney that "inmate Krom has been directed to immediately cease from sending any further communication to…and if they became aware he was continuing to send letters to… disciplinary action will be taken against inmate Krom."

The result was that Krom continued sending unsolicited, unwanted letters and the Sullivan County District Attorney's office kept receiving complaints from the recipients of his letters. As the sort of disciplinary action that would be taken against Krom was not spelled out, an intelligent mind might wonder just what sort of discipline would force a diagnosed schizophrenic, serving a life sentence, to see the light and change his ways? In any event, as inmate Krom was transferred throughout the correctional system, he obviously had access to pen, paper and postage stamps, since his letter-writing blitz continued.

Having been provided copy of many of Krom's letters to various individuals, the author mulled over whether any worthwhile information that might add to the depth of this story and/or stimulate reader interest, would be gained by a personal interview of Ronald Krom. An inquiry was made to New York State Corrections and a response received spelling out the procedure's required for personal interview of an inmate. One of the requirements was that the inmate be sent a letter requesting his consent to be interviewed. Accordingly, a letter of introduction and request for interview was sent to Krom in care of the Auburn Correctional Facility. Ron Krom quickly responded – more than once – agreeing to be interviewed. After trying without success to decipher and make sense out of what amounted to a splash of gibberish and disconnected prose, it was decided that Krom's mental condition has deteriorated and no useful purpose would be served in giving him a venue to portray delusions of grandeur.

It has been said that life is sometimes cruel and ironic. In a display of cruel irony, an intelligent young woman having great empathy for sufferers of mental illness and devoted to easing their suffering, would have her life cut short by the hands of a mental illness sufferer.

A cruel, senseless, act of depravity ended Trudy's life; however, her spirit lives on in the valley and community so dear to her. On June 8, 1986, more than 100 prominent state and county officials, gathered with Resnick family members, friends and former co-workers of Trudy Resnick Farber at 50 Center Street, Ellenville, New York to dedicate the Trudy Resnick Farber Center For Human Development, a facility providing counseling and assistance to troubled members of the Ellenville community.

Trudy Resnick Center Part 1

Trudy Resnick Center Part 2

Trudy Resnick Center Part 3

Trudy Resnick Farber's memory also lives on in the form of scholarship awards in her name, endowed by Harry and Marcia Resnick and awarded annually to students attending New Paltz State University and Ulster County Community College.

The Honorable Louis B. Scheinman, who demonstrated patience and wisdom in presiding over this case, passed away in 1983.

In a surprising move, Joseph Jaffe would eventually forego politics in Sullivan County and join a successful business firm located in New York City.

Switching sides, Carl Silverstein eventually gave up his position as Sullivan County Legal Aid Attorney and became an Assistant District Attorney in Sullivan County.

Acknowledgements

In alphabetical order:

NYSP Investigator John Bult/Retired – steady, dependable and excellent report writer.

Hon. Maryjean Carroll, Forrestburg Town Justice – who provided helpful contact information.

NYSP Investigator James Chandler/Retired – you were a great cop and good brother.

FBI SA Thomas Davidheiser/Retired – a good friend who put me in touch with agents who worked this case.

Loretta Duarte, Sullivan County Commissioner of Jurors – thanks for the lead.

Marion Ehrhardt, who filled in missing gaps, and all the staff at the Ellenville Public Library and Museum.

Elizabeth "Betty" Ewald, a talented editor who – or is it whom – doesn't make me feel like I flunked Writing 101.

Trudy Resnick Farber – I could not forget you Trudy. I hope I have done justice to your story.

NYSP Investigator Ralph Fuente/Retired – we share a lot of good memories.

Investigator Paul Hans, Sullivan County District Attorney's office/Retired NYSP Investigator – thanks for opening the archives and dusting off the files.

NYSP Investigator Jack Hayes/Retired – thanks for conducting lead.

NYSP Senior Investigator Wilfried Holik/Retired – you were the best at crime scene investigation.

Joseph Jaffe, Managing Director Global Business Intelligence and Investigations/former Sullivan County District Attorney – a prosecution he will never forget.

Theodore Kocijanski – your recollection was very helpful.

Hon. Ronald Kossar – thank you for reaching out to the Resnick family.

Loy Kimmes – your memory is superb. Thanks for the leads.

Stephen Lungen, Sullivan County District Attorney – your assistance made it possible to tell Trudy's story.

FBI SA Leo McGillicuddy/Retired – your work was appreciated more than you know.

NYSP Senior Investigator Donald Scherpf/Retired – you were an excellent police supervisor.

Hon. Louis B. Scheinman/Deceased – how he prevented a mistrial is a work of genius.

Hon. Carl Silverstein/Retired, Defense Counsel and former Sullivan County Assistant District Attorney – you had an impossible case to defend and did the best you could.

NYSP Investigator Carl VanWagenen/Retired – information from the search warrant expert was greatly appreciated.

William Walkerwicz – your input was greatly appreciated.

I offer profound apology to anyone not mentioned who may have contributed to the telling of Trudy's story and extend my sincere appreciation.

Printed in the United States
209528BV00001B/55/P